Lecture Notes in Computer Science 13159

More information about this series at https://link.springer.com/bookseries/558

Stephen Poole · Oscar Hernandez ·
Matthew Baker · Tony Curtis (Eds.)

OpenSHMEM and Related Technologies

OpenSHMEM in the Era of Exascale and Smart Networks

8th Workshop on OpenSHMEM
and Related Technologies, OpenSHMEM 2021
Virtual Event, September 14–16, 2021
Revised Selected Papers

Springer

Editors
Stephen Poole
Los Alamos National Laboratory
Los Almos, NM, USA

Oscar Hernandez
NVIDIA Corporation
Santa Clara, CA, USA

Matthew Baker
Oak Ridge National Laboratory
Oak Ridge, TN, USA

Tony Curtis
Stony Brook University
Stony Brook, NY, USA

ISSN 0302-9743 ISSN 1611-3349 (electronic)
Lecture Notes in Computer Science
ISBN 978-3-031-04887-6 ISBN 978-3-031-04888-3 (eBook)
https://doi.org/10.1007/978-3-031-04888-3

This Springer imprint is published by the registered company Springer Nature Switzerland AG
The registered company address is: Gewerbestrasse 11, 6330 Cham, Switzerland

Preface

OpenSHMEM is a portable specification API that implements a partitioned global address space (PGAS) programming model that focuses on low-latency one-sided communication across nodes within a system. OpenSHMEM is a modern derivative of the SGI SHMEM API, originally developed by Cray Research, Inc., for efficient programming of large-scale systems. Because of its strong following, Open Source Software Solutions, Inc. (OSSS) was licensed to drive a specification called OpenSHMEM that has portable implementations among vendors, research laboratories, and academia. The OpenSHMEM and Related Technologies Workshop (OpenSHMEM Workshop) was established in 2014 when OpenSHMEM 1.1 was released to the community and has enjoyed success in being the main workshop where users, vendors, and researchers share their experiences and publish their latest results. The community has developed the specification to version 1.5, adding new features such as teams to group together subsets of processing elements (PEs), non-blocking atomic memory operations (AMOs), and a profiling interface.

This year's workshop (OpenSHMEM 2021) included topics ranging from new applications, benchmarks, and libraries experiences to new OpenSHMEM implementations on novel hardware, programming models, and low-level communication framework extensions. The workshop agenda can be found at http://www.openshmem.org/workshops/openshmem2021/program.html. This year's keynotes included talks on Bale 3.0, a collection of applications with many-to-many communication patterns; NVSHMEM, an implementation of OpenSHMEM for NVIDIA accelerators; the latest advances of Chapel, an asynchronous PGAS programming language developed by Cray, which now supports multi-resolution aggregated communication to improve the message rates of applications; and Arkouda, a Chapel application that provides Python interfaces to key NumPy and Pandas operations for data science applications.

This book constitutes the proceedings of the 6th OpenSHMEM and Related Technologies Workshop. The conference was held virtually and organized by Los Alamos National Laboratory, having 102 attendees from around the world. In total, 12 papers were selected from the 18 submissions (66% acceptance rate) and presented at the workshop. The Technical Program Committee members and the chairs reviewed all the papers submitted to the workshop. The papers were organized as follows: Applications and Implementations; Tools and Benchmarks; and Programming Models and OpenSHMEM Extensions.

September 2021

Stephen Poole
Matthew Baker
Oscar Hernandez
Tony Curtis

Organization

General Co-chairs

Matthew Baker	Oak Ridge National Laboratory, USA
Oscar Hernandez	NVIDIA Corporation, USA
Stephen Poole	Los Alamos National Laboratory, USA
Tony Curtis	Stony Brook University, USA

Technical Program Co-chairs

Bryant Lam	United States Department of Defense, USA
Nick Park	United States Department of Defense, USA
Michael Raymond	Hewlett Packard Enterprise, USA
Pavel Shamis	Arm Ltd., USA
Manjunath Gorentla Venkata	NVIDIA Corporation, USA

Technical Program Committee

Matthew Baker	Oak Ridge National Laboratory, USA
Pavan Balaji	Facebook, USA
Swen Boehm	Oak Ridge National Laboratory, USA
Camille Coti	University of Oregon, USA
Tony Curtis	Stony Brook University, USA
James Dinan	NVIDIA Corporation, USA
Marcel Fallet	United States Department of Defense, USA
Megan Grodowitz	Arm Ltd., USA
Max Grossman	Georgia Tech, USA
Khaled Hamidouche	Advanced Micro Devices, Inc., USA
Oscar Hernandez	NVIDIA Corporation, USA
Curtis Hughey	United States Department of Defense, USA
Bryant Lam	United States Department of Defense, USA
Alex Margolin	Huawei, Israel
Naveen Namashivayam	Hewlett Packard Enterprise, USA
Dhabaleswar Panda	Ohio State University, USA
Nick Park	United States Department of Defense, USA
Stephen Poole	Los Alamos National Laboratory, USA
Wendy Poole	Los Alamos National Laboratory, USA
Swaroop Pophale	Oak Ridge National Laboratory, USA

Howard Pritchard	Los Alamos National Laboratory, USA
Michael Raymond	Hewlett Packard Enterprise, USA
Thomas Rolinger	United States Department of Defense, USA
Gilad Shainer	NVIDIA Corporation, USA
Pavel Shamis	Arm Ltd., USA
Sameer Shende	University of Oregon, USA
Min Si	Argonne National Laboratory, USA
Jessica Steffy	United States Department of Defense, USA
Mitsuhisa Sato	RIKEN, Japan
Manjunath Gorentla Venkata	NVIDIA Corporation, USA
Brody Williams	Texas Tech University, USA

Logistics

Tony Curtis	Stony Brook University, USA
Valerie Hartman	Los Alamos National Laboratory, USA
Beth Kaspar	Los Alamos National Laboratory, USA

Web Chair

Tony Curtis	Stony Brook University, USA

Contents

Applications and Implementations

A Study in SHMEM: Parallel Graph Algorithm Acceleration with Distributed Symmetric Memory

Michael Ing(✉) and Alan D. George

Department of Electrical and Computer Engineering,
University of Pittsburgh, NSF Center for Space, High-Performance, and Resilient Computing (SHREC), Pittsburgh, USA
{mci10,alan.george}@pitt.edu

Abstract. Over the last few decades, the Message Passing Interface (MPI) has become the parallel-communication standard for distributed algorithms on high-performance CPUs. MPI's minimal setup overhead and simple API calls give it a low barrier of entry, while still providing support for more complex communication patterns. Communication schemes that use physically or logically shared memory provide a number of improvements to HPC-algorithm parallelization by reducing synchronization calls between processors and overlapping communication and computation via strategic programming techniques. The OpenSHMEM specification developed in the last decade applies these benefits to distributed-memory computing systems by leveraging a Partitioned Global Address Space (PGAS) model and remote memory access (RMA) operations. Paired with non-blocking communication patterns, these technologies enable increased parallelization of existing apps. This research studies the impact of these techniques on the Multi-Node Parallel Boruvka's Minimum Spanning Tree Algorithm (MND-MST), which uses distributed programming for inter-processor communication. This research also provides a foundation for applying complex communication libraries like OpenSHMEM to large-scale apps. To provide further context for the comparison of MPI to the OpenSHMEM specification, this work presents a baseline comparison of relevant API calls as well as a productivity analysis for both implementations of the MST algorithm. Through experiments performed on the National Energy Research Scientific Computing Center (NERSC), it is found that the OpenSHMEM-based app has an average of 33.9% improvement in overall app execution time scaled up to 16 nodes and 64 processes. The program complexity, measured as a combination of lines of code and API calls, increases from MPI to OpenSHMEM implementations by ∼25%. These findings encourage further study into the use of distributed symmetric-memory architectures and RMA-communication models applied to both additional hardware systems and scalable HPC apps.

Keywords: MPI · RMA · OpenSHMEM · PGAS · HPC · MST

This research was supported by SHREC industry and agency members and by the IUCRC Program of the National Science Foundation under Grant No. CNS-1738783.

S. Poole et al. (Eds.): OpenSHMEM 2021, LNCS 13159, pp. 3–20, 2022.
https://doi.org/10.1007/978-3-031-04888-3_1

1 Introduction

To maximize parallel processing and acceleration, programmers must minimize overhead and synchronization bottlenecks. For distributed-memory systems the current standard is the Message Passing Interface (MPI) due to its ubiquity and support of many communication methods. Using handshake-based point-to-point *send* and *receive* calls and primitive collectives like *broadcast* and *gather*, MPI supports parallelization of numerous kernels and algorithms [14].

The remote memory access (RMA) model introduces new possibilities for further acceleration of distributed parallel apps. Its support for non-blocking and one-sided communication patterns can reduce synchronization bottlenecks in MPI that stem from multiple sequential handshake communications. The increased flexibility afforded by RMA comes with added complexity, requiring the programmer to manually synchronize parallel processes independently to avoid race conditions and invalid memory accesses. Nevertheless, RMA models can lead to increased acceleration by minimizing communication bottlenecks and maximizing the amount of uninterrupted parallel computation for the target of the communication call [6].

In the last few decades, an older concept of distributed symmetric memory, or "SHMEM", has been revisited as an alternative to MPI, resulting in a new specification called OpenSHMEM. Utilizing a partitioned global address space (PGAS) and adhering to the RMA communication model, this specification attempts to support one-sided, non-blocking communication without adding extensive setup overhead or complex API calls. Many OpenSHMEM API calls are modeled after MPI methods, allowing for a low barrier of entry for parallel programmers while still affording increased parallelization [9]. This research contrasts the two-sided MPI specification to the one-sided OpenSHMEM variant, evaluating RMA acceleration benefits and quantifying any increased complexity or loss in productivity.

This comparison starts at the API level and then extends to the app level using a parallelized graph-processing algorithm based on Boruvka's algorithm [13]. The OpenSHMEM specification is applied to an existing MPI implementation of the algorithm and directly compared. A focus on overall execution time and productivity provides a basic framework for the continued study and development of the OpenSHMEM specification at multiple levels of complexity.

In summary, this research contributes:

- An evaluation of OpenSHMEM API calls based on existing distributed-communication standards.
- A discussion of OpenSHMEM programming techniques that lead to parallel acceleration and corresponding levels of increased complexity.
- Analysis of OpenSHMEM optimizations on a Parallel MST app.

2 Background

The core of this research focuses on evaluating productivity and performance of parallel communication libraries with distributed apps. The concepts presented in this section illustrate the scope of the app with respect to that goal.

2.1 PGAS

To take advantage of the benefits of both shared-memory and distributed-memory architectures, the PGAS model implements a global address space, local and remote data storage, one-sided communication, and distributed data structures [15]. Global addressing allows individual processors to simultaneously access the same spot in symmetric memory. This one-sided communication leads to increased programming flexibility and communication-computation overlap. But not everything can be stored in symmetric memory. Data stored locally (in "private" memory) can be more rapidly accessed, forcing programmers to decide what data needs to be remotely accessible and what can be kept local. This decision point creates an efficient compromise between performance and ease of access at the expense of more vigilant design [15]. Support for distributed data structures allows more data to be stored, opening the door for complex program compatibility.

2.2 SHMEM

In 2010, SHMEM was standardized into the OpenSHMEM specification by the PGAS community, unifying development efforts and expanding its viability for widespread use [3]. Analogous to the popular MPI specification, OpenSHMEM universalized functions and standardized important aspects of the model including types, collectives, API-call structure and communication protocols. OpenSHMEM has been supported across numerous platforms by multiple libraries, including Cray SHMEM, OSHMEM, and SHMEM-UCX.

2.3 Minimum Spanning Tree

The baseline algorithm used for this research is Boruvka's algorithm, one of the simplest and oldest MST solutions. It starts with multiple small components composed of individual vertices and their lowest-weight edges. These small components are then merged along their lightest available edges to form larger components. This process continues until only a single component remains, which is the MST [2]. The bottom-up nature of this algorithm makes it amenable to parallelization, since vertices can be separately tracked by different processors, and computation can be distributed. The time complexity of Boruvka's algorithm can be improved through utilization of clever data structures and parallelization [11].

3 Related Research

The OpenSHMEM specification has been explored on the API and app levels, including graph processing. This research extends this investigation by analyzing the specification on both levels for an MST graph-processing app, and evaluating the impact on productivity.

3.1 OpenSHMEM API Calls

Jose and Zhang tested OpenSHMEM API call performance across four different OpenSHMEM libraries, including UH-SHMEM (University of Houston), MV2X-SHMEM (MVAPICH2X), OMPI-SHMEM, and Scalable-SHMEM (Mellanox Scalable) [8]. They compared point-to-point, collective, and atomic performance on an Infiniband Xeon cluster, scaling up to 1 MB in message size and up to 4 K processes for collective operations. This work found that MV2X-SHMEM demonstrates consistently lower latencies compared to other OpenSHMEM libraries, as well as a smaller memory footprint per process. Jose and Zhang also compare the performance of two kernels, Heat Image and DAXBY. They find that MV2X-SHMEM again outperforms other libraries, demonstrating consistent execution time improvement that scales with number of processes.

3.2 OpenSHMEM Graph Processing

OpenSHMEM has been used for graph processing in other contexts, as seen in the work of Fu et al. [5] on "SHMEMGraph", a graph processing framework that focuses on the efficiency of one-sided communication and a global memory space. In order to address communication imbalance, computation imbalance, and inefficiency, the SHMEMGraph framework introduces a one-sided communication channel to support more flexible *put* and *get* operations as well as a fine-grained data serving mechanism that improves computation overlap. The resulting framework was used to test four large web-based graphs on five representative graph algorithms, finding 35.5% improvement in execution time over the state-of-the-art MPI-based Gemini framework [5].

3.3 Productivity Studies

To evaluate and compare the productivity of the algorithm using different communication paradigms, multiple metrics are needed. Measuring both overall lines of code (LOC) and number of communication-specific API calls strikes a balance between increased complexity and overall workload. Development time has also been used to measure productivity with HPC toolsets as seen in [16], but this metric is more subjective and difficult to measure and compare. The OpenSHMEM specification's growing similarities to MPI further legitimize these metrics, making a direct comparison of productivity more viable and informative.

3.4 Parallel MST

Work done by Yan and Cheng have developed a system to find minimum spanning tree data structures on distributed processors called Pregel [10]. This system is "vertex-centric", focusing on messages sent between vertices to keep communication simple and efficient [17]. Based on the bulk synchronous parallel model (BSP), Pregel was theoretically able to achieve performance improvements for graph processing apps by increasing the number of parallel communications that could simultaneously execute.

This approach has inconsistency issues due to varying vertex degree in large-scale graphs, leading to unequal communication backlog and bottlenecks. Two improvements were made in the form of vertex mirroring for message combining as well as the introduction of a request-response API, resulting in the aptly named Pregel+ [17]. Running Pregel+ against modern competitive graph processing systems like Giraph and GraphLab demonstrated the effectiveness of these two techniques, resulting in reduced communication cost and reduced overall computation time for the new Pregel+ implementation [17].

The algorithm used in this research is based on and uses source code from Panja and Vadhiyar [13], who describe the operation of the parallelized, distributed minimum spanning tree graph algorithm. The algorithm is explained in detail in Sect. 4.4. This research validates the algorithm's performance compared to Pregel+, and shows positive performance improvements for overall execution time on a scaling number of parallel processes from 4 to 16. This work was thus deemed acceptable for use as a state-of-the-art scalable distributed parallel algorithm.

4 Experiments

This section details the nature of experiments performed, data collected, and optimizations implemented. API-level experiments, app datasets, supercomputing testbeds, and MND-MST algorithm optimizations are examined in detail.

4.1 API Level

To frame and analyze results for a larger app, it is important to analyze differences of the baseline, API-level performance. This evaluation is done by directly comparing relevant API calls between MPI and OpenSHMEM. Point-to-point and collective communications are averaged over 500 iterations and these tests are scaled up in message size, with some of the collective operations scaling up in number of parallel processes. Microbenchmark tests for both MPI and OpenSHMEM are created by the MVAPICH project from Ohio State University, with some adjustments made to scale to appropriate sizes [12]. Point-to-point benchmarks were executed using two processors and scaling from 1 byte up to 4 MB in message size. Collective benchmarks were similarly scaled up to 4 MB, and the number of nodes was scaled from 2 to 64. All API-level benchmarks used one PE per node.

4.2 Datasets

The datasets used for the app consist of large web-based graphs formed by web-crawling [1]. Created by the Laboratory for Web Algorithmics, these graphs are undirected, weighted and have significantly more edges than vertices, making them ideal for large-scale parallel processing and MST calculations. Although not all fully connected, consistent MSTs can still be calculated effectively for execution time comparison. These graphs range in size from 1.8 million vertices to over 100 million vertices, with edge counts reaching nearly 4 billion. These large graphs have execution times on the order of tens of seconds, allowing for better detection of difference in execution time at scale. Execution times for MPI and SHMEM implementations can be directly compared because the use of different communication libraries have no effect on the way the algorithm is executed. Edges are still processed, removed, and exchanged in the same way, and various implementations differ only in the order and method of communication of edges and components.

Table 1. Graph details

Webgraph Dataset (E/V = Edge-to-vertex ratio)					
Name	Size (GB)	Vertices	Edges	Max deg	E/V
uk-2014	0.15	1.77e6	3.65e7	6.59e4	20.66
gsh-2015	4.70	3.08e7	1.20e9	2.18e6	39.09
ara-2005	4.90	2.27e7	1.28e9	5.76e5	56.28
uk-2005	7.25	3.95e7	1.87e9	1.78e6	47.46
it-2004	8.80	4.13e7	2.30e9	1.33e6	55.74
sk-2005	15.00	5.06e7	3.90e9	8.56e6	77.00

4.3 Testbed

All data was produced by utilizing 2.3 GHz Haswell nodes on the Cori partition of the National Energy Research Scientific Computing Center (NERSC), a U.S. Department of Energy Office of Science User Facility at Lawrence Berkeley National Laboratory. This supercomputer has over 2,300 nodes each with 128 GB of DDR4 memory [4]. The OpenMPI 4.0.3 and Cray-OpenSHMEMX 9.1.0 libraries were used for data collection. Each configuration of runtime parameters averaged execution times over 15 runs. OpenMP sections allocated 4 threads per node.

4.4 Algorithm

This research's algorithm is a parallelized version of the classic Boruvka's algorithm for finding minimum spanning trees, based on [13].

The parallelized version of the algorithm is split into four major parts: graph partitioning, independent computation, merging, and post-processing. During graph partitioning the input graph is read in parallel by each PE and divided into equal parts. The independent computation step allows each PE to run Boruvkas algorithm locally, while the merging step is used for clean-up of individual components and internal edges. The post-processing step combines all remaining components and edges into a smaller number of PEs, where a final round of computation can be done to construct the full MST. Please see [13] for a more detailed description on the algorithm steps and basic functionality.

4.5 Algorithm Variables

Runtime parameters including post-processing mode, MST Threshold, number of nodes, and PE count were tuned during data collection for optimal performance. Post-processing occurs after computation and merging, and was set to either "single" or "leader" mode. The "single" mode consists of having each node send all leftover components to PE 0 before final computation, while the "leader" mode splits PEs into groups of 4 for more parallel computation. It was found that the "single" mode led to better execution due to lower overhead, so all final data was collected using the "single" post-processing method. The MST threshold determined the point at which component consolidation and post-processing was performed, based on the number of new MST edges. This threshold was optimized to be 24% of the total number of MST edges.

Strong scaling was performed by altering the number of nodes and processing elements per job, scaling nodes from 1 to 16 and PEs from 4 to 64. NERSC nodes were limited to 118 GB per node, and 64 PEs per node [4]. Data for multiple node-PE configurations was collected to further evaluate the scalability of both implementations. Node-PE configurations were also influenced by memory limits and allocations, including that of the private heap, the symmetric heap (SH), and a separate "collective symmetric buffer" (CB) used for SHMEM collective communications. The two symmetric buffers were set before running jobs and were allocated per PE. NERSC memory limitations for individual nodes coupled with large graph sizes required fine-tuning of these parameters for optimal execution. Some failures resulted from symmetric memory (heap and the collective buffer) that was too small to handle communication volume, while others were caused by over-allocation that infringed on private memory. Some node-PE configurations were even rendered impossible, as there wasn't enough memory available to support both symmetric memory for communication and private memory for graph data storage. Webgraphs that were larger in size like the uk-2005 graph tended to require larger symmetric heap sizes to execute properly.

4.6 SHMEM Optimizations

A number of techniques are used to optimize the OpenSHMEM-based app beyond simple one-to-one API call replacement. By leveraging partitioning, non-blocking communication and RMA, SHMEM enables programmers to reduce communication overhead and accelerate parallel execution without introducing overwhelming complexity. The first major OpenSHMEM optimization occurs during the exchanging of ghost information after independent computation, including external vertices and their corresponding edges. In the baseline MPI approach, this step consists of a series of handshake *MPI_send* and *MPI_recv* calls, first exchanging the message size before sending the full data structure of vertices and ghost edges to be updated. Each PE then locally updates the corresponding data structure to reflect changes in component sizes.

This relatively straightforward communication can be improved with the use of OpenSHMEM. First, the message size can be sent using one-sided *put* and *get* operations followed by a *shmem_wait_until* synchronization API call. The message size is used for data partitioning. These communications allow each PE to operate independently while sending the message size, which leads to more efficient execution. Second, the ghost information can be communicated via RMA without the need for any synchronization which eliminates handshaking overhead and slowdown from synchronization.

Finally, the OpenSHMEM implementation takes advantage of partitioning, which is essentially overlapping communication and computation. Although the message size communication is relatively small (only a single int or long data value), the ghost information itself can consist of thousands or even tens of thousands of edges. Such a large message can be divided and sent between PEs in chunks, each overlapped with the updating of the local PE data structure. Rather than using a single *get* operation to send the entire message, a non-blocking *get* operation of a smaller chunk size is executed. While the smaller non-blocking RMA operation executes, the PE updates the local data structure for the previous data chunk. In this way communication and computation are overlapped by using a *shmem_quiet* for synchronization.

The other prime target for OpenSHMEM optimization is the exchanging of component data during the merging step. In the MPI implementation, sizes of exchanged vertices and edges are communicated for each pair of processors. These sizes are then used to exchange portions of several different data structures between the pair of processors using a series of synchronous send-receive communications. The OpenSHMEM implementation avoids the handshake overhead entirely by using non-blocking communication calls as well as RMA, which allows each PE to operate independently and retrieve the required information simultaneously. Partitioning is also used to overlap this communication with some of the ending data structure updating and copying. Used together, these techniques take advantage of the large amount of data that must be communicated between PEs and overlaps it with data structure update overhead to maximize uninterrupted computation. The original MPI algorithm uses blocking communication with no overlap, so both PEs must communicate all data before running computation. The optimized OpenSHMEM implementation uses non-blocking communication-computation overlap, with a pre-defined number of partitions. The data to be communicated is divided into equal chunks and communicated chunk-by-chunk asynchronously, with each communication overlapped with computation and later confirmed by a synchronization call (*shmem_quiet*). Although MPI and OpenSHMEM both have the capability for non-blocking communication and computation overlap, the OpenSHMEM implementation benefits from RMA communication calls and fewer lines of code. Non-blocking two-sided MPI also requires the use of additional *MPI_Request* and *MPI_Status* objects for synchronization, which adds overhead.

These same techniques are applied to the post-processing step of the algorithm. Data structures are gathered and combined in a similar manner to the merge step, except that they are gathered into a smaller number of PEs for final computation. For the baseline MPI implementation, all communications require handshakes between a pair of processors. For the "single" mode PE 0 must execute a series of send-receives with every other PE, resulting in a handshake bottleneck. The RMA nature of the OpenSHMEM specification allows each PE to simultaneously get data from PE 0 via a series of one-sided communication operations. To support these communications, the OpenSHMEM implementation adds an additional *all-reduce* collective call to first calculate address offsets. At the cost of an extra API call and an extra data structure, this technique removes the handshake bottleneck with PE 0 and allows this entire series of communications to execute asynchronously.

5 Results

All data collected are presented in this section, including microbenchmark performance and an app-level comparison of OpenSHMEM and MPI. Additional algorithm tuning data and productivity comparisons are also examined.

5.1 API Level

The results of the API-level OSU microbenchmarks executed on NERSC are shown in Tables 2 and 3. To provide proper context for the distributed MST algorithm, communication calls that are most often used in the algorithm are presented in these tables, including *get*, *put*, *all-reduce*, and *barrier-all* operations. To compare one-sided and two-sided point-to-point operations, the MPI benchmarks run 2 two-sided handshake communications and then divide the round trip time by two. The barrier operation measures the latency for the indicated number of processes to call *barrier*.

For point-to-point calls, the OpenSHMEM *put* and *get* operations show comparable latencies at all sizes, with *get* operations slower at low message sizes and faster at high message sizes. This crossover occurs around a message size of 4KB. The MPI basic communication calls show execution latencies that are similarly comparable to both *put* and *get* communication latencies. At smaller message sizes (≤4 KB), *put* latencies are lower by an average of 0.091 µs, and *get* latencies are higher by an average of 0.531 µs. This latency gap widens at larger message sizes to 3.56 µs higher for *put* and 3.75 µs lower for *get* per operation, but is still a relatively insignificant difference for app execution time.

Table 2. MPI and OpenSHMEM microbenchmark data. Latencies in μs.

Point-to-point Microbenchmarks			
Size	**MPI 2-sided**	**SHMEM put**	**SHMEM get**
64 bytes	1.18	**1.13**	1.71
1 KB	1.46	**1.28**	2.09
32 KB	8.27	5.46	**5.13**
256 KB	31.47	30.73	**28.24**
2 MB	217.49	230.23	**212.70**
4 MB	430.84	461.23	**424.56**

Barrier Microbenchmark		
Nodes	**MPI 2-sided**	**OpenSHMEM**
2	**1.24**	1.48
4	5.16	**2.15**
8	7.12	**2.62**
16	12.72	**6.41**
32	13.10	**4.62**
64	14.48	**6.64**

Table 3. MPI and OpenSHMEM all-reduce. Latencies in μs

OpenSHMEM						
Size	**N=2**	**N=4**	**N=8**	**N=16**	**N=32**	**N=64**
64 bytes	5.20	10.70	13.99	29.41	26.27	29.30
1 KB	6.11	13.62	21.67	28.92	32.22	37.79
32 KB	18.59	47.79	72.73	95.59	93.05	101.88
256 KB	127.90	214.39	270.90	358.52	274.18	288.69
2 MB	974.60	1167.45	1456.71	1547.68	1454.02	1488.44
4 MB	1966.46	2342.73	2712.33	2876.35	3127.96	3070.97

MPI						
Size	**N=2**	**N=4**	**N=8**	**N=16**	**N=32**	**N=64**
64 bytes	1.36	5.52	5.60	9.06	13.59	24.06
1 KB	1.98	13.02	10.16	18.11	23.27	19.12
32 KB	20.69	171.23	82.76	185.84	280.24	432.05
256 KB	89.35	410.93	403.74	888.88	1113.13	745.60
2 MB	618.35	2994.57	3344.70	3774.10	2609.00	3459.31
4 MB	1217.65	5026.94	4760.20	4891.37	5215.68	4848.71

Collective operations shown in Tables 2 and 3 are scaled in message size and number of processes. The OpenSHMEM *barrier-all* latencies increase at a slower rate than the MPI counterparts, scaling by a factor of 4.47 from 2 to 64 nodes, while MPI scales by a factor of 11.66. The *all-reduce* latencies display more variation. At lower message sizes (≤4 KB) the OpenSHMEM latencies are on average 74.18% slower than MPI, but at larger message sizes are 28.7% faster on average than MPI. As the number of processes increases, the difference in latency between the MPI and OpenSHMEM calls decreases. There is an average of 111.8% absolute difference in latency from MPI to OpenSHMEM for 2 processes, but only 63.9%, 75.8%, and 71.5% average absolute difference for 4, 8, and 16 processes, respectively. In addition, OpenSHMEM latencies are higher than MPI counterparts for large message sizes (≥8 KB) with 2 processes, but are on average lower when running with more processes. There is also a range of message sizes (32 bytes to ~2 KB) where OpenSHMEM latencies are significantly larger than MPI, with an average percent increase of 118.3%.

5.2 MST Algorithm

The scaled execution time data for both implementations of the MND-MST algorithm are presented with raw execution times in Figs. 1, 2, 3, 4, 5, and 6. Data for these experiments was collected for all 6 webgraphs using NERSC Haswell nodes on the Cori partition, and was scaled up to 16 nodes and up to 64 PEs. MPI results are denoted by the blue bars, and SHMEM results are denoted by the orange bars. The yellow bar displays the best overall MPI performance, and the green bar displays the best overall SHMEM performance. As mentioned previously, not all node-PE configurations were executable on NERSC due to memory limitations. These are represented by blank bars.

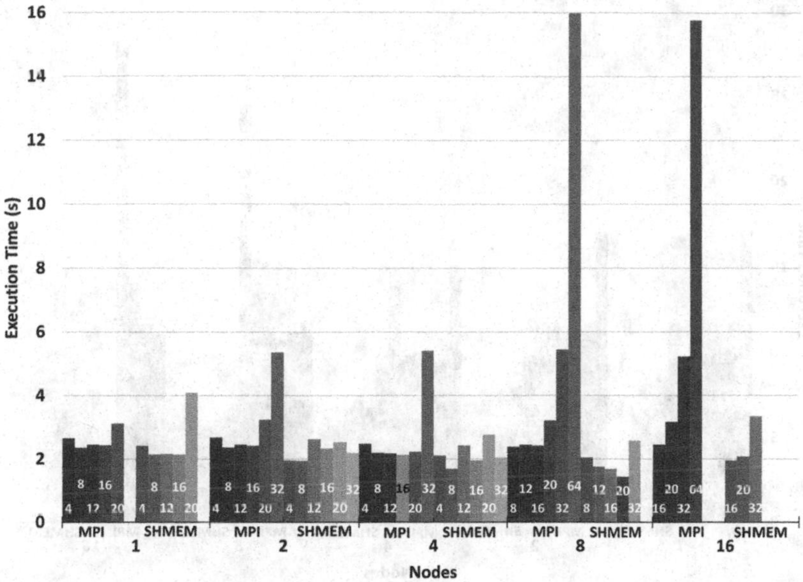

Fig. 1. MPI vs. OpenSHMEM performance for the uk-2014 webgraph. Bar labels denote PEs. Blue = MPI, Yellow = Best MPI, Orange = SHMEM, Green = Best SHMEM. (Color figure online)

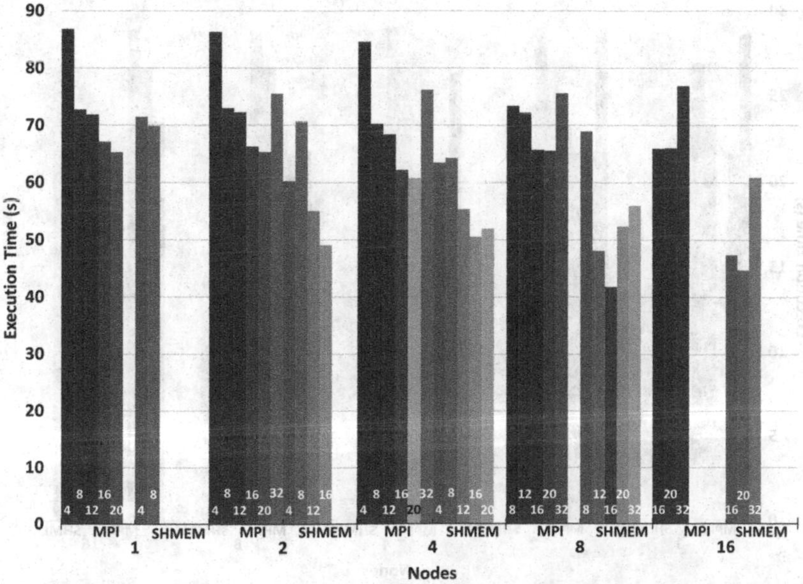

Fig. 2. MPI vs OpenSHMEM performance for the gsh-2015 webgraph. Bar labels denote PEs. Blue = MPI, Yellow = Best MPI, Orange = SHMEM, Green = Best SHMEM. (Color figure online)

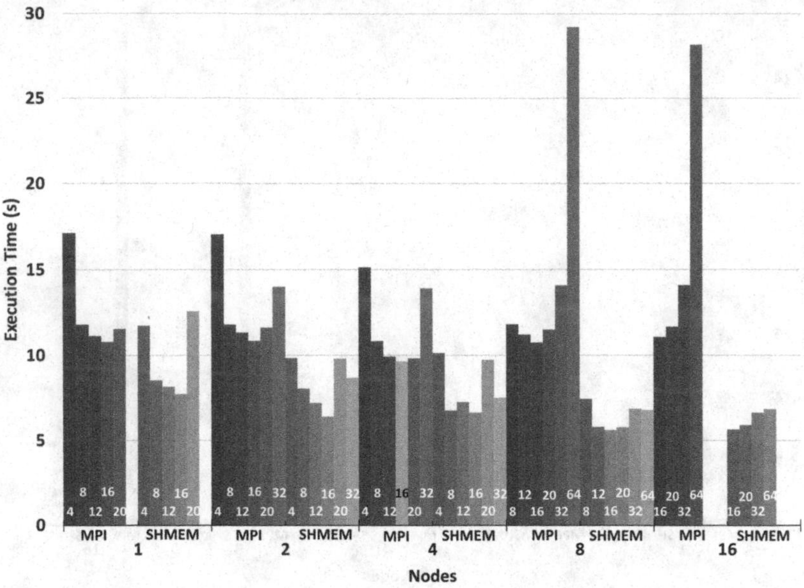

Fig. 3. MPI vs. OpenSHMEM performance for the ara-2005 webgraph. Bar labels denote PEs. Blue = MPI, Yellow = Best MPI, Orange = SHMEM, Green = Best SHMEM. (Color figure online)

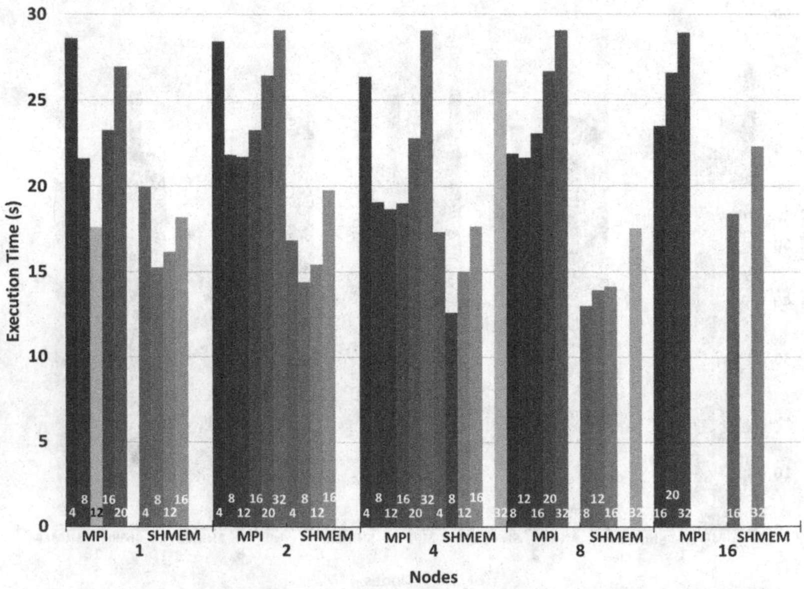

Fig. 4. MPI vs. OpenSHMEM performance for the uk-2005 webgraph. Bar labels denote PEs. Blue = MPI, Yellow = Best MPI, Orange = SHMEM, Green = Best SHMEM. (Color figure online)

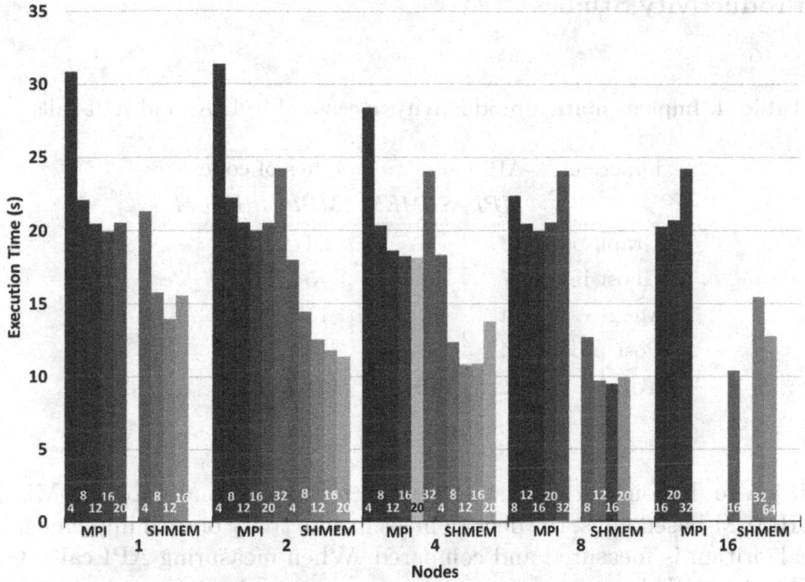

Fig. 5. MPI vs. OpenSHMEM performance for the it-2004 webgraph. Bar labels denote PEs. Blue = MPI, Yellow = Best MPI, Orange = SHMEM, Green = Best SHMEM. (Color figure online)

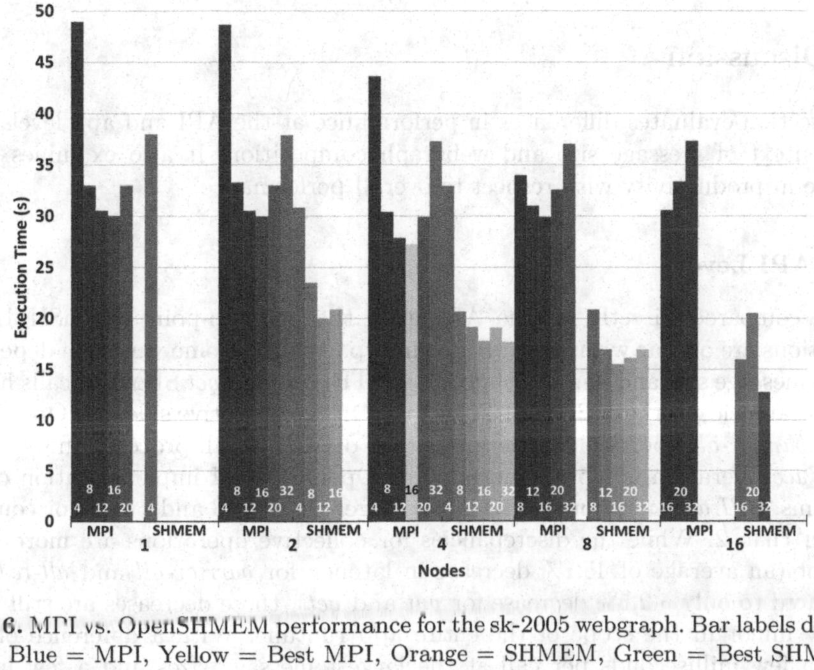

Fig. 6. MPI vs. OpenSHMEM performance for the sk-2005 webgraph. Bar labels denote PEs. Blue = MPI, Yellow = Best MPI, Orange = SHMEM, Green = Best SHMEM. (Color figure online)

5.3 Productivity Studies

Table 4. Implementation productivity, measured in LOC and API-calls.

Function	API calls		Lines of code	
	MPI	*SHMEM*	*MPI*	*SHMEM*
Graph part	3	6	247	273
Ghost info	7	12	54	91
Merge	14	25	117	185
Post proc	24	29	128	160
Total	**82**	**110**	**1188**	**1402**

In addition to demonstrating scaling and performance results for the MPI and OpenSHMEM-based apps, the development productivity of each implementation of the algorithm is measured and compared. When measuring API calls, OpenSHMEM and MPI share a common setup structure each with corresponding *init* and *finalize* calls. For the sake of simplicity, these along with *shmem_malloc* and *shmem_free* calls are ignored in API counts to avoid dilution. The OpenSHMEM-based app shows an increase in LOC by 18.01%, and an increase in API calls by 34.15% as shown in Table 4.

6 Discussion

This section evaluates differences in performance at the API and app levels, in the context of message size and webgraph composition. It also examines the change in productivity with respect to overall performance.

6.1 API Level

When compared directly on the API-level, the point-to-point OpenSHMEM operations are on-par with their MPI counterparts, with some variation depending on message size and number of processes. The *put* and *get* SHMEM calls have similar latencies to the MPI Send-Recv pair. On the collective side, the OpenSHMEM *barrier-all* operation outperforms that of MPI for all process counts. The *all-reduce* operation is more nuanced. The OpenSHMEM implementation outperforms *MPI_allreduce* for message sizes larger than 4KB and processor counts greater than 2. While the discrepancies for collective operations are more significant (an average of 45.1% decrease in latency for *barrier-all* and *all-reduce* compared to only ~2.5% decrease for *put* and *get*), these decreases are still relatively minor in the scope of the entire app runtime. With a difference of at most a few milliseconds per call at the largest message sizes and a few hundred API calls in the entire app at runtime, the performance improvement from

SHMEM API calls is on average less than 2% of the total execution time. This minor improvement alone isn't enough to justify an increase in programming complexity that comes with the OpenSHMEM specification. Instead, it is the combination of one-sided and non-blocking communication patterns with strategic programming techniques that lead to concrete, noticeable speedup over MPI.

6.2 Productivity Studies

The use of communication-computation overlapping techniques and flexible one-sided communication patterns comes with additional program complexity, demonstrated by the ~34% increase in API-calls and ~18% increase in LOC for the OpenSHMEM implementation. To combine these metrics into a single result, we averaged both increases to find a combined increased complexity of ~25%. To produce significant performance improvement and justify this increase in complexity, these programming paradigms must also be thoroughly understood and implemented by the programmer, with the added risk of manual synchronization.

It is important to note that a portion of this increase can be attributed to the use of custom MPI types which are currently not supported by OpenSHMEM. Due to the "shmem_TYPE_OP()" format of SHMEM calls, certain lines were doubled to ensure that the right datatype was being used. Another portion of the increased overhead is caused by the use of "pWrk" and "pSync", two array data structures used to perform certain OpenSHMEM communications including many collective operations [3].

The majority of the differences in productivity can be attributed to the merge and post-processing portions of the algorithm, due to the high number of communication operations present. In addition, the optimized OpenSHMEM-based app uses partitioning and non-blocking communication, which adds additional complexity in the form of synchronization calls (*shmem_barrier* and *shmem_quiet*).

Finally, certain symmetric variables and data structures had to be introduced to keep symmetric memory locations consistent between processors. With MPI, variables of the same name are stored in separate locations across processors and can thus be of different sizes. However, any pointer or variable declared in the symmetric memory must be the same size across every PE to avoid invalid accesses. For this reason, new "maximum value" variables were introduced to ensure symmetric variables had consistent sizes across PEs, which had to be calculated via collective communication. This addition introduced more overhead in the form of additional API calls as well as lines of code.

One drawback of using OpenSHMEM is that the OpenSHMEM specification version 1.4 only supports "to-all" communication for many collective API-calls, meaning all processes receive data from every communication [9]. This fact is due to the use of the symmetric heap present across all PEs, and leads to more overhead for corresponding OpenSHMEM calls. In addition, performing any "to-one" collective operation equivalent to an *MPI_Reduce* or *MPI_Gather* must be programmed manually, using sequential point-to-point operations. As a result, all "to-one" communications in the algorithm were replaced with "to-all" communications, unless noted otherwise.

6.3 MST Algorithm

The changes in API calls alone do not provide a significant amount of performance improvement, and increase the programming complexity of the app. To fully exploit the benefits of the OpenSHMEM specification, the programmer must utilize strategic programming techniques, non-blocking communication, and RMA to maximize uninterrupted computation time.

The result of the added overhead and nuanced programming strategies is promising, with performance improvements from MPI to OpenSHMEM averaging over 30% for all node-PE configurations. Some graphs seemed to perform better with OpenSHMEM; the it-2004 and sk-2005 webgraphs averaged nearly 40% improvement in execution while gsh-2015 and uk-2014 showed an average improvement of 20%. This variation in performance correlates roughly with file size and number of edges, with the largest two webgraphs (sk-2005 and it-2004) showing the best improvement and the smallest two webgraphs (gsh-2015 and uk-2014) showing the least improvement. The correlation coefficient between average percent decrease in execution time and both file size and number of edges is 0.71. Performance improvement is even better correlated with edge-to-vertex ratio, with a correlation coefficient of 0.86. This improvement is likely due to the larger number of edges per vertex to analyze, which results in a larger volume of communication and more potential for performance gain from optimizations.

At all node counts, both MPI and OpenSHMEM implementations display the best performance improvement at either 16 or 20 PEs with the exception of the uk-2005 webgraph. When measuring percent decrease in execution time compared to the 1 node, 4 PE configuration, both implementations show optimum performance with a PE count of 16, with an average percent improvement of 28.46% for MPI and 32.94% for OpenSHMEM. The worst performance for both implementations is at 64 PEs, followed closely by 4 PEs. PE counts of 8 to 20 see more consistent performance improvement.

For node scaling, MPI shows optimum performance with 4 nodes at an average of 22.16% improvement, while OpenSHMEM peaks at 8 nodes, with an average of 37.48% decrease. These results are calculated relative to 1 node and 4 PEs. MPI displays worst performance with 16 nodes, while OpenSHMEM displays worst performance when using 1 node. With too few or too many nodes, graph data can either be too distributed or not distributed enough, resulting in extra communication overhead or inadequate parallelization. The variability of scaling results is due to the partitioning of the graphs by the processes, and is highly dependent on the format of the graph itself. While some graphs are amenable to more PEs and increased vertex subdivision, other graphs might not be able to mask the increased communication overhead with independent computation or data partitioning.

7 Conclusions

At the app level, PGAS communication models such as OpenSHMEM show promising results in terms of consistent scaled performance improvement, in spite of limited latency difference between API calls. Through the utilization of strategic programming techniques and flexible RMA communications, the OpenSHMEM specification demonstrated significant improvement over MPI on a parallel graph app, with percent increase in programming complexity equal to or lower than percent increase in performance. The performance improvement from MPI to OpenSHMEM also demonstrates positive correlation with increasing webgraph size and edge-to-vertex ratio, indicating that OpenSHMEM has promising scaling potential on HPC apps. As the specification continues to be developed, more complex communication schemes will be supported, increasing the range of apps and problems that can adopt this growing model.

This research provides a foundation for studying the OpenSHMEM specification at a higher level. The baseline API-call comparison provides context for evaluating the presented RMA programming optimizations, and the examination of productivity quantifies the increased workload for prospective developers. As apps and databases increase in scale, distributed-computing systems will become even more prominent. In turn, the OpenSHMEM specification will continue to grow in viability as a means for parallel performance improvement.

8 Future Work

The speedup displayed from using OpenSHMEM optimizations is promising, and scales well. It has presently only been applied to the baseline version of the algorithm which focuses on CPUs. Panja and Vadhiyar also describe a hybrid version of the algorithm, leveraging GPUs to achieve higher levels of acceleration, with the added cost of host-device communication overhead and complexity. There is significant potential for further development on this implementation. NVIDIA has recently released its own version of the OpenSHMEM library for GPUs, called NVSHMEM, which uses GPUDirect RDMA (GDR). This technology allows GPUs to directly communicate with one another, avoiding the CPU communication bottleneck [7]. In addition to the acceleration displayed in this work with non-blocking RMA communication, the application of the NVSHMEM library to the MST algorithm could lead to further latency reduction.

While NVSHMEM has not yet been applied to larger apps, it is our hope to continue to expand this work to the hybrid GPU algorithm, potentially combining OpenSHMEM and NVSHMEM libraries. This extension would more robustly explore the performance improvement potential of the MND-MST algorithm, and would combine two SHMEM libraries at a larger scale.

References

1. Boldi, P., Vigna, S.: The WebGraph framework I: compression techniques. In: Proceedings of the Thirteenth International World Wide Web Conference (WWW 2004), pp. 595–601. ACM Press, Manhattan, USA (2004)

2. Borúvka, O.: O jistém problému minimálním [about a certain minimal problem] **5**(3), 37–58 (1926)
3. Chapman, B., et al.: Introducing openshmem: shmem for the PGAS community. In: Proceedings of the Fourth Conference on Partitioned Global Address Space Programming Model. PGAS 2010, Association for Computing Machinery, New York, NY, USA (2010). https://doi.org/10.1145/2020373.2020375
4. Friesen, B.: Cori system - nersc documentation (2020). https://docs.nersc.gov/systems/cori/
5. Fu, H., Gorentla Venkata, M., Salman, S., Imam, N., Yu, W.: Shmemgraph: efficient and balanced graph processing using one-sided communication. In: 2018 18th IEEE/ACM International Symposium on Cluster, Cloud and Grid Computing (CCGRID), pp. 513–522 (2018). https://doi.org/10.1109/CCGRID.2018.00078
6. Gropp, W.D., Thakur, R.: Revealing the performance of MPI RMA implementations. In: Cappello, F., Herault, T., Dongarra, J. (eds.) Recent Advances in Parallel Virtual Machine and Message Passing Interface, pp. 272–280. Springer, Heidelberg (2007)
7. Hsu, C.H., Imam, N.: Assessment of nvshmem for high performance computing. Int. J. Network. Comput. **11**(1), 78–101 (2021). https://doi.org/10.15803/ijnc.11.1_78
8. Jose, J., Zhang, J., Venkatesh, A., Potluri, S.: A comprehensive performance evaluation of openshmem libraries on infiniband clusters. In: OpenSHMEM Workshop (2014)
9. Laboratory, O.R.N., Laboratory, L.A.N.: Openshmem application programming interface version **1**, 4 (2017)
10. Malewicz, G., et al.: Pregel: a system for large-scale graph processing. In: Proceedings of the 2010 ACM SIGMOD International Conference on Management of Data. p. 135–146. SIGMOD 2010, Association for Computing Machinery, New York, NY, USA (2010). https://doi.org/10.1145/1807167.1807184
11. Nesetril, J.: A few remarks on the history of MST-problem. Archivum Math. **33**(1), 15–22 (1997)
12. Panda, D.K., Subramoni, H., Chu, C.H., Bayatpour, M.: The mvapich project: transforming research into high-performance MPI library for HPC community. J. Comput. Sci. 101208 (2020). https://doi.org/10.1016/j.jocs.2020.101208
13. Panja, R., Vadhiyar, S.: MND-MST: A multi-node multi-device parallel boruvka's mst algorithm. In: Proceedings of the 47th International Conference on Parallel Processing. ICPP 2018, Association for Computing Machinery, New York, NY, USA (2018). https://doi.org/10.1145/3225058.3225146
14. Schulz, M., et al.: MPI: a message passing interface standard 2019 draft spec (2019)
15. Stitt, T.: An Introduction to the Partitioned Global Address Space (PGAS) Programming Model. OpenStax CNX (2020). http://cnx.org/contents/82d83503-3748-4a69-8d6c-50d34a40c2e7@7
16. Wang, G., Lam, H., George, A., Edwards, G.: Performance and productivity evaluation of hybrid-threading HLS versus HDLS. In: 2015 IEEE High Performance Extreme Computing Conference (HPEC), pp. 1–7 (2015). https://doi.org/10.1109/HPEC.2015.7322439
17. Yan, D., Cheng, J., Lu, Y., Ng, W.: Effective techniques for message reduction and load balancing in distributed graph computation. In: Proceedings of the 24th International Conference on World Wide Web, pp. 1307–1317. WWW 2015, International World Wide Web Conferences Steering Committee, Republic and Canton of Geneva, CHE (2015). https://doi.org/10.1145/2736277.2741096

OpenFAM: A Library for Programming Disaggregated Memory

Sharad Singhal[1](✉), Clarete R. Crasta[3], Mashood Abdulla[2], Faizan Barmawer[2], Dave Emberson[1], Ramya Ahobala[2], Gautham Bhat[2], Rishi kesh K. Rajak[2], and P. N. Soumya[2]

[1] Hewlett Packard Enterprise, San Jose, CA 95002, USA
{sharad.singhal,emberson}@hpe.com
[2] Hewlett Packard Enterprise, Bangalore 560 048, Karnataka, India
{mashood.abdulla,sfaizan,ramya.ahobala,gautham.bhat-k, rishikesh.rajak,soumya.p.n}@hpe.com
[3] Hewlett Packard Enterprise, Highland, NY 12528, USA
clarete.riana@hpe.com

Abstract. HPC architectures are increasingly handling workloads such as AI/ML or high performance data analytics where the working data set cannot be easily partitioned, or does not fit into node local memory. This poses challenges for programming models such as OpenSHMEM, which require data in the working set to fit in the symmetric heap. Emerging fabric-attached memory (FAM) architectures enable data to be held in external memory accessible to all compute nodes, thus providing a new approach to handling large data sets. Unfortunately, most HPC libraries do not currently support FAM, and programmers use file system or key-value store abstractions to access data that is resident off-node, resulting in lower application performance because of the deep software stack necessary in the data path.

The OpenFAM API treats data in FAM as memory-resident, and provides memory management and data operation APIs patterned after OpenSHMEM. In this paper, we discuss the design of an open-source reference implementation of the API, and demonstrate its efficiency using micro-benchmarks on a 32-node EDR InfiniBand cluster. We conclude with a discussion of future work and relation to OpenSHMEM.

Keywords: Fabric attached memory · Programming API · Disaggregated memory · OpenFAM implementation

1 Introduction

High performance computing (HPC) clusters have been traditionally optimized for workloads where the problem can be partitioned and parallelized. Increasingly, these clusters are being used for problems such as high performance data analytics or machine learning [1–3] where data cannot be partitioned easily. In addition, such workloads require very large working sets, causing an imbalance in the compute-to-memory ratios within the clusters [4, 5].

S. Poole et al. (Eds.): OpenSHMEM 2021, LNCS 13159, pp. 21–38, 2022.
https://doi.org/10.1007/978-3-031-04888-3_2

Emerging fabric-attached memory (FAM) architectures [5] provide a new approach to handling large data sets in HPC applications by supporting external memory accessible to all compute nodes over a high-speed, low-latency fabric. These architectures are enabled by the emergence of high-speed optical networks [6] and storage class memory (SCM) [7]. Although currently expensive, SCM offers the potential to significantly reduce the latency to persistence, thus allowing higher performance for applications that require large working sets. In addition, since FAM represents a separate failure domain than compute nodes, FAM-based architectures can provide support for reducing downtime and checkpoint-restart overheads [8] in long-running HPC jobs. Finally, by holding shared data in FAM, applications can reduce contention at the network interfaces on compute nodes, which currently have to serve data to other nodes when using one-sided operations.

Although there is significant effort in the systems research community to explore these architectures (see Sect. 6), most HPC libraries do not currently support FAM, making these architectures inaccessible to application writers. Programmers thus overlay file system or key-value store abstractions [9, 10] for data that is resident off-node, reducing the true potential of these architectures. In contrast, the OpenFAM API [11] treats data in FAM as memory-resident, and provides memory management and data operation APIs patterned after OpenSHMEM [12]. The API offers the following benefits to the HPC programmer:

- The API is natural to HPC programmers used to writing applications using one-sided operations such as those defined in OpenSHMEM.
- It allows an application to allocate FAM, and provides APIs to allow those allocations to be retained after the application terminates. This allows FAM-resident data sets to be shared among applications without the need to constantly move data to and from slower storage tiers, thus enabling much more efficient HPC workflows [13, 14].
- It associates access permissions with individual allocations to restrict sharing as necessary among users, thus providing user-level control over visibility of FAM-resident data.

In this paper, we describe an open-source reference implementation [15] of the OpenFAM API. We start with a brief review of the OpenFAM API, followed by the architecture of the reference implementation. We then present a performance characterization of the implementation by evaluating the time taken within the implementation for different operations. We follow with a discussion of some of the limitations we are working with, and relationship to OpenSHMEM. The paper concludes by describing related work, and a summary.

2 The OpenFAM API

We first provide a brief review of the OpenFAM API. A more detailed description is present in [11]. The API is targeted for use in a clustered environment where each compute node runs a separate OS instance, but also has access to fabric-attached memory that is addressable using a global address space. The API assumes a two-level hierarchy for fabric-attached memory: *Regions* represent large data containers, and have non-functional characteristics such as resilience or persistence associated with them. Each region is treated as a separate heap by memory managers, which can allocate *data items* within the region that are directly accessible by applications. Data items inherit the non-functional characteristics of the region within which they are allocated. Both regions and data items have access permissions associated with them to allow finer-grained access control, and can be named to enable different parts or invocations of the application (or different applications) to access a given region or data item as necessary.

Rather than exposing the global address space directly to the applications, the OpenFAM API uses descriptors (opaque handles) to address FAM. The methods in the API are grouped based on the following categories:

- *Initialization and finalization*: These operations include initialization, finalization, and aborting a running application.
- *Data path operations*: Data path operations include blocking and non-blocking versions of `get` (copy data from FAM to local node memory), `put` (copy data from local node memory to FAM), and corresponding `gather` and `scatter` operations. An additional API allows a copy to be made from one part of FAM into another part of FAM.
- *Memory mapping operations*: If supported by the underlying fabric, this set of APIs allow FAM to be mapped directly into the process address space and accessed by the CPU. Cache coherence is maintained among processors within a node, but is not provided across nodes accessing FAM.
- *Atomics*: This group of operations include both fetching (e.g., `fetch_add()` or `compare_swap()`) and non-fetching (e.g., `set()`) operations on FAM, with memory side controllers ensuring atomicity in case the operation is performed concurrently by multiple processing elements (PEs).
- *Memory ordering and collectives*: This group includes `fence()` and `quiet()` with semantics similar to those defined in OpenSHMEM. Unlike OpenSHMEM, OpenFAM only defines a `barrier` operation; other collectives are not defined in the API.
- *Memory management*: These operations include region creation, destruction, and resizing, as well as data item allocation and deallocation.
- *Query and access control operations*: These operations include the ability to look up allocations by name, and change access permissions for data items or regions.

Most methods defined in the API follow a consistent pattern for providing byte-level access to FAM-resident data, where local memory is addressed using local pointers while FAM is addressed using a descriptor, a byte offset from the start of a data item, and a length field specifying the number of bytes at that offset. For example, the `get_blocking` call is specified as

```
void fam_get_blocking(void *local, Fam_Descriptor *descriptor,
uint64_t offset, uint64_t nbytes);
```

Here `local` represents the address of the destination buffer in the calling process, `descriptor` is the associated reference to the source FAM data item, and the operation is specifying that `nbytes` be copied starting at `offset` from the start of the data item in FAM to the local destination buffer. Other methods follow the same pattern.

3 The OpenFAM Reference Implementation

The overall architecture of the OpenFAM reference implementation [15] is shown in Fig. 1. It consists of about 50,000 lines of C++ code (including tests). The implementation assumes that FAM is provided to compute nodes over a high speed RDMA network, and is implemented using memory servers, which serve allocations to applications running on the compute nodes. Applications are compiled with the OpenFAM library, and are deployed across the compute nodes as processing elements (PEs) using a workload manager such as SLURM [16]. The PEs treat the memory within the compute nodes as "private", while considering memory served by memory servers as "global." Once allocated by a PE, all other PEs within the application (or within other applications) can access data items from the memory servers using RDMA and atomics operations.

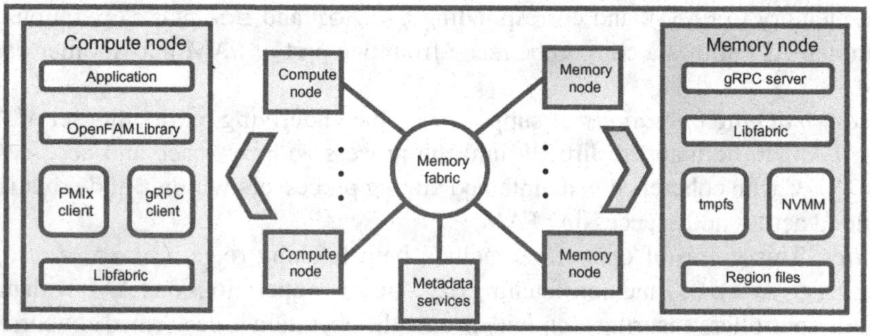

Fig. 1. Architecture of the OpenFAM reference implementation

The OpenFAM implementation includes a *client library* that is linked to the PEs, a *memory management service* that runs on the memory nodes, and two additional services (the *client interface service* and the *metadata management service*) that manage cluster configuration information and metadata required for allocations respectively.

The *OpenFAM client library.* The client library exposes the OpenFAM API to the application, and is used by the PEs to access FAM using libfabric [17]. In addition, the client library includes a PMIx client [18] to communicate with the workload manager, and a gRPC client [19] to communicate with the OpenFAM metadata services.

The memory management service. The allocated memory is served to the PEs from memory servers. The PEs interact directly with memory servers via the underlying fabric using RDMA for data path operations such as `get`, `put`, or atomics using the topology details available from the client interface service. The service currently supports several fabric interconnects including Ethernet, InfiniBand, and Omnipath. The memory management service hosts NVMM [20] and libfabric components. NVMM is responsible for creation of heaps, as well as the allocation and deallocation of data items. Memory-mapped files provide parts of OpenFAM regions that are allocated within a memory node for individual data items. For data path operations, upon validation of permissions, FAM is mapped from the memory server, registered onto libfabric and the key is shared with PEs. The PEs then access FAM in the memory servers directly using libfabric. The metadata management service coordinates region allocations across memory servers to enable regions to span memory nodes. In addition to serving FAM to the clients, the memory management service also supports RDMA operations among memory servers for operations such as `fam_copy()`.

The client interface service. The client interface service (CIS) provides a layer of abstraction between PEs and metadata and memory services. All PEs interact with the CIS for region and data item allocation, lookup and other metadata and memory operations. The CIS stores cluster information such as addresses for nodes hosting other services, as well as memory node information. This service minimizes the burden on the OpenFAM client to track and maintain cluster-wide configuration information.

The metadata management service. Region, data item, and memory server metadata information is hosted in the metadata management service. This service also serves as a resource manager. It provides a list of memory servers used for hosting regions. It also identifies memory servers when data items are allocated. Our initial design uses hash-based addresses for selecting memory servers when regions are created. In the future, we can also enable other user-defined selection policies. The metadata management service hosts the key-value store (KVS) used to track permissions and data item allocations. In the current implementation, the radixtree module [21] provides the KVS service, but other KVS implementations such as etcd, pmemkv or persistent concurrent hash maps can be plugged in if needed.

Depending on configuration parameters, the client interface service and the metadata management service can be co-located with the memory management service or run as separate executables. Examples demonstrating the use of the API as well as example applications (SpMV and PageRank) are available at [22] and [23] respectively.

4 Performance Measurements

The OpenFAM reference implementation can be configured to run on both scale-up servers and scale-out clusters. We next describe performance results (throughput and latency) measured for both blocking and non-blocking OpenFAM data path operations (`get`, `put`, `scatter`, `gather`), as well as for atomics operations using the cluster environment. We were specifically interested in scalability as memory servers are added to the system during testing. In each case, 16 single-threaded PEs were used to generate requests, while the number of memory servers was changed from 1–16. For large transfers, we measured the aggregate throughput as the number of memory servers increased. For small transfers and atomics, we used round-trip latency measurements, since they are more representative of performance. To reduce the effect of the network when measuring latency, the PEs and the memory servers were distributed in the cluster to minimize the number of switch-hops between the PEs and the memory servers.

The OpenFAM reference implementation can be compiled to turn profiling on and off. When turned on, each API logs the time taken within itself as the test is conducted. Once the test completes, the logs are used to compute averages, which are presented in this section.

4.1 Data Path Performance

Data path performance was measured using 48 nodes from a 96-node InfiniBand cluster. The cluster interconnect provides 12.5 GBps link bandwidth, and is configured in a fat-tree. Each node has 40 Xeon Gold 6248 cores (80 hyper threaded cores) with 128 GB memory, and runs RHEL 8.3. For data path (e.g., `get`, `put`, `gather`, and `scatter`) operations, tests were run using 34 nodes from the InfiniBand cluster. Metadata services were hosted on two nodes, and 16 nodes hosted PEs (one per node). The remaining 16 nodes were used as memory servers, and number of memory servers (1, 2, 4, 8, and 16) was varied within the tests. A single region was configured to span all memory servers, so data items could be distributed across the memory servers. The workload was distributed across memory servers using two configurations:

Even: For this distribution, each PE allocated data items equally on all memory servers, starting from a different memory server (in a round robin fashion) and wrapped around when number of PEs exceed the number of memory servers. Thus each PE concurrently accessed data from all memory servers. The number of data items and accesses were chosen to maintain an even balance across the memory servers.

Random: In this case, data items from each PE were randomized across memory servers. Because the number of available memory servers is small during testing, a random assignment distributes data unevenly across memory servers, thus resulting in an imbalance of workload on the memory servers.

Each PE allocated 112 data items (4 MiB each), and performed 100 operations on each data item. The average throughput was then computed from the instrumentation logs and reported in the tests. In the second set of tests, small transfer performance was measured by reducing the data item size to 256 bytes. In this case, average latency was measured instead of aggregate throughput as the performance metric.

Figures 2 and 3 show the total achieved throughput when the data items are allocated evenly as the number of memory servers is increased from 1 to 16.

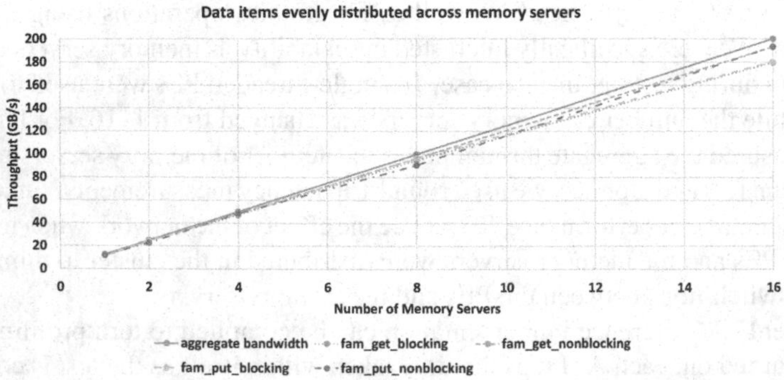

Fig. 2. Overall throughput achieved for put/get calls in the even configuration

The Figures also show the aggregate available bandwidth with the number of memory servers. From the Figures, we observe that the total achieved throughput scales linearly with memory servers and is close to the aggregate bandwidth (12.5 GBps × number of memory servers). For 16 servers, throughput ranges from 179.6 GBps for `fam_get_blocking` to 193.1 GBps for `fam_put_nonblocking`.

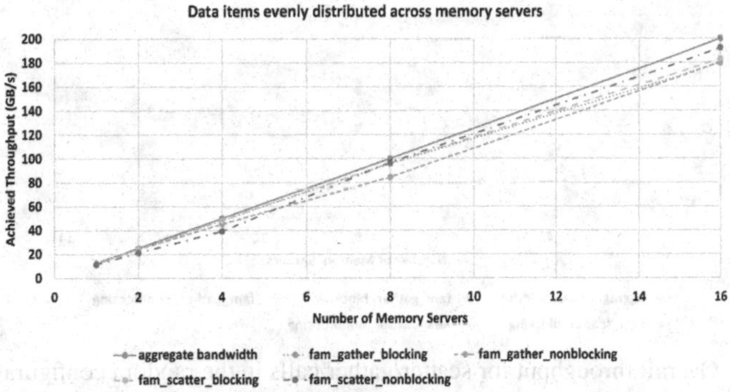

Fig. 3. Overall throughput for scatter/gather calls in the even configuration.

Figures 4 and 5 show the total achieved throughput when data items are allocated randomly across available memory servers. Again, the overall aggregate bandwidth available is shown for reference. Unlike the even configuration, we see a significant drop in aggregate throughput as memory servers are added, with a maximum throughput of 134.5 GBps for `fam_put_nonblocking` with 16 memory servers.

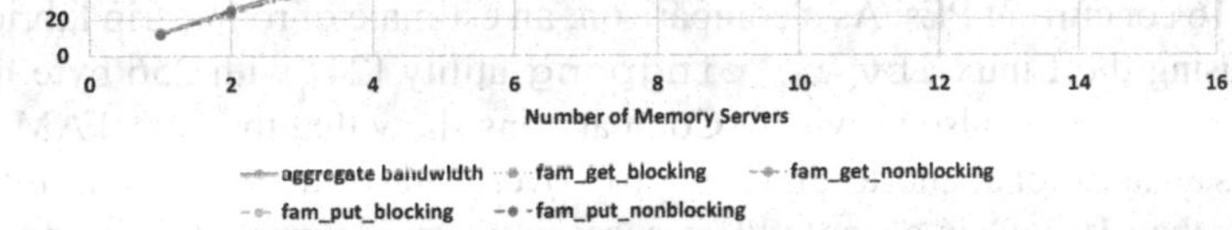

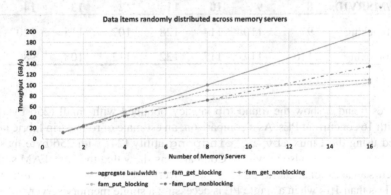

Fig. 4. Overall throughput for put/get calls in the random configuration.

Table 1 shows the number of data items allocated in each memory server with the random configuration for `get` and `put` blocking calls when 16 memory servers are used. It is clear from the table that there is a significant difference in the number of data items allocated (and hence the number of accesses) on different memory servers. Because performance in the implementation is primarily limited by the link bandwidth at the network interfaces on the memory servers, the overall performance drops because of in-cast observed by the more-heavily loaded memory servers. We see similar patterns with `gather` and `scatter` as well.

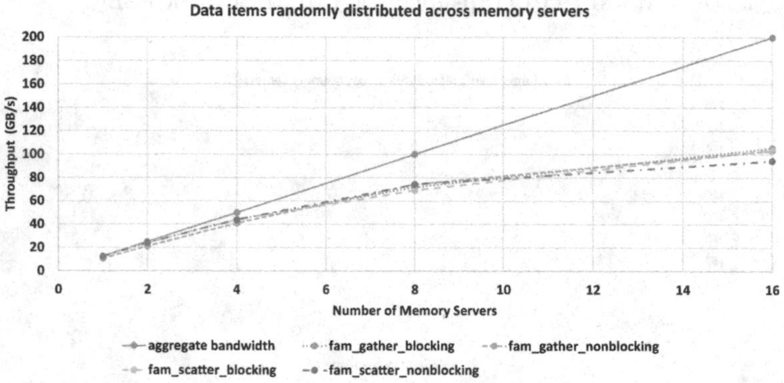

Fig. 5. Overall throughput for scatter/gather calls in the random configuration.

Table 1. Number of data items allocated across memory servers for random placement

API/MSRVIDs	0	1	2	3	4	5	6	7
get_blocking	100	112	130	101	113	121	91	128
put_blocking	105	101	116	114	112	112	107	129
API/MSRVIDs	**8**	**9**	**10**	**11**	**12**	**13**	**14**	**15**
get_blocking	97	110	114	128	107	115	120	105
put_blocking	110	117	117	122	112	108	98	112

Figures 6 and 7 show the round trip latency obtained with small (256 byte) data items with 16 concurrent PEs. As a comparison, an estimate of round-trip fabric latency (obtained using the Linux `ibv_rc_pingpong` utility [24] with 256 byte messages between two servers) is also provided. Comparisons show that the OpenFAM software stack incurs an additional end-to-end roundtrip overhead (primarily within libfabric) of slightly less than 1 μs when a single PE is accessing a single memory server.

We note that in all cases (including both the even and the random placement of data items) round-trip latencies are below 10 μs, and are comparable, supporting our hypothesis that the drop in throughput for random workload placement is caused by in-cast at the memory servers due to workload imbalance.

We also repeated the same experiments with different mixtures of `get` and `put` workloads, and found that the aggregate throughput is consistent with the above results when the fraction of `get` versus `put` is varied.

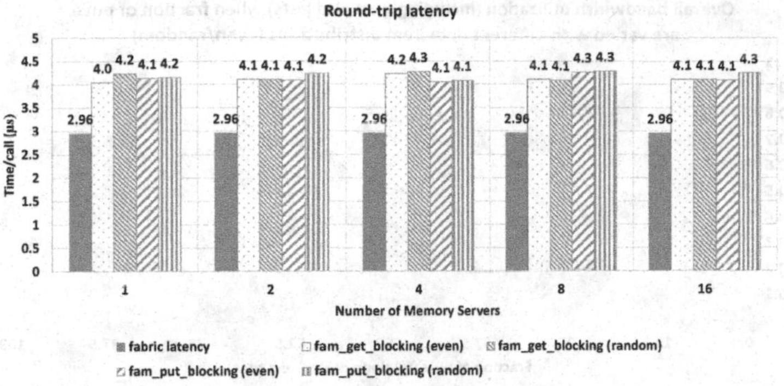

Fig. 6. Observed round trip latency for blocking put/get calls

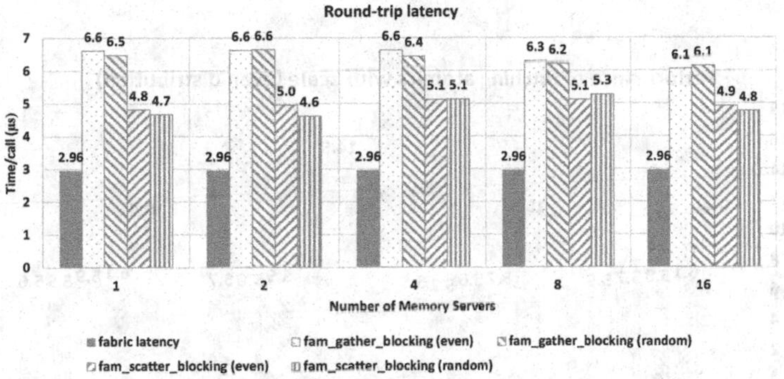

Fig. 7. Observed round trip latency for blocking scatter/gather calls

Figure 8 shows the aggregate bandwidth utilization (aggregate throughput/aggregate bandwidth) obtained with 16 PEs targeting 16 memory servers concurrently using 4 MiB transfers, while the fraction of PEs doing (blocking) `get` versus `put` requests is varied. As in the previous tests, the implementation achieves an aggregate throughput close to the aggregate fabric bandwidth when the workload is evenly distributed across memory servers. The random case, once again, shows lower utilization, but performance is better when the PEs are evenly balanced across `get` and `put` traffic, thus reducing the contention for the network in the random case.

We next measured the performance of fetching atomic operations. Results are shown in Figs. 9 and 10. Error bars on the graphs represent standard errors.

We observe that all latencies are below 10 µs, except the case when all 16 PEs are accessing a single memory server, indicating that the memory server is overloaded. For a single memory server, the random distribution of workload (where the workload is unbalanced) shows larger latency than the even case when the server is heavily loaded.

To understand the scaling better, we repeated the last experiment by varying the number of PEs accessing a single memory server concurrently. The results are shown in Fig. 11. It is clear from the figure that as concurrency is increased, latency goes up, showing additional contention at the memory server for atomics operations.

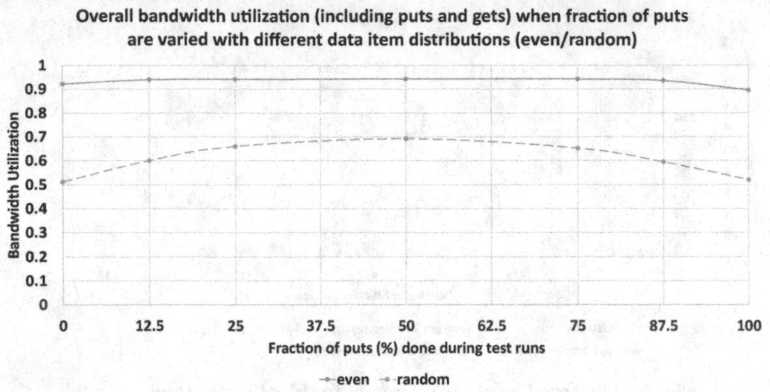

Fig. 8. Overall bandwidth utilization for different mixture of put and get calls

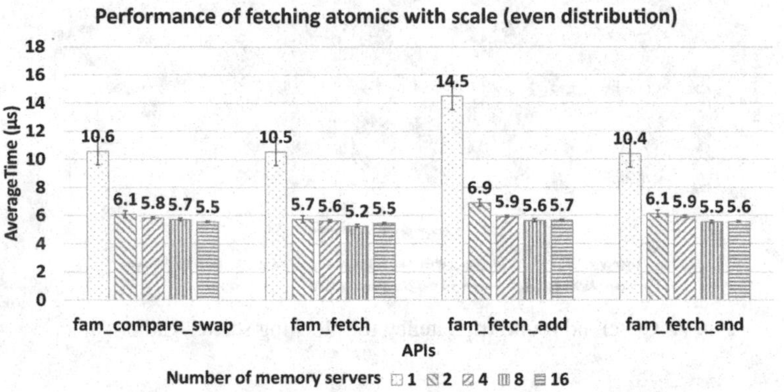

Fig. 9. Observed round-trip latency for fetching atomics with even distribution

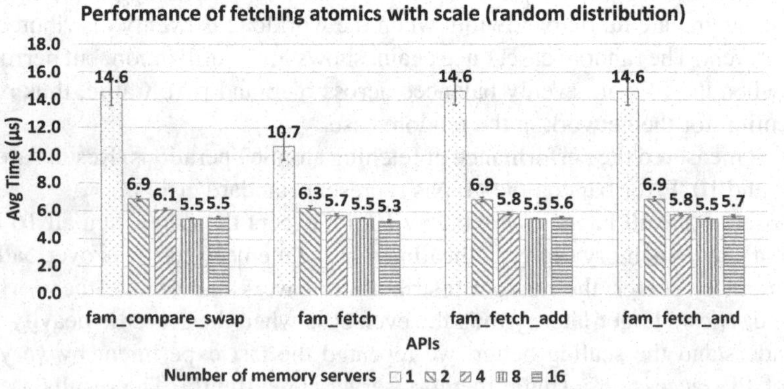

Fig. 10. Observed round-trip latency for fetching atomics with random distribution

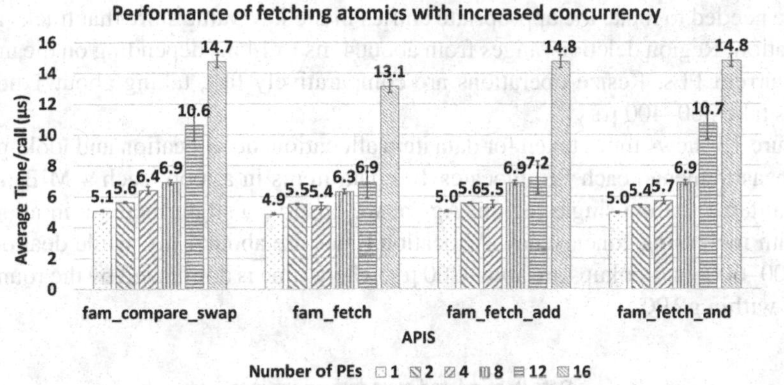

Fig. 11. Performance of fetching atomics with increasing concurrency.

4.2 Meta Data Operations

Metadata operations in OpenFAM include memory management operations (such as allocation and deallocation of data items, and creation, deletion and resizing of regions), permission management, and region naming and lookup. In this section, we focus on performance for the region- and data item-related memory operations associated with allocation and deallocation of memory, and lookups, since they are more frequently used in applications. We used OpenFAM in its scale-up configuration on a MC990x server with Intel Xeon E7-8890 v3 CPUs running at 2.50 GHz for these measurements. The server contains 11.13 TB of memory and 288 cores running Centos Linux Server 7.6.

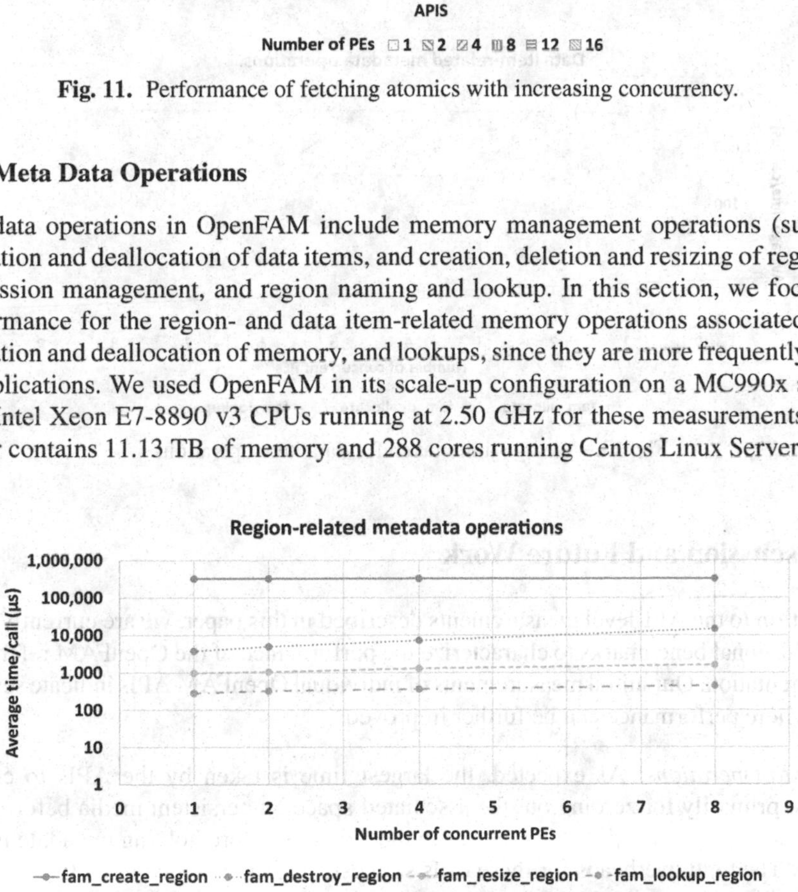

Fig. 12. Average time taken for region operations

Figure 12 shows the average time taken for region creation, deletion, resizing, and lookup operations. For region creation and deletion, each PE creates 100 regions, each 256 MiB in size, spanning 16 memory servers. For region re-sizing, each PE starts with a 1 MiB region, and increments its size by 1 MiB 100 times. We observe that region creation is the most expensive operation (~320 ms). The time is largely dominated by the time needed to make the appropriate entries in the key-value store that tracks region information. Region deletion ranges from about 4 ms to 14 ms depending on the number of concurrent PEs. Resize operations are comparatively fast, taking about 1 ms, and lookups take 300–400 μs.

Figure 13 shows times taken for data item allocation, de-allocation and lookups. For these measurements, each PE allocates 100 data items in a loop, each 4 MiB in size. All data items share a single region. Again, we observe a slight increase in allocation time with increasing concurrency. Allocation times are about 4 ms, while deallocation takes 400–600 μs. Lookups are about 300 μs, where time is dominated by the round-trip latency within gRPC.

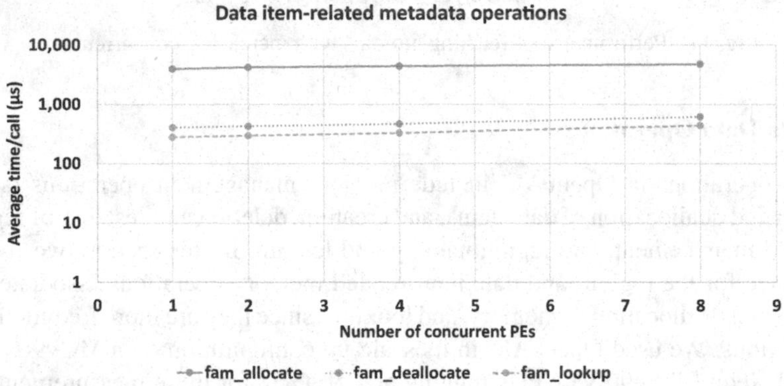

Fig. 13. Average times taken for data item operations

5 Discussion and Future Work

In addition to the API-level measurements described in this paper, we are currently running additional benchmarks to characterize the performance of the OpenFAM reference implementation. Our initial measurements of individual OpenFAM APIs indicate several areas where performance can be further improved.

Metadata Operations. As expected, the largest time is taken by the APIs to create regions, primarily for zeroing out the associated space on persistent media before files are memory-mapped and making entries in the key-value store holding metadata information. The high overheads for these calls suggests that the practice in HPC programs of allocating all space at the beginning of the application before the compute intensive parts should be followed when using OpenFAM as well. In addition, data item allocation requires several milliseconds, primarily to check for permissions, the overheads associated with nested gRPC calls, and the book-keeping required for tracking allocations. Currently, the library uses the default parameters for gRPC, which may require tuning. In addition, it is possible to also use two-sided APIs provided by libfabric to make the RPC calls much more efficient.

Data Item Striping. The difference observed by us between the cases where the workload is evenly balanced across memory servers versus where the memory servers are unevenly loaded (the random case) will most likely be reduced as the number of memory servers are increased. In addition, we are exploring how individual data items can be interleaved across memory servers in addition to regions. For large data items, interleaving may help improve performance in larger clusters.

Large Atomic Transfers. The OpenFAM API does not define atomic transfers for large data items. As part of the reference implementation, we have extended the API to add support for large atomic transfers, e.g., `fam_put_atomic()` [25]. These APIs take advantage of the fact that FAM is actually provided by memory servers, which have memory-side compute available. This enables the memory server to queue accesses to overlapping transfers from different PEs, and use reverse RDMA to complete the operations. Atomic transfers allow programs to automatically serialize overlapping requests at the memory server, and avoid torn reads or writes without requiring explicit locks or barriers. In addition, the queuing mechanism provides crash-consistency, where an all-or-nothing guarantee can be provided in case of failure during the transfer. While functionally complete, we are currently optimizing the code for this capability and will report on it in the future.

Exposing a Global Address Space. OpenFAM uses descriptors for addressing fabric attached memory instead of a global address space. While this has advantages in that it hides the details of the cluster from the programmer, it makes the API distinct from the remote addressing used in other HPC APIs such as OpenSHMEM. A programmer wishing to use both PE to PE communication as well as to access FAM within the same program has to be cognizant of the two different addressing models. We are currently exploring how FAM can be exposed using a single 64-bit address, thus making it simpler for the programmer to use OpenFAM with other libraries that use a PGAS model for addressing remote memory.

Co-existence of OpenFAM and OpenSHMEM. We are also exploring how OpenSHMEM programs can access FAM. OpenSHMEM provides guidelines to allow other APIs to co-exist with OpenSHMEM, and those guidelines can also be used to develop programs that use both OpenSHMEM and OpenFAM. The OpenFAM API drew heavily from the OpenSHMEM 1.3 API. Since then, the OpenSHMEM community has included the notion of teams to allow subsets of PEs to coordinate accesses to remote data. In addition, the community is considering proposals on memory spaces [26] to enable different types of memory (e.g., HBM or accelerator memory) to be defined within the OpenSHMEM programming model. While FAM can also be defined as a memory type, it fundamentally differs from remote memory defined in the symmetric heap, in that FAM is not associated with any PE, and one-sided operations on FAM from a given PE do not require any involvement of other PEs that "own" the remote memory. We are tracking the memory spaces effort in OpenSHMEM to understand how FAM may be supported using extensions to the memory spaces APIs.

System and Hardware Evolution. OpenFAM was designed to operate in the near-term using commodity servers with RDMA NICs as memory servers. However, given that the

API primarily uses one-sided operations, the CPUs on the memory servers are relatively under-utilized. This offers significant potential to optimize the memory server hardware using specialized NICs and memory controllers. It also offers the possibility of extending the OpenFAM API to support memory-side operations, which can further reduce round-trips over the fabric. We are exploring some of these choices for our future work.

6 Related Work

A significant amount of research exists on using distributed memory over RDMA networks, and associated challenges. Intel's DAOS [10] has been designed to work directly with persistent memory. At its core DAOS uses a key-value store abstraction, and can work with both SCM and SSD back-ends. Intel has layered a number of APIs on top of DAOS including a file-system API. Much like a distributed file system, DAOS has built in mechanisms for data protection and resilience. Like OpenFAM, DAOS does not directly expose a global address space, although one can be layered on top of DAOS. I/O extensions to OpenSHMEM are described in [9], which extends OpenSHMEM to support workflows that need to persist data among analysis applications. This work is close in spirit to OpenFAM, and uses extensions to the OpenSHMEM API by introducing file-spaces. Unlike OpenFAM, however, it uses a file abstraction for remote memory.

AsymNVM [27] provides another solution for fabric-attached persistent memory. In the proposed architecture, NVM devices (i.e., back-end nodes) can be shared by multiple servers (i.e., front-end nodes) and provide recoverable persistent data structures. The focus is on providing a framework where high-performance data structures can be built using FAM, and the framework focuses on data structure updates; crash consistency and replication; and data management.

Distributed Shared Persistent Memory (DSPM) [28] is a framework for using persistent memory in data center environments. Like OpenFAM, DSPM provides load-store capability to distributed memory with additional functions for naming and reliability. Unlike OpenFAM, DSPM is implemented as a kernel module, and provides mechanisms for transparent caching of memory pages. The key ideas are to integrate distributed memory caching and data replication techniques and to exploit application hints. Similar mechanisms are described in [29], where rather than paging, cache-lines are tracked and flushed to fabric attached memory to reduce the amount of network overhead and write amplification.

DeACT [30] considers issues when using FAM as virtual memory, and focuses on the necessary address translations required to do so. By defining fast caching of translations in a trusted kernel, it leverages translation units at a hardware level. However, results presented are based on simulations, and require hardware support for FAM. Remote regions [31] enables a process to export parts of its memory to remote hosts, and to access memory exported from remote hosts using a file interface. The abstraction provides a simpler interface to RDMA and other remote memory technologies compared to the existing RDMA verbs interface.

Megalloc [32] provides a distributed SCM allocator that exposes FAM as a shared address space on a cluster using RDMA. It is similar to the NVMM allocator used within

OpenFAM. Memory ordering and persistence in presence of failure is addressed in [33] by using logging mechanisms to provide ordering, atomicity, and persistence protection guarantees. Crash consistency is also the focus of [34], which explores different ways to organize distributed persistent memory and build data stores using it.

AIFM [35] considers APIs that enable application developers to directly allocate fabric attached memory, and provides a runtime that handles swapping objects in and out, prefetching, and memory evacuation. Swapping is done at individual application-level memory objects, rather than the virtual memory (VM) abstraction of pages. When AIFM detects memory pressure, its runtime swaps out objects and turns all pointers to the objects into remote pointers. When the application dereferences a remote pointer, a lightweight green threads runtime restores the object to local memory. The runtime's low context switch cost permits other green threads to make productive use of the wait cycles, which hides remote access latency and maintains high throughput.

Research has also explored distributed database systems that use RDMA underneath. For example, [36] reviews many existing databases and makes the case that RDMA networks move the bottlenecks to the CPU, thus making traditional replication techniques used in transactional databases obsolete. Clover [37] is a recent high performance key-value store that uses one-sided RDMA to persistent disaggregated memory for its operation. While OpenFAM's use of disaggregated persistent memory can be used to build a key-value store, or support multi-application workflows, OpenFAM was designed to access disaggregated memory using a heap abstraction for direct use by the application, rather than as a storage or database engine.

We may be able to use ideas from related research to extend the memory-mapped APIs in OpenFAM to a cluster environment, to provide transparent caching in OpenFAM for additional performance improvements, or to develop additional capabilities that expose disaggregated memory at a higher level of abstraction with OpenFAM as a substrate.

7 Summary

Emerging workloads such as machine learning and high performance data analytics are increasingly being deployed on HPC clusters. However, in many instances these workloads have datasets that are not easily partitioned, or are too large to fit within node memory. Fabric-attached memory provides an approach to dealing with such workloads.

However, most HPC programming models do not currently support fabric-attached memory, and programmers use file system or key-value store abstractions to access data in FAM. The OpenFAM API was designed for accessing FAM, and is patterned after the OpenSHMEM API. While it has differences from the OpenSHMEM API, it provides one-sided operations similar to those in OpenSHMEM.

In this paper, we describe an open-source reference implementation of the OpenFAM API, and present measurements characterizing the performance of the implementation. The implementation has been tested using scale-up systems, as well as on InfiniBand and Omnipath clusters. For an evenly balanced system, the implementation provides <10 μs round-trip latency for fabric atomics and short transfers, and aggregate throughput close to the fabric bandwidth for large transfers.

We are continuing to improve and optimize the reference implementation and expect to enhance it for scalability as well as to test it using more extensive benchmarks in our future work.

References

1. Wasi-ur-Rahman, M., Lu, X., Islam, N.S., Rajachandrasekar, R., Panda, D.K.: High-Performance design of YARN mapreduce on modern HPC clusters with lustre and RDMA. In: 2015 IEEE International Parallel and Distributed Processing Symposium, May 2015, pp. 291–300 (2015). https://doi.org/10.1109/IPDPS.2015.83
2. Ramirez-Gargallo, G., Garcia-Gasulla, M., Mantovani, F.: TensorFlow on state-of-the-art HPC clusters: a machine learning use case. In: 2019 19th IEEE/ACM International Symposium on Cluster, Cloud and Grid Computing (CCGRID), May 2019, pp. 526–533 (2019). https://doi.org/10.1109/CCGRID.2019.00067
3. Verbraeken, J., Wolting, M., Katzy, J., Kloppenburg, J., Verbelen, T., Rellermeyer, J.S.: A survey on distributed machine learning. ACM Comput. Surv. **53**(2), 30:1–30:33 (2020). https://doi.org/10.1145/3377454
4. Memory Bandwidth and System Balance in HPC Systems Archives. SC16. http://sc16.supercomputing.org/tag/memory-bandwidth-and-system-balance-in-hpc-systems. Accessed 21 June 2021
5. Peng, I., Pearce, R., Gokhale, M.: On the memory underutilization: exploring disaggregated memory on HPC systems. In: 2020 IEEE 32nd International Symposium on Computer Architecture and High Performance Computing (SBAC-PAD), September 2020, pp. 183–190 (2020). https://doi.org/10.1109/SBAC-PAD49847.2020.00034
6. De Sensi, D., Di Girolamo, S., McMahon, K.H., Roweth, D., Hoefler, T.: An in-depth analysis of the slingshot interconnect. In: SC20: International Conference for High Performance Computing, Networking, Storage and Analysis, November 2020, pp. 1–14 (2020). https://doi.org/10.1109/SC41405.2020.00039
7. Weiland, M., et al.: An early evaluation of Intel's optane DC persistent memory module and its impact on high-performance scientific applications. In: Proceedings of the International Conference for High Performance Computing, Networking, Storage and Analysis, New York, NY, USA, November 2019, pp. 1–19 (2019). https://doi.org/10.1145/3295500.3356159
8. Keeton, K., et al.: MODC: resilience for disaggregated memory architectures using task-based programming. In: Workshop on Resources Disaggregation and Serverless, April 2021. https://wuklab.github.io/words/
9. Grodowitz, M., Shamis, P., Poole, S.: OpenSHMEM I/O extensions for fine-grained access to persistent memory storage. In: Nichols, J., et al. (eds.) SMC 2020. CCIS, vol. 1315, pp. 318–333. Springer, Cham (2020). https://doi.org/10.1007/978-3-030-63393-6_21
10. DAOS and Intel® Optane™ Technology for High-Performance Storage. Intel. https://www.intel.com/content/www/us/en/high-performance-computing/daos-high-performance-storage-brief.html. Accessed 27 Aug 2020
11. Keeton, K., Singhal, S., Raymond, M.: The OpenFAM API: a programming model for disaggregated persistent memory. In: Pophale, S., Imam, N., Aderholdt, F., GorentlaVenkata, M. (eds.) OpenSHMEM and Related Technologies. OpenSHMEM in the Era of Extreme Heterogeneity. LNCS, vol. 11283, pp. 70–89. Springer, Cham (2019). https://doi.org/10.1007/978-3-030-04918-8_5
12. OpenSHMEM Specification 1.5. http://openshmem.org/site/Specification. Accessed 05 Sep 2020

13. Becker, M., et al.: Accelerated genomics data processing using memory-driven computing. In: 2019 IEEE International Conference on Bioinformatics and Biomedicine (BIBM), November 2019, pp. 1850–1855. https://doi.org/10.1109/BIBM47256.2019.8983296
14. Becker, M., et al.: Scaling genomics data processing with memory-driven computing to accelerate computational biology. In: Sadayappan, P., Chamberlain, B.L., Juckeland, G., Ltaief, H. (eds.) High Performance Computing. Lecture Notes in Computer Science, vol. 12151, pp. 328–344. Springer, Cham (2020). https://doi.org/10.1007/978-3-030-50743-5_17
15. OpenFAM. https://github.com/OpenFAM. Accessed 06 Sep 2020
16. Yoo, A., Jette, M., Grondona, M.: SLURM: simple linux utility for resource management. In: Feitelson, D., Rudolph, L., Schwiegelshohn, U. (eds.) JSSPP 2003. LNCS, vol. 2862, pp. 44–60. Springer, Heidelberg (2003). https://doi.org/10.1007/10968987_3
17. Libfabric Programmer's Manual. https://ofiwg.github.io/libfabric/. Accessed 05 Sep 2020
18. "PMI v2 API - Mpich. https://wiki.mpich.org/mpich/index.php/PMI_v2_API. Accessed 21 June 2021
19. "gRPC: A high performance, open source universal RPC framework. gRPC. https://grpc.io/. Accessed 05 Sep 2020
20. HewlettPackard/gull. Hewlett Packard Enterprise (2021). https://github.com/HewlettPackard/gull. Accessed 21 June 2021
21. HewlettPackard/meadowlark. Hewlett Packard Enterprise (2021). https://github.com/HewlettPackard/meadowlark. Accessed 21 June 2021
22. OpenFAM API Examples. OpenFAM (2021). https://github.com/OpenFAM/OpenFAM/tree/master/examples/api. Accessed 03 Sep 2021
23. OpenFAM Example Applications. OpenFAM (2021). https://github.com/OpenFAM/OpenFAM/tree/master/test/apps. Accessed 03 Sep 2021
24. "ibv_rc_pingpong(1) - Linux manual page. https://man7.org/linux/man-pages/man1/ibv_rc_pingpong.1.html. Accessed 21 June 2021
25. Large Atomic Transfer Library for OpenFAM. OpenFAM (2021). https://github.com/OpenFAM/OpenFAM_ATL. Accessed 06 July 2021
26. OpenSHMEM Memory Spaces. GitHub: OpenSHMEM (2021). https://github.com/openshmem-org/specification/wiki/Memory-Spaces. Accessed 21 June 2021
27. Ma, T., Zhang, M., Chen, K., Song, Z., Wu, Y., Qian, X.: AsymNVM: an efficient framework for implementing persistent data structures on asymmetric NVM architecture. In: Proceedings of the Twenty-Fifth International Conference on Architectural Support for Programming Languages and Operating Systems, New York, NY, USA, March 2020, pp. 757–773 (2020). https://doi.org/10.1145/3373376.3378511.
28. Shan, Y., Tsai, S.-Y., Zhang, Y.: Distributed shared persistent memory. In: Proceedings of the 2017 Symposium on Cloud Computing, Santa Clara, California, September 2017, pp. 323–337 (2017). https://doi.org/10.1145/3127479.3128610
29. Calciu, I., et al.: Rethinking software runtimes for disaggregated memory. In: Proceedings of the 26th ACM International Conference on Architectural Support for Programming Languages and Operating Systems, New York, NY, USA, pp. 79–92. Association for Computing Machinery (2021). https://doi.org/10.1145/3445814.3446713. Accessed 14 May 2021
30. Kommareddy, V.R., Hughes, C, Hammond, S.D., Awad, A.: DeACT: Architecture-Aware Virtual Memory Support for Fabric Attached Memory Systems, August 2020. http://arxiv.org/abs/2008.00171. Accessed 09 Nov 2020
31. Aguilera, M.K., et al.: Remote regions: a simple abstraction for remote memory, pp. 775–787 (2018). https://www.usenix.org/conference/atc18/presentation/aguilera. Accessed 02 May 2020

32. Yu, S., Xiao, N., Deng, M., Xing, Y., Liu, F., Chen, W.: Megalloc: fast distributed memory allocator for NVM-based cluster. In: 2017 International Conference on Networking, Architecture, and Storage (NAS), August 2017, pp. 1–9 (2017). https://doi.org/10.1109/NAS.2017.8026865
33. Giles, E., Doshi, K., Varman, P.: Bridging the programming gap between persistent and volatile memory using WrAP. In: Proceedings of the ACM International Conference on Computing Frontiers, New York, NY, USA, May 2013, pp. 1–10. https://doi.org/10.1145/2482767.2482806.
34. Tsai, S.-Y., Zhang, Y.: Building Atomic, Crash-Consistent Data Stores with Disaggregated Persistent Memory, January 2019. https://arxiv.org/abs/1901.01628v1. Accessed 12 May 2020
35. Ruan, Z., Schwarzkopf, M., Aguilera, M.K., Belay, A.: AIFM: high-performance, application-integrated far memory, pp. 315–332 (2020). https://www.usenix.org/conference/osdi20/presentation/ruan. Accessed 22 June 2021
36. Zamanian, E., Yu, X., Stonebraker, M., Kraska, T.: Rethinking database high availability with RDMA networks. Proc. VLDB Endow. **12**(11), 1637–1650 (2019). https://doi.org/10.14778/3342263.3342639
37. Tsai, S.-Y., Shan, Y., Zhang, Y.: Disaggregating Persistent Memory and Controlling Them Remotely: An Exploration of Passive Disaggregated Key-Value Stores, pp. 33–48 (2020). https://www.usenix.org/conference/atc20/presentation/tsai. Accessed 30 Oct 2020

OpenSHMEM over MPI as a Performance Contender: Thorough Analysis and Optimizations

Min Si[1(✉)], Huansong Fu[2], Jeff R. Hammond[3], and Pavan Balaji[4]

[1] Argonne National Laboratory, Lemont, USA
minsi.atwork@gmail.com
[2] Amazon, Seattle, USA
[3] NVIDIA Corporation, Santa Clara, USA
jeff_hammond@acm.org
[4] Facebook, Menlo Park, USA

Abstract. OpenSHMEM is a Partitioned Global Address Space (PGAS) style programming model for one-sided scalable communication over distributed-memory systems. The community has always focused on high levels of performance for specific communication operations such as RMA, atomics, and collectives and encourages native implementations directly porting onto each network hardware in order to pursue minimal instructions from the application to the network hardware. OSHMPI is an OpenSHMEM implementation on top of MPI, which aims to provide portable support of the OpenSHMEM communication over mainstream HPC systems. Because of the generalized functionality of MPI, however, OSHMPI incurs heavy software overheads in the performance-critical path.

Why does OpenSHMEM over MPI not perform well? In order to answer this question, this paper provides an in-depth analysis of the software overheads of the OSHMPI performance-critical path, from the aspects of both the semantics and the library implementation. We also present various optimizations in the MPI and OSHMPI implementations while maintaining the full MPI functionality. For remaining performance overheads that fundamentally cannot be avoided based on the MPI-3.1 standard, we recommend extensions to the MPI standard to provide efficient support for OpenSHMEM-like PGAS programming models. We evaluate the optimized OSHMPI by comparing with the native implementation of OpenSHMEM on an Intel Broadwell cluster with the Omni-Path interconnect. The evaluation results demonstrate that the optimized OSHMPI/MPI environment can deliver performance similar to that of the native implementation.

1 Introduction

OpenSHMEM is a widely used Partitioned Global Address Space (PGAS) style programming model for distributed-memory systems. As the fundamental principle of the OpenSHMEM model, the community has heavily focused on high

S. Poole et al. (Eds.): OpenSHMEM 2021, LNCS 13159, pp. 39–60, 2022.
https://doi.org/10.1007/978-3-031-04888-3_3

levels of performance for specific one-sided or collective communication patterns through explicit data transfer operations. The intent of the OpenSHMEM specification is to get to "close to zero instructions" from the application to the network hardware. For instance, each data transfer operation has the unique typed version (i.e., separate function for each basic type such as `shmem_int_put` and `shmem_double_put`). These functions embed the data type information as a constant value at OpenSHMEM library compile time. Consequently the library code can be highly optimized for each type without any type check overhead. Following such a principle, the community has developed native implementations that are highly optimized for different vendor platforms (e.g., SGI SHMEM, Cray SHMEM). Alternatively, some OpenSHMEM implementations tend to gain portability by porting onto low-level network frameworks (e.g., Sandia OpenSHMEM (SOS) over Open Fabrics Interfaces (OFI) and OSHMEM over Unified Communication X (UCX)). Nevertheless, these implementations still optimize for a specific platform (e.g., SOS/OFI is optimized primarily for the Intel Omni-Path architecture) and require the user to manually find the appropriate solution.

OpenSHMEM over MPI is the way to gain broader portability and vendor support. In fact, MPI is recognized as the de facto standard for communication on distributed-memory systems and supported by all major high-performance computing (HPC) vendors and common parallel computing platforms. More importantly, the MPI ecosystem covers powerful performance and debugging tools, all of which are now available for use in OpenSHMEM programs. OSHMPI [11] is the OpenSHMEM implementation built on top of the MPI-3 one-sided communication model (also as known as RMA). However, it is treated primarily as a functionality reference rather than as a serious performance contender. The general belief in the community is that such a heavy software stack (e.g., OSHMPI/MPI/OFI) often generates bulky communication instructions and may even cause significant performance loss.

Why does OpenSHMEM over MPI RMA not perform well? The primary goal of this paper is to answer this question through a detailed deep-dive and scientifically thorough analysis. From a high-level overview, we believe the performance loss can be caused by two reasons. First, many MPI implementations do not optimize the one-sided communication routines. Second, the MPI standard provides more generalized functionality than that of OpenSHMEM. The generalization makes various complex algorithms possible to write, but it comes with additional cost. For instance, a user can specify arbitrarily complex non-contiguous derived datatypes in a call to `MPI_Put`. MPI has to always check even if such a functionality is not needed, such as in the context of OpenSHMEM over MPI where only basic datatypes are used.

To diagnose all performance issues, we systemically analyze all instructions generated for the OpenSHMEM over MPI context. Based on the analysis, we further optimize the OSHMPI and MPI implementation to enable a fast path for the OpenSHMEM context while still maintaining the full MPI functionality. For any overhead that fundamentally cannot be removed, we recommend extensions to the MPI standard to enhance support for the generic PGAS over MPI scheme. We employ a refactored version of the OSHMPI library and the MPICH implementation with the `ch4:ofi` configuration to demonstrate the performance study. MPICH provides a highly optimized MPI implementation by reducing the software overhead and using techniques such as static builds and link-time interprocedural optimization (IPO) inlining. It enables a very fast MPI Put/Get path for both OFI and UCX [16].

To correctly capture and evaluate only the performance overhead of the OpenSHMEM over MPI approach, we compare our implementation with the SOS implementation of OpenSHMEM on an Intel Omni-Path platform where both implementations are built on top of the same underlying OFI framework. The experimental results demonstrate that the optimized OSHMPI/MPICH can deliver performance similar to that of native implementations.

Scope of this Paper: While OpenSHMEM defines several kinds of communication routines, this paper focuses on the fundamental limits in implementing the most performance-critical and essential RMA routines in OpenSHMEM on top of MPI RMA. We believe similar observations can be extended to other functions.

2 Background

In this section we compare the semantics of the one-sided models in OpenSHMEM and MPI and briefly introduce the design of OSHMPI as the reference OpenSHMEM over MPI implementation.

2.1 Semantics Overview

Both OpenSHMEM and MPI define the one-sided communication model. The semantics, however, have several key differences. We summarize the differences below.

Memory Exposure: OpenSHMEM defines the concept of symmetric data objects including symmetric heap and global/static variables. The symmetric data is remotely accessible for all processes. Unlike OpenSHMEM, MPI requires the user to explicitly expose a remotely accessible memory region called *window*. Each window object is associated with a *communicator* (i.e., a group of processes). This semantics allows the user to benefit from *communication virtualization*. For instance, a user can create multiple communicators with the same group of processes. With each communicator, the user can also create multiple windows for the same memory buffer. The communication with each communicator (or window) is fully isolated. We note that OpenSHMEM specification 1.5 introduces the teams concept that provides similar communication virtualization. In this paper, we focus only on the implementation of the default symmetric data objects.

Operation Expression: In OpenSHMEM, the RMA operation routines directly deal with the absolute virtual address of the remote buffer, and the data type of each operation is encoded in the function interface (e.g., `shmem_int_put`). The interface of MPI RMA operations has two differences. First, it requires the relative *displacement* of the remote buffer rather than an absolute virtual address. This was designed to meet the requirements of various networks, some of which require relative offset whereas others require an absolute virtual address. The second difference is that both basic data types (e.g., *integer* or *float*) and complex user-defined data layout (e.g., *vector* or *struct*) are specified as a datatype input parameter. This allows an MPI RMA operation to carry arbitrary data layout.

2.2 OSHMPI

As indicated in the semantics comparison, MPI provides more generalized functionalities than OpenSHMEM does. Thus, the one-sided communication of OpenSHMEM can be fully expressed by using MPI RMA. OSHMPI-1.0 is a reference implementation of OpenSHMEM 1.2 over MPI-3 [11]. As the basis of this study, we redeveloped the OSHMPI library to fully support OpenSHMEM 1.4 and released it as OSHMPI-2.0b1.[1] We give here a brief overview of its high-level design.

OSHMPI internally creates two MPI windows at OpenSHMEM initialization, one for symmetric heap and the other for global/static variables. Every process locks the two windows by calling `MPI_Win_lock_all` immediately after window creation. Thus, each OpenSHMEM Put/Get operation can be implemented by using the corresponding MPI operation followed with a call to `MPI_Win_flush_local`.[2] The `shmem_quiet` synchronization can be implemented by using `MPI_Win_flush_all`[3] and `MPI_Win_sync`.[4] At finalization, OSHMPI unlocks the internal windows on all processes and frees the windows before making a call to `MPI_Finalize`.

3 Related Work

In this section we describe the related work in the following three categories.

Native OpenSHMEM Implementations: The original implementations of SHMEM were native implementations directly on top of hardware such as the Cray T3D [5]. Subsequent native implementations included QSHMEM for the Quadrics Elan network [15]. Many SGI platforms offered an optimized native implementation of SHMEM, including ccNUMA systems. Cray SHMEM is the

[1] https://github.com/pmodels/oshmpi/releases/tag/v2.0b1.

[2] Flush_local locally completes all outstanding RMA operations initiated by the calling process to the remote process specified by rank on the window.

[3] Flush_all ensures all outstanding RMA operations issued by the calling process to any remote process on the window will have completed both at the local and at the remote side.

[4] Win_sync synchronizes memory updates on the specific window.

highly optimized native implementation for Cray XC and XK series supercomputers. It is directly implemented on top of the low-level DMAPP API. Cray OpenSHMEMX [13] is a OpenSHMEM specification version 1.4 compliant native implementation for current and future-generation Cray systems. On InfiniBand (IB) platforms, three OpenSHMEM implementations are commonly used. OSHMEM [3] is an implementation of OpenSHMEM API that is distributed within the Open MPI distribution. It is implemented on top of the low-level UCX communication framework. Scalable-SHMEM [2] is the native implementation for Mellanox IB and works with the OpenFabrics RDMA for Linux stack (OFED). MVAPICH2-X is the hybrid MPI+PGAS release of MVAPICH library and is highly optimized for IB systems [12]. On Intel Omni-Path systems, SOS [14] is the primary native implementation. It is implemented on top of the low-level OFI communication framework. Our analysis for the OSHMPI/MPICH stack utilizes the same OFI framework. Thus we choose SOS as the representative of OpenSHMEM native implementations and compare it with our implementation in this paper.

Other PGAS over MPI Implementations: MPI is often used as the portable underlying communication runtime of high-level PGAS libraries. Dinan et al. [7] analyzed the semantic mismatch between the ARMCI communication interface of Global Arrays and MPI-2 RMA and evaluated the performance of Global Arrays applications on the resulting implementation, ARMCI-MPI [1], on three different HPC platforms. Since the introduction of MPI-3, ARMCI-MPI is able to use RMA quite naturally, and the current implementation maps ARMCI's one-sided operations directly to MPI's. DASH [9] is a C++ template library following a PGAS-like programming model. DART-MPI [18] is a portable implementation of the DASH runtime based on the MPI-3 shared memory support and RMA operations. OpenCoarrays is a library that supports the Fortran 2008 coarrays PGAS model using MPI (and possibly other communication protocols), which is used by GCC Fortran today [8]. The Intel Fortran implementation of coarrays is based on MPI-3 one-sided communication [4]. Bonachea and Duell [6] analyzed the usage of the MPI-1 two-sided model and MPI-2 RMA for Global Address Space (GAS) languages such as Unified Parallel C (UPC) and Co-Array Fortran (CAF). Their analysis showed that those MPI-1 and MPI-2 models are unsuitable for GAS languages. Yang et al. [17] then demonstrated that the more comprehensive MPI-3 RMA framework can be used as the runtime of CAF with a broader goal of enabling a single application to use both MPI and CAF with high interoperability. All these previous studies focused on the complete functionality and high-level performance. In contrast, our work pursues more fine-grained semantics-mismatch and overhead analysis together with a comprehensive performance fine-tuning. None of these aspects are covered by previous studies. We also note that the outcome from our work may also apply to the other PGAS over MPI libraries.

Software Overhead Analysis: Raffenetti et al. [16] analyzed the software overhead of the MPICH implementation of MPI. Their analysis focused primarily on the instruction-overhead critical paths including MPI send/and MPI Put operations, and the optimizations were proposed for general MPI applications. In contrast, this paper focuses on the OpenSHMEM context that gives more restricted semantics than that of the underlying MPI layer, thus exposing different overheads and optimization opportunities. Our analysis covers both the instruction-overhead critical MPI Put/Get operations and the time-consuming synchronization routines. We note that our work is based on the MPICH implementation that includes all optimizations presented in [16].

4 Analysis of Performance Loss in Contiguous RMA

Although OSHMPI is functional, many of the generalized features of MPI are unnecessary for the support of OpenSHMEM and even cause performance loss, especially in the performance-critical Put/Get routines in comparison with a native implementation of OpenSHMEM. We demonstrate and analyze the performance loss in the rest of this section. We note that we present only the instruction analysis of the Put path, but the observations can be fully applied also to the Get path. Thus, we omit the description of Get.

Our analysis and optimizations are based on the OSHMPI-2.0b1 and MPICH-3.3[5] releases. OSHMPI-2.0b1 fully supports the OpenSHMEM 1.4 specification and enables function inlining for all OSHMPI internal routines. We utilize the `ch4:ofi` configuration of MPICH that provides highly optimized MPI RMA [16]. In the remainder of this paper OSHMPI refers to the OSHMPI-2.0b1 version and MPICH refers to the `ch4:ofi` configuration of MPICH-3.3 unless otherwise specified. To emphasize the extra software overhead caused by the MPI layer, we compare the internal implementation and the instructions of OSHMPI/MPICH with those of SOS 1.4.2 release as the representative of native implementations. Our analysis utilizes a basic latency scenario where one process performs `shmem_putmem` followed with a call `shmem_quiet` to the remote process. We discuss their internal implementations and analyze the overhead separately.

shmem_putmem: It issues a Put operation to the remote process, and returning from this function ensures the source buffer can be reused. In other words, the Put operation is locally completed. A native implementation of `shmem_putmem` usually consists of only a few internal steps. For instance, SOS implements this routine with two steps: (1) preparing OFI write parameters and making a call to `ofi_inject_write` or `ofi_write`,[6] and (2) waiting the local completion of the outstanding write by calling `fi_cntr_read` and `fi_cntr_wait`.[7] In contrast, OSHMPI/MPICH involves a number of additional steps, as demonstrated in Fig. 1. We separate these steps into three phases and describe each step below.

[5] http://www.mpich.org/downloads/.

[6] `ofi_inject_write` is used for data smaller than 64Bytes, and `ofi_write` is used for other data sizes. The latter only initiates a write to remote memory, but the former also guarantees local completion.

[7] `fi_cntr_read` reads an OFI event counter that is updated at operation completion, and `fi_cntr_wait` is its blocking version.

```
shmem_putmem(dest, source, nelems, pe) {
    translate_win_and_disp(dest, &win, &disp); // (1)

    /* nonblocking put */
    MPI_Put(source, nelems, src_dtype=MPI_BYTE, pe, disp, nelems,
        dest_dtype=MPI_BYTE, win) {
        win_get_ptr(win, &win_ptr); // (2)

        trans_rank_to_netaddr(pe, win_ptr->comm, &nw_addr); // (3)

        decode_dtype(src_dtype, &src_size, &src_contig,...); // (4)
        decode_dtype(dest_dtype, &src_size, &dest_contig,...);
        if (src_contig && dest_contig && bytes <= ofi_max_bytes) { // (5)
            prepare_ofi_write_parameters(...); // (6)
            dest_vaddr = disp + win_ptr->abse; // (7)
            ofi_inject_write(...);
        }
    }

    /* ensure local completion of nonblocking put */
    MPI_Win_flush_local(pe, win) {
        win_get_ptr(win, &win_ptr); // (8)
        wait_ofi_completion(...); // (9)
        target_ptr = win_find_am_target(win_ptr, pe); // (10)
        do {
            MPI_full_progress(); // (11)
        } while (target_ptr && target_ptr->local_cmpl_cnts != 0);
    }
}
```

Fig. 1. Pseudo code of `shmem_putmem` implementation in OSHMPI/MPICH

- *Phase-1: MPI parameter preparation.* The OSHMPI layer translates the `dest` buffer address to its corresponding window handle (i.e., either the window for symmetric heap or the one for global/static variables) and the relative displacement (step (1) in Fig. 1).
- *Phase-2: MPI Put.* It then makes a call to `MPI_Put` with the `MPI_BYTE` datatype. The implementation of `MPI_Put` can be further divided into six steps. It first gets the internal object pointer of the `win` handle (step (2)). The internal object is used to store window attributes such as the initial address, size, and displacement unit of remote memory regions associated with this window. It next translates the remote process's rank in the window's communicator to its physical network address (step (3)). The network address will be used when posting an OFI write. Because the ranks in each communicator can be arbitrarily reordered, the address lookup is an expensive operation. It then decodes the source and destination datatypes to obtain the data layout such as data sizes and whether the data is contiguous (step (4)). After that, it checks whether both source and destination datatypes are contiguous and other OFI conditions are met (step (5)). If so, it then prepares OFI write paramcters (step (6)), calculates the absolute virtual address of the destination buffer (step (7)), and makes a call to `ofi_inject_write` or `ofi_write` similarly to the implementation of SOS.
- *Phase-3: Local completion.* Because `MPI_Put` is a nonblocking operations, we need to issue `MPI_Win_flush_local` on the corresponding window to ensure its local completion. The internal implementation of flush_local can be broken into four steps. It first gets the internal object pointer of the `win` handle (step (8)). It next waits for the completion of any outstanding writes in OFI by calling a loop of `fi_cntr_read` and `fi_cntr_wait` (step (9)). It then checks

whether there is a target active message object associated with the remote rank (step (10)). This step is necessary for MPICH because some RMA operations (e.g., Put with very sparse noncontiguous data or Accumulates with a network-unsupported reduce operation) cannot be offloaded to hardware and have to fall back to the active-message-based approach. If the target active message object exists, it then triggers MPI full progress until all outstanding active messages on the target process are locally completed; otherwise, it makes the full progress once (step (11)). MPICH ensures that the full progress is always triggered in blocking communication calls in order to guarantee prompt progress for all MPI communication types such as point-to-point, collectives, and internal active messages.

Obviously, these additional steps in OSHMPI/MPICH generate a significant number of CPU instructions on the performance critical operation path. We used the Intel SDE tool to emulate instructions generated from the OpenSHMEM latency program statically linked with the OSHMPI and MPICH libraries and that linked with SOS. The instructions were generated with `nelem`=4 in `shmem_putmem`. Table 1 summarizes the instruction counts generated by each internal step of OSHMPI/MPICH (see the Original Count column) and that of SOS. As expected, OSHMPI/MPICH consumes more significant instructions than does SOS. The total instruction count of OSHMPI/MPICH is 333 whereas SOS consumes only 71, without counting the instructions of the underlying OFI library. We especially emphasize the instructions caused by the requirement of MPI semantics (rows are highlighted in gray), which are completely unnecessary for the SOS implementation.

Table 1. `shmem_putmem` instruction count analysis with parameter `nelem`=4. Gray rows indicate instructions caused by the requirement of MPI semantics. The others instructions in MPI and SOS are implementation-specific; we omit the description.

OSHMPI Internal Step	Orig Cnt	Opt Cnt	SOS Internal Step	Cnt
OSHMPI: calling overhead	14	16	SOS: calling overhead	16
(1) OSHMPI: trans win and disp	12	5	-	-
MPI_Put: calling overhead	9	0	-	-
(2) MPI_Put: get win obj	14	9	-	-
(3) MPI_Put: trans rank to network address	17	5	-	-
(4) MPI_Put: decode dtypes	22	0	-	-
(5) MPI_Put: check OFI conditions	13	7	SOS: check OFI conditions	7
(6) MPI_Put: prepare OFI param	14	8	SOS: prepare OFI param	24
(7) MPI_Put: compute dest_vaddr, mr_rkey	8	1	-	-
Flush_local: calling overhead	8	0	-	-
(8) Flush_local: get win obj	7	8	-	-
(9) Flush_local: wait OFI completion	38	17	SOS: wait OFI completion	-*
(10) Flush_local: find targets with active msg	59	0	-	-
(11) Flush_local: MPI full progress	81	2	-	-
MPI: others	15	15	SOS: others	24
OSHMPI total	333	93	SOS total	71

* SOS skips completion waiting for data smaller than 64 bytes because it uses **`fi_inject_write`**, which ensures local completion at return. Such an optimization cannot be done in MPICH because flush_local cannot determine whether other RMA operations (Get or large Put) has been issued. Thus, it has to always check the OFI completion counters (step (9)).

shmem_quiet: We then perform a similar analysis for the `shmem_quiet` routine. This ensures completion of all remote memory access and memory updates. In SOS, the synchronization is done by waiting for OFI completion counters. OSHMPI, however, has to take several MPI calls to ensure the semantics correctness required by `shmem_quiet`. Figure 2 demonstrates the internal implementation of `shmem_quiet` in OSHMPI/MPICH. OSHMPI internally calls `MPI_Win_flush_all` and `MPI_Win_sync` at quiet. Because OSHMPI creates two windows, one for symmetric heap (`symm_heap_win`) and the other for global/static variables (`symm_data_win`), it must call the two MPI functions twice.

In flush_all, MPICH first gets the internal object pointer of the `win` handle (step (1)). It next waits for OFI completion (step (2)). It then traverses all target objects that are associated with the specific window to ensure any outstanding active-message-based operations in this window are completed remotely (step (4)). While waiting for the active message completion, it iteratively makes MPI full progress. Similar to flush_local, the full progress is made at least once (step(3)). The next MPI function is win_sync, which is used for memory synchronization.

```
shmem_quiet() {
    /* ensure remote completion */
    MPI_Win_flush_all(win=symm_heap_win) {
        win_get_ptr(win, &win_ptr); // (1)
        wait_ofi_completion(...); // (2)

        target_am_all_cmpl = TRUE;
        do {
            MPI_full_progress(); // (3)

            // (4)
            /* traverse targets that received active message to ensure
               remote completions on all targets */
            for (pe = 0; pe < win_ptr->comm_ptr->local_size; pe++) {
                target_ptr = win_find_am_target(win_ptr, pe);
                if (target_ptr && target_ptr->remote_cmpl_cnts) != 0) {
                    target_am_all_cmpl = FALSE; break;
                }
            }
        } while (!target_am_all_cmpl);
    }
    /* ensure memory updates */
    MPI_Win_sync(win=symm_heap_win) { // (5)
        memory_barrier();
    }
    MPI_Win_flush_all(win=symm_data_win) { // (6)
        /* same as above */
    }
    MPI_Win_sync(win=symm_data_win) { // (7)
        /* same as above */
    }
}
```

Fig. 2. Pseudo code of `shmem_quiet` implementation in OSHMPI/MPICH

Table 2 summarizes the instruction count of `shmem_quiet` generated by OSHMPI/MPICH (see the Original Count column). The dominant cost in the OSHMPI/MPICH path comes from the MPI full progress and the traversal of target objects (steps (3–4)) in `MPI_Win_flush_all`, both are required by MPI semantics. Such a cost is even doubled because OSHMPI internally maintains two windows. As a result, OSHMPI/MPICH consumes 544 instructions whereas SOS consumes only 91. We note that the result captures the instructions taken by the Put latency program where only one Put is issued prior to a quiet. Thus, OSHMPI/MPICH does not issue any active-message-based operation and makes the MPI full progress only once.

Table 2. `shmem_quiet` instruction count analysis. Gray rows highlights instructions caused by the requirement of MPI semantics. The others instructions in MPI and SOS are implementation-specific; we omit the description.

OSHMPI Internal Step	Orig Cnt	Opt Cnt	SOS Internal Step	Cnt
OSHMPI: calling overhead	15	15	SOS: calling overhead	15
Flush_all: calling overhead	4	0	-	-
(1) Flush_all: get win obj	7	7	-	-
(2) Flush_all: wait OFI completion	14	14	SOS: wait OFI completion	51
(3) Flush_all: MPI full progress	81	2	-	-
(4) Flush_all: traverse targets with active msg	130	0	-	-
Win_sync: calling overhead	4	0	-	-
(5) Win_sync: memory barrier	1	1	-	-
(6) Flush_all for global/static var	267	3	-	-
(7) Win_sync for global/static var	5	0	-	-
MPI: others	16	2	SOS: others	25
OSHMPI total	544	44	SOS total	91

5 Optimizations for Fast RMA

Based on the overhead analysis in the preceding section, we then investigate ways to optimize the `shmem_putmem` and `shmem_quiet` in the OSHMPI/MPICH environment. We note that although our optimizations and discussion are based on the MPICH implementation, most address general issues also exist in other MPI implementations.

5.1 Basic Datatype Decoding with IPO Link-Time Inlining

Each OpenSHMEM RMA operation directly encodes the datatype in the function calls and supports only the standard RMA types. The datatype information is treated as a constant in the native implementations. Unlike OpenSHMEM, MPI allows the user to specify arbitrary datatypes such as the basic datatype `MPI_INT` or a complex user-defined derived datatype (e.g., vector, struct). The datatype description is encoded into the `MPI_datatype` object passed to MPI calls as an input variable. MPICH cannot optimize the datatype decoding process at compile time because the value of the datatype variable is unknown. Because of such a semantics limitation, the constant information of datatypes was lost in OSHMPI/MPICH and caused 22 additional instructions at the RMA fast path (see Table 1 step (4)). Many of these instructions are expensive pointer dereferences (i.e., to extract the attributes of the datatype object).

The interprocedural (IPO) optimization technique allows compiler to optimize code across source files and libraries at link time. This feature is provided by mainstream modern compilers such as the Intel compiler and the LLVM family. One of the IPO features is to inline functions across libraries and apply constant propagation for all inlined functions.

We note that IPO is extremely time-expensive when the optimizing space is large. Thus, we need to carefully define the inlining scope. Specifically, we make the following two configurations: (1) We inline only OSHMPI and MPICH libraries at link time, and (2) we explicitly exclude any *non-performance-critical* path in OSHMPI such as `shmem_init`. After applying IPO link-time inlining, we observe that MPICH can recognize the basic datatype defined for each RMA operation as a constant (e.g., `MPI_INT` is for `shmem_int_put`).

Once the datatype parameter becomes a constant, we then reconstruct the MPI datatype decoding routine to eliminate pointer dereferences. Specifically, we embed the required datatype attributes into the object handle rather than storing them as object fields. Such an approach works for basic datatypes because they require only two essential attributes when issuing an RMA operation: datatype kind (i.e., basic or derived) and size in bytes. The former is to distinguish a basic datatype from more complex derived datatypes; thus the fast-path code can be chosen. The latter is required for issuing the corresponding network data transfer. MPI implementations such as MPICH, MVAPICH, and Cray MPI represent the object handle as a 32-bit integer. It allows us to reserve a few bits for the two attributes. We note that the handle-embedded approach might be more complicated for MPI implementations whose object handle is represented as address pointers (e.g., OpenMPI). However, most architectures require some level of alignment for all pointer allocations (typically 4-byte or 8-byte alignment). Thus, even though the pointer uses 64 bits to represent the address, the two or three least significant bits are unused for alignment reasons. Therefore, the MPI implementation can reserve those bits to embed such information.

The attribute extraction now becomes bit-and and bit-shift instructions operated on the datatype handle. Thanks to IPO, these instructions can be fully eliminated by the compiler since the handle is recognized as a constant value at link time. Hence, no instruction is generated for datatype decoding in our optimized OSHMPI/MPICH, just as that in native implementations.

5.2 Fast Window Attributes Access

MPI implementations usually maintain an internal data object for each window. The object stores window attributes such as the associated communicator, network address, network endpoint (`ep`), remote window's memory registration key (`mr_rkey`), and remote window's displacement unit (`disp_unit`). At each RMA operation, the MPI implementation has to load these window attributes to prepare necessary parameters for network data transfer as well as for optimizations (e.g., one may compare the target rank with the rank of the local process in the communicator and perform local copy if they are identical). Accessing each attribute field is essentially a pointer dereference, however, and may involve expensive memory access overhead. Such an overhead can be significant especially when multilevel pointer dereferences are involved (e.g., accessing any attribute of the window's internal communicator is a two-level dereference).

Table 3. Pointer dereferences and instruction counts caused by window attributes access inside `MPI_Put`.

Internal step	#Ptr Deref	Instr Cnt
1. Translate rank to network address	2	8
2. Check target_rank for self message optimization	2	3
3. Prepare OFI parameters (ep, base, mr_rkey, disp_unit)	4	13
4. OFI counter update for tracking completion	1	4

Table 3 shows the pointer dereferences and relevant instructions taken inside each internal step of an `MPI_Put` call. We note that the network address translation (step 1) is required by the MPI semantics because the process's rank can be arbitrarily reordered in different communicators. Thus, MPICH has to maintain a lookup table to translate the process's rank in each communicator to the physical network address. The lookup table implementation was highly optimized in MPICH especially for common communicator patterns [10]. Figure 3a shows the assembly code generated for this step within the context of an OSHMPI-issued Put. The communicator is duplicated from `COMM_WORLD` (i.e., defined as the `DIRECT_INTRA` communicator mode). Thus it can utilize the fast lookup path with only 8 instructions. In order to load the communicator mode of the window and choose the fast code path, however, two pointer dereferences cannot be avoided (lines 1–2). We observed a similar situation in step 2. That is, in order to check whether the target process is the process itself (i.e., a self message), MPICH has to access the communicator's internal field, causing a two-level dereference (see lines 1–2 in Fig. 4a). We note that most MPI implementations contain this step in every RMA operation because it allows a self-message to be directly transferred in the MPI layer through `memcpy`. Steps 3 and 4 are required by the semantics of OFI data transfer and also can be found in a native implementation of OpenSHMEM. Thus, our optimization focuses only on the former two steps.

Similar to the object handle of datatypes, we noticed unused bits also in the window handle. Thus, we can identify whether the communicator is the `DIRECT_INTRA` mode when creating the window, and we can reserve a "window attribute" bit from the window handle to store such information. When issuing an RMA operation, we first check the value of the "window attribute" bit rather than loading the communicator's mode through pointer dereferences. We note that the window handle has already been loaded into the CPU register when converting to the internal window object; thus, checking a bit of the handle is very lightweight. In the context of OSHMPI, the windows are always created over the simplest `DIRECT_INTRA` communicators. Thus, the optimization can effectively eliminate the communicator dereferences in steps 1 and 2 for all RMA operations. Figures 3b and 4b show the optimized assembly code.

```
/* load win->comm */
mov r9, qword ptr [rdi+0x70]
/* load comm->mode */
mov edx, dword ptr [r9+0x1b8]
/* mode == DIRECT_INTRA? */
cmp rdx, 0xb
jnbe 0x41db85
jmp qword ptr [rdx*8+0x769560]
/* load table */
mov rax, qword ptr [rip+0x60522f]
/* shift to table[target_rank] */
add rax, 0x28
jmp 0x41db85
```

(a) Original version

```
/* handle & DIRECT_INTRA_MASK? */
test ebx, 0x2000000
jz 0x41cfb5
/* load table */
mov rax, qword ptr [rip+0x647740]
/* shift to table[ target_rank ] */
add rax, 0x28
jmp 0x41d203
```

(b) Optimized version

Fig. 3. Translating rank to network address in Put operation with optimization of embedded window attributes.

```
/* load win->comm */
mov rdx, qword ptr [rdi+0x70]
/* comm->rank == target_rank? */
cmp dword ptr [rdx+0x50], 0x1
jz 0x41dc32
```

(a) Original version

```
/* load global comm_world_rank */
mov edx, dword ptr [rip+0x6278a0]
/* comm_world_rank == target_rank? */
cmp edx, 0x1
jnz 0x41d238
```

(b) Optimized version

Fig. 4. Checking self-message in Put operation with optimization of embedded window attributes.

5.3 Avoiding Virtual Address Translation

Unlike OpenSHMEM, MPI defines generic relative offset (i.e., *displacement*) to describe the address of the remote RMA buffer. This allows MPI to be compatible with different requirements for remote memory access performed by the network hardware. For instance, some networks require the relative offset of the remote buffer (e.g., the OFI/psm2 provider for Intel Omni-Path), but others may require an absolute virtual address of the remote buffer (e.g., the OFI/gni provider for Cray Aries interconnect and UCX for InfiniBand networks). When utilizing MPI RMA in OSHMPI, however, we always must translate the remote absolute virtual address defined in OpenSHMEM to the corresponding relative displacement for every RMA operation. For networks that prefer absolute virtual address, a consequent translation (i.e., from relative displacement to virtual address) has to be performed again in the MPI layer. Obviously, such a translation is redundant.

Unfortunately, we cannot eliminate the redundant translation if we treat the MPI standard as a constant. To demonstrate the more efficient approach, we extended the MPI standard with a set of new functions called `MPI_Put|Get_abs` that can directly take the absolute virtual address as the input parameter. Figure 5 gives the API definition. Compared with the standard `MPI_Put|Get`, the only change is `target_vaddr`, which was originally a *displacement*.

This way allows us to avoid the intermediate remote address translation in OSHMPI and MPICH for networks that prefer absolute virtual address (e.g., Cray Aries and InfiniBand). However, we noticed that such an optimization can cause an extra translation in the MPI layer for networks that require relative

```
int MPI_Put_abs(const void *origin_addr, int origin_count,
                MPI_Datatype origin_datatype,
                int target_rank, MPI_Aint target_vaddr, int target_count,
                MPI_Datatype target_datatype, MPI_Win win);
int MPI_Get_abs(void *origin_addr, int origin_count,
                MPI_Datatype origin_datatype,
                int target_rank, MPI_Aint target_vaddr, int target_count,
                MPI_Datatype target_datatype, MPI_Win win);
```

Fig. 5. API definition of the *abs* extension for `MPI_Put|Get`.

offset (e.g., Intel Omni-Path) at each of the extended *abs* function. To eliminate such a translation, we require the user of MPI to use either only the basic RMA functions or only the extended functions for each window. The user should choose the preferred mode based on the application context. For instance, in OSHMPI the abs functions are clearly more suitable. We then defined a window info hint "`rma_abs`" (value is `true` or `false`) to indicate whether the window is exclusively used by the extended abs operations. If `rma_abs` is `true` and the underlying network requires relative offset, then MPICH internally registers `MPI_BOTTOM` as the base address of the virtual memory region on each process. For each RMA operation, the relative offset can be calculated by (`target_vaddr`−`MPI_BOTTOM`). Because `MPI_BOTTOM` is a predefined constant in MPI, the arithmetic calculation instructions can be fully eliminated by the compiler.

5.4 Optimizing MPI Progress

MPI implementations usually make expensive "full progress" in various MPI blocking functions. The full progress guarantees that all types of MPI communication (i.e., point-to-point, collectives, and active message based RMA) can be promptly progressed. For instance, for an active message based communication, the remote process has to trigger the MPI progress in an MPI call to complete the exchange of internal data packets. The MPI progress also internally triggers low-level network progress by making network synchronization calls such as `fi_cq_read` for OFI or `ucp_worker_progress` for UCX. These calls ensure prompt progress for any internal software emulation (e.g., active message based RDMA) or data processing (e.g., to move data out from a preregistered internal buffer) at the low-level network libraries.

Both OpenSHMEM RMA and quiet operations involve the MPI full progress in OSHMPI/MPICH. Table 4 analyzes the instructions that are taken for progress-relevant internal steps in `shmem_putmem` and `shmem_quiet`. We note that these steps are expensive not only in instruction counts but also in time because they force memory synchronization with the network hardware.

The expensive progress steps are required for general MPI programs. *Are they necessary also in the special OSHMPI context*? To answer this question, we systemically analyze the MPI progress requirements below.

For MPI Point-to-Point/Collectives: Both MPI point-to-point and collectives require two-sided communication between local and remote processes. Thus, the remote process must ensure prompt progress, For instance, the eager protocol

Table 4. Progress-relevant internal steps in `shmem_putmem` and `shmem_quiet` in OSHMPI/MPICH.

shmem_putmem	Instr Cnt
Flush_local: wait completion of outstanding RMA operations	38
Flush_local: MPI full progress	24

shmem_quiet	Instr Cnt
Flush_all: wait completion of outstanding RMA operations	14
Flush_all: MPI full progress	24

designed for small point-to-point messages requires the receiver process to copy data from the MPI internal buffer to the user receive buffer in order to complete the data transfer. This step may be performed in the progress routine on the receiver process. For collectives, for example, a process involved in an `MPI_Bcast` call may receive the data from the root process and then need to forward the data to another member process. Such a protocol is commonly used to overlap multiple data transfer in collective algorithms. The data receiving and forwarding steps are performed by the progress routine on each member process. The point-to-point and collective semantics require all processes involved in the communication to make the call. Hence, a process need perform such steps only when a collective or point-to-point call has been made.

For Active-Message-Based MPI RMA: MPI implementations may utilize internal active messages for an RMA operation if the underlying network hardware cannot efficiently handle it. For instance, a pack+AM+unpack-based approach may be chosen for a noncontiguous Put if the data layout is very sparse. An `MPI_Accumulate` has to be implemented by using an active message if the network hardware cannot guarantee atomic updates to the remote buffer with the specified datatype or if the MPI implementation chooses to use only CPU-based atomicity in order to be compatible with direct load/store-based intranode Accumulates. Nevertheless, the MPI implementation always must assume that the process may receive an active message from the other processes because the above situations may potentially occur. Consequently, the progress routine always has to be performed to promptly handle any incoming active message.

One may consider that the MPI implementation may predict whether active messages will be used by remote processes and skip the progress routine when possible. Such an approach, unfortunately, is complex because of two limitations. First, we need information from both the user program and the underlying network. To be specific, the user program must provide the (1) operation type (i.e., for atomic operations), (2) the basic datatype and data layout (e.g., contiguous or sparse noncontiguous), and (3) the data length for each operation. The network library must provide the (4) supported data layout for each operation together with (5) the data length limitation (e.g., for ordered message or for atomic message). By combining all the information, a correct prediction can be made. We note that many of these information are required to check whether an MPI Accumulate can directly leverage native network atomics or requires active message. For simple Put/Get, only (2) and (3) are essential. Nevertheless, to disable the active message progress on a remote process, we have to check all information. Second, a process requires all the other processes in the window to share their local information in advance before any communication occurs (ideally at window creation). The network-provided information is usually identical on all processes; thus each process can simply query it locally. The user information, however, may vary on each process. More important, the user has to specify such information before communication occurs, likely through MPI info hints. The hint may become significantly complex if the user program involves several different combinations of (1–3) in a window. Clearly, such an approach is impractical for MPI users.

Alternatively, we apply an engineer approach to resolve this issue. Specifically, we assume that all RMA operations can be handled directly by a network library when starting an MPI program. Thus, we trigger the active message progress with a very low frequency. For instance, we trigger the progress once only every 100 times RMA flush calls are made. This allows MPICH to catch any unexpected incoming active message. Once an active message is received, we then revert to normal frequency (i.e., trigger progress at least once at each RMA flush call). The mechanism exposes two MPI control variables (CVAR) for flexible user adjustment. Specifically, we define `MPIR_CVAR_CH4_RMA_ENABLE_DYNAMIC_AM_PROGRESS` to enable or disable the optimization (`false` by default) and `MPIR_CVAR_CH4_RMA_AM- _PROGRESS_LOW_FREQ_INTERVAL` to set the interval of progress polling at the low frequency mode. The former is `true` at `shmem_init` in OSHMPI. We expect that the active message progress is always triggered with the low frequency for OpenSHMEM programs because all OpenSHMEM RMA and atomic operations can be handled via native network operations.

For OFI/UCX Internal Progress: The first step of each MPI flush call in Table 4 already triggers necessary network progress for RMA data transfer. Thus, it is unnecessary to make MPI full progress again for such a purpose.

To summarize, the MPI full progress can be safely skipped in both `MPI_Win-_flush_local` and `MPI_Win_flush_all`, thus significantly reducing overhead for both `shmem_putmem` and `shmem_quiet` functions in OSHMPI/MPICH.

5.5 Reducing Synchronization in OSHMPI

Although we have eliminated the MPI full progress step in the flush calls, the overhead of an `MPI_Win_flush_local` or `MPI_Win_flush_all` is still expensive because the first step of each call always makes a call to network synchronization. We note that such synchronization is required to complete a network data transfer even in OpenSHMEM native implementations. In OSHMPI, however, we may unnecessarily trigger the synchronization call (i.e., `MPI_Win_flush_all`) twice at `shmem_quiet`, one for the window of symmetric heap and the other for that of global/static data objects. If only one of the windows contains outstanding operations, we need trigger the synchronization call only on that "active" window. Thus, we set a flag for each window in OSHMPI to keep track of the existence of outstanding operations. The same optimization applies to `MPI_Win_sync`.

5.6 Other Implementation-Specific Optimizations

The instruction analysis also provides useful guidance for us to reduce unnecessary instructions at the performance critical paths. These optimizations are MPICH-specific. Specifically, we apply four optimizations in MPICH: (1) eliminating repeated `MPI_PROC_NULL` check,[8] (2) removing unused signal checks in MPI full progress, (3) statically triggering subprogressing hooks (e.g., for collectives) instead of dynamic function pointer access, and (4) optimizing the hash search for checking the existence of target active message objects.

6 Evaluation

In this section we evaluate the performance of OSHMPI/MPICH on the Argonne Bebop cluster.[9] Each Bebop node uses two sockets of the 18-core Intel Xeon E5-2695 v4 processor (Broadwell) and is connected with the Intel Omni-Path interconnect. We used the Intel compiler (version 17.0.4) and libfabric-1.7.0 as the OFI network low-level library. We configured OSHMPI with the `ch4:ofi` configuration of MPICH and compared it with the SOS 1.4.2 release.[10] We linked both the MPICH and SOS libraries with the same underlying libfabric library. We also measured the OFI native Put latency by using a customized version of the `fi_pingpong` test included the libfaric official release. It mimics the data transfer pattern of `osu_oshm_put`. We use it to demonstrate the ideal performance of OFI-based data transfer. For each measurement we collected the execution time of 10 runs and report the average and the standard deviation (shown as error bars in the graphs). The error bars are very small for most results (less than 5%) and thus can barely be seen.

6.1 Instruction Analysis

We first break down the instruction counts of optimized `shmem_putmem` and `shmem_quiet` following the same approach as that used in Sect. 4. We statically linked

[8] `MPI_PROC_NULL` is an MPI predefined dummy process rank. An MPI RMA operation using `MPI_PROC_NULL` as the remote rank is a no-op.

[9] https://www.lcrc.anl.gov/systems/resources/bebop.

[10] We have made the following changes in SOS to ensure a fair comparison with OSHMPI/MPICH: (1) disable the OFI domain thread (set domain attribute `data_progress = FI_PROGRESS_MANUAL` at `shmem_init`) to reduce latency overhead at large data transfer; (2) reduce frequent calls to expensive `fi_cntr_wait` at `shmem_quiet`; and (3) disable bounce buffer optimization in the latency test because it increases latency overhead for medium data sizes (set environment variable `SHMEM_BOUNCE_SIZE=0`).

the latency program against the OSHMPI and MPICH libraries with IPO link-time optimization. We explicitly disabled inline functions in the latency program layer to make a fair comparison with SOS. In other words, both OSHMPI and SOS are unaware of the variable values defined in the latency program layer (e.g., `nelem`) and thus treat them as variables at compile time. Consequently, only the information defined in OSHMPI (e.g., datatype) is passed into MPICH via link-time inlining.

The Optimized Count columns in Tables 1 and 2 summarize the instruction counts generated by `shmem_putmem` and `shmem_quiet`, respectively. Roughly speaking, the instruction overhead of `shmem_putmem` is reduced to 93 and the overhead of `shmem_quiet` is reduced to 44 with all these optimizations. We especially highlight the following instruction-saving aspects. First, thanks to IPO link-time optimization, the instruction count of all cross-library overheads (e.g., calling overhead of `MPI_Put` and `Flush_local` in `shmem_putmem`) are now reduced to zero. It also helped eliminate the datatype decoding overhead (step (4) of `shmem_putmem`) with an embedded datatype handle as described in Sect. 5.1. We note that IPO allows more instructions to be saved throughout the implementation (i.e., partially reduced instructions in steps (5–6) and (9) of `shmem_putmem`). We omit the discussion in this paper. Second, the optimization of fast window attribute access reduces the network address translation (step (3)) to only 5 instructions, matching with the instructions demonstrated in Fig. 3b. Third, the instructions for computing `dest_vaddr` (step (7)) are optimized via the *abs* extension of MPI RMA functions. Fourth, we emphasize the highly optimized progress routines (step (11) in `shmem_putmem` and step (3) in `shmem_quiet`). Because we avoid unnecessary polling for non-RMA routines and utilize a dynamic approach to deal with the active message challenge (see detail in Sect. 5.4) together with implementation code refactoring (see Sect. 5.6), the optimized version now consumes only 2 instructions for the MPI full progress step. Fifth, as shown in Table 2, skipping unnecessary window synchronization (see Sect. 5.5) is straightforward and effective. When only either symmetric heap or global/static variable is used for communication, such an optimization can reduce 269 instructions including expensive low-level network synchronization calls. The remaining 3 instructions are used to check the window flag.

6.2 Latency

We next evaluated the latency of optimized OSHMPI/MPICH. We used the `osu_oshm_put` and `osu_oshm_get` tests from the OSU microbenchmark suite (version 5.6.2) to measure the latency of Put and Get, respectively.

Figures 6a and 6b report the Put latency. For both the intrasocket and internode results, we also include the OFI native Put latency (denoted by OFI) to indicate the ideal performance. The original OSHMPI/MPICH latency has a clear gap between that of SOS and OFI, It consumes about 1 µs latency for a 1-byte message, whereas OFI and SOS require only 0.54 µs and 0.66 µs, respectively. The optimized version significantly reduces the cost. The achieved latency is almost identical to that of SOS. The improved latency is mainly contributed by the optimization of MPI full progress in MPICH and reduced window synchronization in OSHMPI. Similar observations can be made in the internode results. Our optimizations reduce 0.4 µs latency of OSHMPI/MPICH with a 1-byte message. The achieved latency is the same as that of SOS and OFI. For other message sizes, we observe a similar trend.

The Get latency reported in Figs. 6c and 6d shows less gap between the original OSHMPI/MPICH and other implementations. Nevertheless, the optimized OSHMPI/MPICH can achieve a lower latency that is the same as that of SOS.

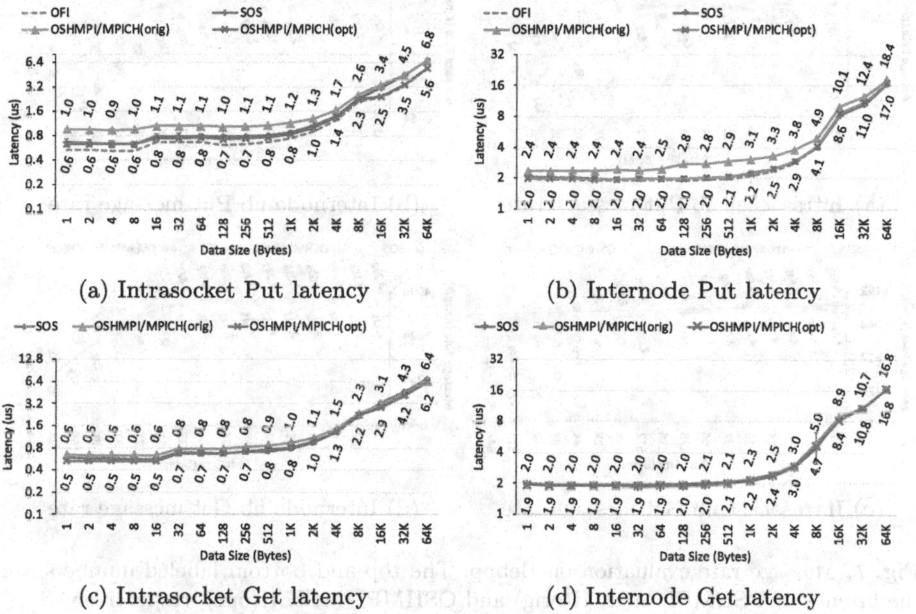

(a) Intrasocket Put latency

(b) Internode Put latency

(c) Intrasocket Get latency

(d) Internode Get latency

Fig. 6. Latency evaluation on Bebop. The top and bottom labeled numbers are the latency of OSHMPI/MPICH(orig) and OSHMPI/MPICH(opt), respectively.

6.3 Message Rate

The third set of experiments focus on message rate. We used the `osu_oshm_put_mr_nb` and `osu_oshm_get_mr_nb` tests from the OSU microbenchmark suite. The communication pattern involves multiple calls to the nonblocking `shmem_putmem_nbi` (`shmem_getmem_nbi` for the Get test) followed by a call to `shmem_quiet`. Thus, these tests present the overhead of the lightweight nonblocking RMA calls.

Figures 7a and 7b report the message rate of nonblocking Put. We observe that the optimized OSHMPI/MPICH significantly improves the message rate of Put. It achieves an average improvement of 2.1× for intrasocket Put with varying data size and 1.6× for internode Put. Since OSHMPI `shmem_putmem_nbi` internally contains only an `MPI_Put`, we confirm that the improvement is contributed by the fast path optimizations (i.e., datatype decoding, fast window attribute access, and RMA abs extension). The optimized message rate is almost identical to that of SOS.

We observe a similar trend with nonblocking Get. However, the gap between the original OSHMPI/MPICH and SOS is much less than that of nonblocking Put. Thus, the improvement ratio is reduced. We report an average improvement of 10.3% for intrasocket Get with varying data size and 7.3% for internode Get.

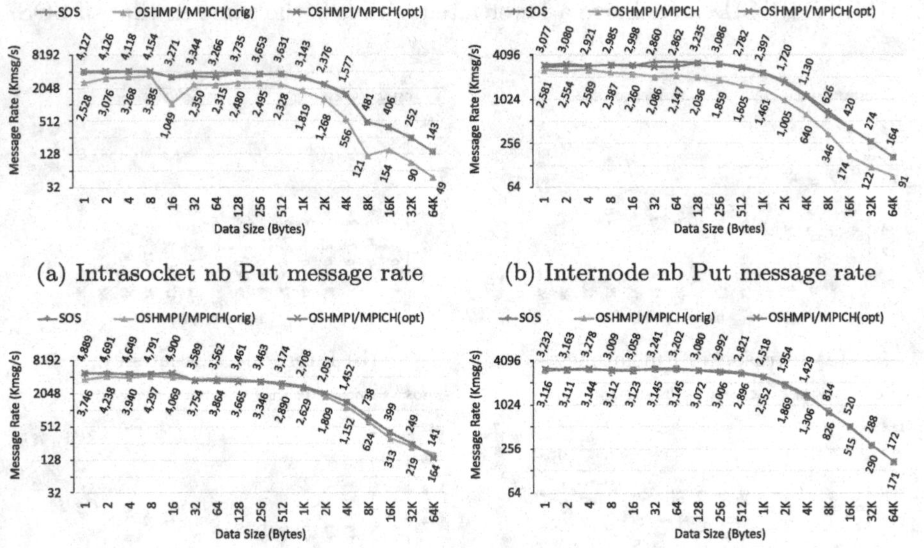

(a) Intrasocket nb Put message rate (b) Internode nb Put message rate

(c) Intrasocket nb Get message rate (d) Internode nb Get message rate

Fig. 7. Message rate evaluation on Bebop. The top and bottom labeled numbers are the latency of OSHMPI/MPICH(orig) and OSHMPI/MPICH(opt), respectively.

7 Conclusion and Future Work

OpenSHMEM and MPI are two widely used communication models for distributed-memory systems. The OpenSHMEM functionalities can be implemented by using MPI. For instance, mapping the essential OpenSHMEM RMA operations to MPI Put/Get with appropriate MPI window synchronization is straightforward. However, a general belief in the community is that such an OpenSHMEM over MPI implementation will not deliver the same level of performance as that of native OpenSHMEM implementations. This is mainly caused by the additional instructions generated for OpenSHMEM to MPI mapping. Therefore, OpenSHMEM over MPI is often used only as a short-term solution for platforms where a native OpenSHMEM is not yet available. In this paper we demonstrated that OpenSHMEM over MPI can actually become a performance contender. We showcased the OSHMPI and MPICH implementations and focused on the essential RMA routines. We first made a thorough analysis to understand the instruction overhead generated in the RMA critical path of the OSHMPI and MPICH layers. Based on the observed performance bottlenecks, we further optimized several key aspects including datatype decoding, MPI window attribute access, virtual destination address translation, and the expensive MPI progress. Our evaluation was performed on an Intel Broadwell cluster with the Intel Omni-Path interconnect. We compared the optimized OSHMPI/MPICH with the native OpenSHMEM implementation on that platform. We concluded that the optimized OSHMPI/MPICH can deliver the same level of performance in both latency and message rate as that of a native OpenSHMEM implementation.

Although the analysis and optimizations focused on the RMA routines, most can be easily adapted also for other OpenSHMEM routines. As future work, we plan to optimize atomics and collective routines in the OSHMPI and MPICH environment. Furthermore, we note that our performance evaluation used only microbenchmarks on the Intel Omni-Path platform. We therefore also plan to look into the performance of miniapplications and evaluate other platforms.

Acknowledgment. This research was supported by the United States Department of Defense (DoD). This material was based upon work supported by the United States Department of Energy, Office of Science, Advanced Scientific Computing Research (SC-21), under contract DE-AC02-06CH11357. The experimental resource for this paper was provided by the Laboratory Computing Resource Center on the Bebop cluster at Argonne National Laboratory.

References

1. ARMCI-MPI. https://github.com/pmodels/armci-mpi
2. Mellanox ScalableSHMEM User Manual. Technical report, Mellanox Technologies Ltd. (2012)
3. Open MPI: Open Source High Performance Computing. https://www.open-mpi.org/
4. Essential Guide to Distributed Memory Coarray Fortran with the Intel Fortran Compiler for Linux (2018). https://software.intel.com/content/www/us/en/develop/articles/distributed-memory-coarray-fortran-with-the-intel-fortran-compiler-for-linux-essential.html
5. Barriuso, R., Knies, A.: SHMEM User's Guide for C. Technical report, Cray Research Inc. (1994)
6. Bonachea, D., Duell, J.: Problems with using MPI 1.1 and 2.0 as compilation targets for parallel language implementations. Int. J. High Perform. Comput. Netw. **1**(1–3), 91–99 (2004)
7. Dinan, J., Balaji, P., Hammond, J.R., Krishnamoorthy, S., Tipparaju, V.: Supporting the global arrays PGAS model using MPI one-sided communication. In: 2012 IEEE 26th International Parallel and Distributed Processing Symposium, pp. 739–750 (2012)
8. Fanfarillo, A., Burnus, T., Cardellini, V., Filippone, S., Nagle, D., Rouson. D.: OpenCoarrays: open source transport layers supporting Coarray Fortran compilers. In : Proceedings of the 8th International Conference on Partitioned Global Address Space Programming Models, PGAS 2014, Association for Computing Machinery, New York, NY, USA (2014)

9. Fürlinger, K., et al.: DASH: data structures and algorithms with support for hierarchical locality. In Euro-Par Workshops (2014)
10. Guo, Y., et al.: Memory compression techniques for network address management in MPI. In 2017 IEEE International Parallel and Distributed Processing Symposium (IPDPS), pp. 1008–1017 (2017)
11. Hammond, J.R., Ghosh, S., Chapman, B.M.: Implementing OpenSHMEM using MPI-3 one-sided communication. In: Poole, S., Hernandez, O., Shamis, P. (eds.) OpenSHMEM 2014. LNCS, vol. 8356, pp. 44–58. Springer, Cham (2014). https://doi.org/10.1007/978-3-319-05215-1_4
12. Jose, J., Kandalla, K., Luo, M., Panda, D.K.: Supporting hybrid MPI and OpenSHMEM over InfiniBand: design and performance evaluation. In: 2012 41st International Conference on Parallel Processing, pp. 219–228 (2012)
13. Namashivayam, N., Cernohous, B., Pou, D., Pagel, M.: Introducing cray OpenSHMEMX - a modular multi-communication layer OpenSHMEM implementation. In: Pophale, S., Imam, N., Aderholdt, F., Gorentla Venkata, M. (eds.) OpenSHMEM 2018. LNCS, vol. 11283, pp. 41–55. Springer, Cham (2019). https://doi.org/10.1007/978-3-030-04918-8_3
14. Weeks, H., Dosanjh, M.G.F., Bridges, P.G., Grant, R.E.: SHMEM-MT: a benchmark suite for assessing multi-threaded Shmem performance. In: Gorentla Venkata, M., Imam, N., Pophale, S., Mintz, T.M. (eds.) OpenSHMEM 2016. LNCS, vol. 10007, pp. 227–231. Springer, Cham (2016). https://doi.org/10.1007/978-3-319-50995-2_16
15. Parzyszek, K., Nieplocha, J., Kendall, R.A.: A generalized portable SHMEM library for high performance computing. Technical report, Ames Lab., Ames (2000)
16. Raffenetti, K., et al.: Why is MPI so slow?: Analyzing the fundamental limits in implementing MPI-3.1. In: Proceedings of the International Conference for High Performance Computing, Networking, Storage and Analysis, SC 2017, pp. 62:1–62:12. ACM, New York (2017)
17. Yang, C., Bland, W., Mellor-Crummey, J., Balaji. P.: Portable, MPI-interoperable Coarray Fortran. In: Proceedings of the 19th ACM SIGPLAN Symposium on Principles and Practice of Parallel Programming, PPoPP 2014, pp. 81–92. Association for Computing Machinery, New York (2014)
18. Zhou, H., Idrees, K., Gracia, J.: Leveraging MPI-3 shared-memory extensions for efficient PGAS runtime systems. In: Träff, J.L., Hunold, S., Versaci, F. (eds.) Euro-Par 2015. LNCS, vol. 9233, pp. 373–384. Springer, Heidelberg (2015). https://doi.org/10.1007/978-3-662-48096-0_29

Tools and Benchmarks

SKaMPI-OpenSHMEM: Measuring OpenSHMEM Communication Routines

Camille Coti[1,2(✉)] and Allen D. Malony[2]

[1] LIPN, CNRS UMR 7030, Université Sorbonne Paris Nord, Paris, France
camille.coti@lipn.univ-paris13.fr
[2] University of Oregon, Eugene, USA
malony@cs.uoregon.edu

Abstract. Benchmarking is an important challenge in HPC, in particular, to be able to tune the basic blocks of the software environment used by applications. The communication library and distributed runtime environment are among the most critical ones. In particular, many of the routines provided by communication libraries can be adjusted using parameters such as buffer sizes and communication algorithm. As a consequence, being able to measure accurately the time taken by these routines is crucial in order to optimize them and achieve the best performance. For instance, the SKaMPI library was designed to measure the time taken by MPI routines, relying on MPI's two-sided communication model to measure one-sided and two-sided peer-to-peer communication and collective routines. In this paper, we discuss the benchmarking challenges specific to OpenSHMEM's communication model, mainly to avoid inter-call pipelining and overlapping when measuring the time taken by its routines. We extend SKaMPI for OpenSHMEM for this purpose and demonstrate measurement algorithms that address OpenSHMEM's communication model in practice. Scaling experiments are run on the Summit platform to compare different benchmarking approaches on the SKaMPI benchmark operations. These show the advantages of our techniques for more accurate performance characterization.

1 Introduction

The ability to effectively utilize high-performance computing (HPC) systems to their best potential depends heavily on tuned library implementations specific to a machine's processor, memory, and communications components. For distributed memory applications, the communication routines and distributed runtime system should be implemented and optimized in close association with the capabilities of the hardware interconnection network. This poses special challenges for standard communication interfaces designed to be portable across HPC platforms. The performance of low-level communication operations is important, but it is the communication model semantics that ultimately defines the context for correct execution. Both aspects come into play when porting a communications library from one HPC architecture to another.

S. Poole et al. (Eds.): OpenSHMEM 2021, LNCS 13159, pp. 63–80, 2022.
https://doi.org/10.1007/978-3-031-04888-3_4

Benchmarking is a powerful technique for understanding HPC performance. When applied to the development and tuning of scalable distributed systems, especially portable parallel communication libraries, benchmarking can provide valuable insight for identifying high-value settings of parameters and algorithm variants for different use scenarios. The design of a benchmarking methodology and framework that can elaborate communication model behaviors and correctly generate test cases is highly relevant for achieving productive outcomes. It serves to maintain a coherent plan for measurement and analysis during the performance characterization and library tuning process.

The original goal of the research reported in this paper was to develop a benchmarking system for OpenSHMEM that could be use to tune OpenSHMEM implementations across multiple HPC machines. Most important to our work was designing a benchmarking methodology that was consistent with the OpenSHMEM standard and systematic in its processing. Unfortunately, only OpenSHMEM mini-benchmarks existed at the time the research began. While we anticipated that we would have to develop the tests for most of the OpenSHMEM operations, we wondered if we could reuse the high-level structure and methods of the SKaMPI benchmarking system [18]. The paper reports our experience and success in following this strategy.

There are four research contributions deriving from our work. First, we produced a "first of its kind" fully functional benchmarking system for OpenSHMEM, based on the SKaMPI methodology and framework. Second, we show how the SKaMPI methodology and framework could be reused for OpenSHMEM purposes. This outcome could be beneficial to extending SKaMPI with other communication libraries in the future. Third, we describe how the tests of communication routines specific to the OpenSHMEM standard are constructed. Finally, we demonstrate our benchmarking system on the Summit platform and report detailed analysis results.

The rest of the paper is structured as follows. In Sect. 2 we discuss related research work in the performance measurement, analysis, and benchmarking of communication libraries. Here we introduce the former SKaMPI work for MPI. Section 3 looks at the specific problem of measuring OpenSHMEM routines and the challenges of creating a portable benchmarking solution based on SKaMPI for characterization and tuning. Our experimental evaluation is presented in Sect. 4. We show the use of our solution on the DOE Summit system at Oak Ridge National Laboratory (ORNL). Finally, we conclude and describe future directions.

2 Related Works

Measuring the time taken by communications can be performed in two contexts. It can be made on parallel applications, in order to determine how much time the application spends communicating. Various robust *profiling* and *tracing* systems can be used, such as TAU [20], VTune [16], Scalasca [4], Score-P [11], and EZTrace [24]. The objective is to characterize communication performance for the routines actually used by the application.

The other context has to do with analyzing communications performance for the purpose of tuning the communication routines (point-to-point [2] or collective routines [10,13]), and to make sure that they fulfill performance requirements [23] on the system of interest. This *benchmarking* approach is fundamentally different from above, but can lead to important outcomes that contribute to better application communication performance. The *Special Karlsruhe MPI benchmark (SKaMPI)* was created to benchmark MPI communications for supercomputer users and system administrators who want to tune their MPI libraries [12], evaluate and chose algorithms for collective communications [25,26], and ensure performance portability of the MPI library across platforms [17].

Measuring the time spent in communications should consider parameters that might potentially be exploited by applications. Regardless of the communication library used, the *effective bandwidth* can be measured directly [15]. However, each library will have communication routines that will need specific measurement techniques to understand their operation. For instance, peer-to-peer communications are interesting because certain libraries might allow overlap with computation. The measurement methodology to capture phenomena in such cases can be non-trivial. Moreover, designing benchmarking methods that can be applied across communication libraries is a challenge.

SKaMPI overcomes most limitations of previous benchmarks such as PARKBENCH [6] and *mpbench* [14], as described in [18]. For instance, *mpbench* reduces the number of calls to the timer by calling the measured function several times in a loop and measuring the total time taken by the loop. However, some pipelining might occur between consecutive calls; for instance, when measuring tree-based collective operations, or point-to-point communications that do not ensure remote completion when the sender call returns.

In order to eliminate obvious pipelining between some collective operation calls, *mpbench* uses a different root for the operation (for broadcasts and reductions) at every iteration. However, depending on the communication topology used, this might not be enough and in some cases a pipeline can still establish between consecutive calls. Other algorithms have been designed to eliminate inter-call pipelining and perform an accurate measurement of these calls, relying on the synchronizing model of MPI peer-to-peer communications to enforce separation of consecutive collective routines [22], and on the synchronization model of MPI2 one-sided communications [1].

Theoretical models are a close relative to benchmarking and can complement its objectives, in that they utilize empirical values measured on target machines. The representative *LogP* model [3] expresses point-to-point communications using four parameters: the *send and receive overheads*, which are the time to prepare the data to send it over the network and the time to get it from the network and provide it to the application (denoted o_s and o_r), the *wire latency*, which is the time for the data to actually travel through the network (denoted L), and the *gap*, which is the minimum interval between consecutive communications (denoted g). Since o and g can overlap, the LogP model encourages overlapping with computation with communication.

3 Measuring OpenSHMEM Communication Routines

SKaMPI's measuring infrastructure and synchronization algorithms are described and evaluated in [8]. Our objective is to utilize the SKaMPI framework for benchmarking OpenSHMEM communication. However, considering studies of potential clock drift [9], we know that both barrier and window-based process synchronization suffer from drift and the processes might lose their synchronization as the measurement progresses. SKaMPI's window-based clock synchronization can measure operations very accurately, but the logical global clocks drift quickly, so only a small number of MPI operations can be measured precisely. The hierarchical algorithm presented in [9] has a smaller clock drift, but the processes still skew during the measurement. As a consequence, we cannot rely on this synchronization only to perform our measurements, and whenever possible, we need to design measurement strategies that rely on more precise measurements than just a synchronization followed by a call to the measured routine.

Scalable clock synchronization algorithms are presented in [7] and can achieve synchronization in $O(log(P))$ rounds, whereas SKaMPI's algorithm takes $O(p)$ rounds. Adopting a better algorithm is related to the *infrastructure* that supports the measurements and is out of the scope of this paper. However, it is important that we use lightweight timing mechanisms that are non-perturbing relative to the granularity of the artifact being measured. In some fine-grained measurement cases, we had to update SKaMPI timing methods.

3.1 Point-to-Point Communication Routines

Blocking Operations. OpenSHMEM includes two categories of blocking point-to-point communication routines: remote memory access routines and atomic operations. In these two categories, we have two types of routines: those that return as soon as possible and not when the data has actually been delivered, and those that return when the data has been delivered in the destination buffer.

Routines from the latter category can be called *fetching* or *get-based.* Their completion time corresponds to the time elapsed between the call and the return of the communication routine (see Fig. 1a), making them trivial to measure. Routines from the former category can be called *non-fetching* or *put-based.* They are supposed to return as soon as the source buffer can be reused and not when the data has actually been delivered to the destination buffer. Since OpenSHMEM is a one-sided communication model, the target process does not participate in the communication: a global synchronization routine like a barrier cannot ensure completion of the operation, since the target process can enter the barrier and exit before the one-sided operation completes (and, since the order of operations is not guaranteed, before it has even reached the target process).

Completion of the operation can be ensured with `shmem_quiet`. Therefore, we want to measure the time elapsed between the call to the communication routine and the return of `shmem_quiet` (see Fig. 1b). However, calling `shmem_quiet` can have a cost. Therefore, we need to measure the cost of an almost empty call to `shmem_quiet` and with substract it from the measured time.

The `shmem_quiet` routine ensures completion of the outgoing put-based operations. It works on all active communications with remote processes for the calling process. To measure the routine, therefore, we must issue a `shmem_put` for one byte before the `shmem_quiet`. We cannot exclude this `shmem_put` from the measurement, because some communication engines might make it progress and complete before they schedule the communication with all the remote processes involved by `shmem_quiet`. However, it sends a small message and its latency should be combined with the latency of the first part of the `shmem_quiet`, so this `shmem_put` should have a negligible impact on the measurement of `shmem_quiet` (see Fig. 1c).

Some implementations and some networks implement `shmem_put` as a non-blocking communication that only ensures that the sending buffer on the source process is reusable after the call exits (as in OpenMPI[1] [19]). Others implement it like a blocking communication (oshmpi[2] implements it as two `MPI_Isend` followed by a `MPI_Waitall` [5,21]). Hence, measuring the time spent in the call to `shmem_put` is relevant. We provide a function for this.

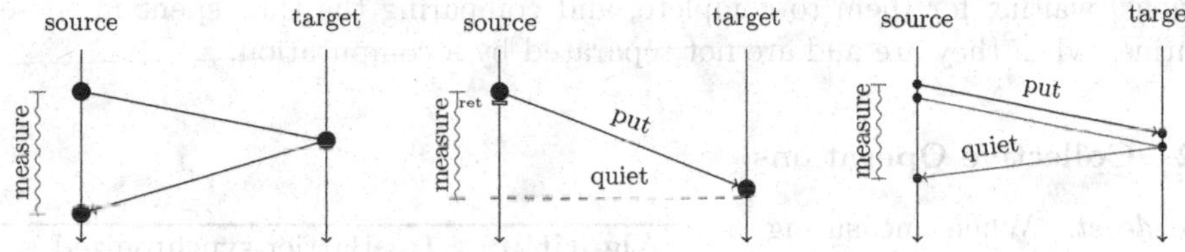

(a) Measure a get. (b) Measure a put. (c) Measure a quiet.

Fig. 1. Different measurement cases for blocking operations.

Non-blocking Operations. With some implementations and some networks, the call to the communication routine can just post the communication and the communication is performed in `shmem_quiet`. Therefore, we can measure the time taken by this call to `shmem_quiet` for a given communication size. In the preamble of the measurement routine, we measure the time to perform a complete non-blocking communication (including the call to `shmem_quiet`) for the same buffer size. Then we post the operation and wait twice the measured time. Then we measure the time spent in `shmem_quiet`. If the library has good overlap capabilities, the communication will be performed during the wait, and the call to `shmem_quiet` will not do anything. Otherwise, the communication will be performed in `shmem_quiet`.

Hence, we are providing four functions to measure non-blocking *put* operations and four functions to measure non-blocking *get* operations:

---

[1] SHA 62362849cae65b2445723e426affc2bb7918a6c8.

[2] SHA 776449f6ea0368b61450b0c37e83463357f6f1bf.

- `Shmem_{Put,Get}_Nonblocking_Full` measures the full completion of a non-blocking operation, with a `shmem_put_nbi` or a `shmem_get_nbi` immediately followed by a `shmem_quiet`.
- `Shmem_{Put,Get}_Nonblocking_Quiet` measures the time spent in `shmem_quiet`, called immediately after `shmem_put_nbi` or `shmem_get_nbi`. If there is no overlap, most of the communication time is expected to be spent here. Otherwise, this call should be fast.
- `Shmem_{Put,Get}_Nonblocking_Post` measures the time spent in the call to `shmem_put_nbi` or `shmem_get_nbi`. This call should be fast and the communication should not be performed here, otherwise the communication cannot be overlapped with computation.
- `Shmem_{Put,Get}_Nonblocking_Overlap` measures the time spent in `shmem_put_nbi` or `shmem_get_nbi` and the time spent in `shmem_quiet`, separated by a computation operation that should take about twice the time to completed the full (non-blocking) communication.

These routines can be used to evaluate the overlapping capabilities of the library, by showing how much time is spent posting the non-blocking communications, waiting for them to complete, and comparing the time spent in these routines when they are and are not separated by a computation.

3.2 Collective Operations

Broadcast. When measuring a broadcast, a major challenge concerns how to avoid a pipeline that might occur between consecutive communications. Therefore, we want to separate consecutive broadcasts, while avoiding external communication costs to be included. An initial possibility consists in separating consecutive broadcast with a barrier, and subtracting the time to perform a barrier (measured separately), as show by Algorithm 1.

Algorithm 1: Barrier-synchronized broadcast measurement.

$t\_bcast \leftarrow 0.0$;
barrier();
for $i \leftarrow 0$ **to** *iterations* **by** 1 **do**
  $t1 \leftarrow$ **wtime()**;
  broadcast($buffer, root$);
  barrier();
  $t2 \leftarrow$ **wtime()**;
  t_bcast ← t_bcast + $(t2 - t1)$;
$t\_bcast \leftarrow t\_bcast / iterations$;
$t\_barrier \leftarrow$ time_barrier();
$t\_bcast \leftarrow t\_bcast - t\_barrier$;

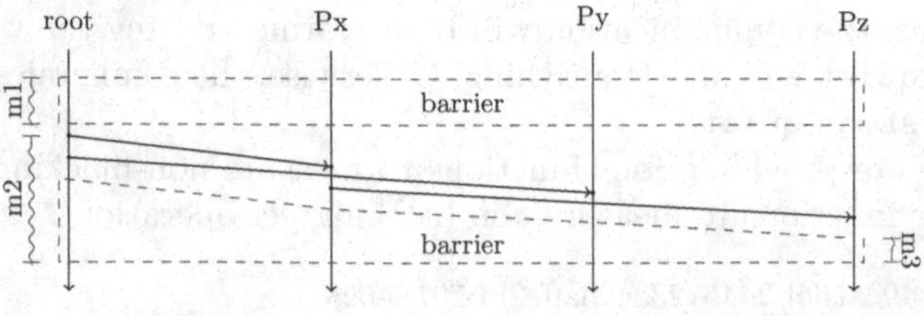

Fig. 2. Barrier-synchronized broadcast.

However, since with some broadcast algorithms, processes might exit early, the barrier performed after the broadcast could become unbalanced and take a time different than a barrier performed by a set of already more or less synchronized processes. For instance, Fig. 2 depicts a case when a process ends after the other ones, so the barrier can be finalized as soon as it enters it and all the other processes are already synchronized ($m3 < m1$). Moreover, a barrier does not truly synchronize the processes. For instance, they can be implemented as a reduction followed by a broadcast using the same root, and depending on which process is the root of these operations, the end of the second barrier in Fig. 2 can create a skew between processes.

Algorithm 2: Active synchronization-based.

```
root ← 0;
for i ← 0 to iterations by 1 do
    t1 ← start_sync();
    broadcast( buffer, root);
    t2 ← stop_sync();
    t_bcast ← t_bcast + (t2 − t1);
t_bcast ← t_bcast/iterations;
```

SKaMPI provides a time-based synchronization, provided by `start_synchronization` and `stop_synchronization` routines. We can measure the broadcast operation as in Algorithm 2.

Algorithm 3: In rounds.

```
t1 ← start_sync();
for root ← 0 to size by 1 do
    broadcast( buffer, root);
e_time ← stop_sync();
t_bcast ← (e_time − s_time)/size;
```

Another possibility to try to avoid overlap and get the full extent of a broadcast by doing broadcasts in rounds. Each process is made the root of a broadcast and multiple broadcasts are performed. However, depending on the broadcast topology, there might still be some overlap between consecutive broadcasts. Algorithm 3 was introduced by [22]. In turns, processes acknowledge completion of their part of the broadcast to the root. The time to perform an acknowledgment is measured prior to the measurement, and subtracted from the total time.

However, this algorithm was designed in a two-sided communication model, with synchronous communications. Conveniently, OpenSHMEM provides a routine that waits until a variable located in the shared heap validates a comparison: `shmem_wait_until`. The first step is used to measure the acknowledgment time (`rt1`) between the root process and each process `task`. The algorithm is using a "large" number of repetitions

Algorithm 4: (Part 1) One-sided communications broadcast measurement.

```
Function initialize(task)
    /* Measure ack                          */
    t1 ← wtime();
    if root == rank then
        ack(task);
        wait_for_ack();
    else if task == rank then
        wait_for_ack();
        ack(root);
    rt1 ← wtime() −t1;
    return rt1;
```

(M). In the algorithm described in [22], this first step is made using an exchange of two-sided send and receive communications. This step is used to measure the time taken by an acknowledgment, later used in the algorithm. Then a first broadcast is performed and process *task* acknowledges it to the root of the broadcast (lines 3 to 8). Then comes the measurement step itself, performed M times for each task (line 24 to 29). The broadcast time is obtained by subtracting the acknowledgment measured in the first exchange step (line 34).

Algorithm 4: (Part 2) One-sided communications broadcast measurement.

```
11 Proc warmup(task)
       /* Warm-up                                   */
12     broadcast( buffer, root);
13     if root == rank then
14         ack(task);
15         wait_for_ack();
16     else if task == rank then
17         wait_for_ack();
18         ack(root);
19     return;
20 for task ← 0 to size by 1 do
       /* Initialize                                */
21     rt1 ← initialize( task);
22     warmup( task);
       /* Measure broadcast                         */
23     t1 ← wtime();
24     for i ← 0 to M by 1 do
25         broadcast( buffer, root);
26         if root == rank then
27             wait_for_ack();
28         else if task == rank then
29             ack(root);
30     t2 ← wtime();
31     if rank == task then
32         rt2 ← t2 − t1;
33         myt ← rt2 − rt1;
34         btime ← max(btime, myt);
35 return btime;
```

We are performing the acknowledgment by incrementing a remote counter using an atomic `fetch_and_inc` operation and waiting for the value of this counter. We are using a `fetch_and_add` operation instead of an `add` operation because, as specified by the OpenSHMEM standard, non-fetching calls may return before the operation executes on the remote process. We can wait for remote completion with a `shmem_quiet`, but we decided to use the simplest operation available; besides, although this operation goes back-and-forth between the source and the target, we are measuring this exchange in the initialization of the measurement routine.

Lemma 1. *even if a remote write operation interleaves between the operations* `shmem_int_wait_until( ack, SHMEM_CMP_EQ, 1 )` *and* `*ack = 0`*, there cannot be two consecutive remote increment of the* `*ack` *variable. In other words,* `*ack` *cannot take any other value than 0 and 1 and acknowledgments sent as atomic increments are consumed by* `shmem_int_wait_until` *before another acknowledgment arrives.*

Proof. If we denote:

- $\prec$ the *happens before* relation between two events, with $a \prec b$ meaning that a happens before b;

- $broadcast_{ay}$: the local operation on process y for the ath broadcast (beginning of the operation);
- $fetch\_inc_{ay}$: the local operation on process y for the ath `shmem_int_atomic_fetch_inc` (on the source process y, beginning of the operation);
- inc_{ay}: the increment of `*ack` on process y for the ath `shmem_int_`atomic_fetch_inc (on the target process y);
- $wait_{ay}$: the ath time process y waits for the value of `*ack` to be modified with `shmem_int_wait_until( ack, SHMEM_CMP_EQ, 1 );`
- $assignment_{ay}$: the ath time process y assigns `*ack` to the value 0, hence consuming previously received acknowledgments.

These operations are represented Fig. 3. Even if `*ack` is incremented remotely which the broadcast operation is still in progress on the root process, it will not be read before the end of the root's participation to the broadcast. Hence, the root cannot begin the next broadcast before it is done with the current one. We need to note the fact that other processes might still be in the broadcast.

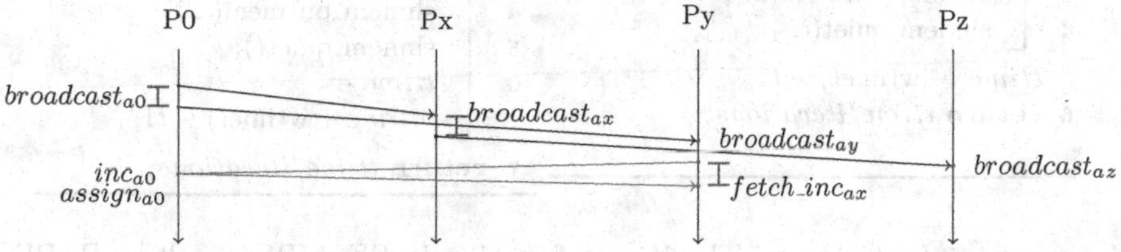

Fig. 3. Broadcast measurement

The next broadcast starts after `*ack` has been set back to 0. We have:
- on the root process:
$broadcast_{1root} \prec inc_{1root} \prec wait_{1root} \prec assignment_{1root} \prec broadcast_{2root} \prec inc_{2root} \prec wait_{2root} \prec assignment_{2root}$
- on any Px
$broadcast_{1x} \prec fetch\_inc_{1x} \prec broadcast_{2x} \prec fetch\_inc_{2x}$

We also know that:

- $fetch\_inc_{1x} \prec inc_{1root}$
- $inc_{1root} \prec assignment_{1root}$

The OpenSHMEM standard states that: "*When calling multiple subsequent collective operations on a team, the collective operations—along with any relevant team based resources—are matched across the PEs in the team based on ordering of collective routine calls*". Hence, for any two processes x and y, $broadcast_{1x} \prec broadcast_{2y}$, so $fetch\_inc_{1x} \prec fetch\_inc_{2y}$.

Therefore, by transitivity of the $\prec$ relation:
$fetch\_inc_{1x} \prec assignment_{1root} \prec inc_{2root} \prec assignment_{2root}$

We can conclude that there cannot be two consecutive `shmem_int_atomic_fetch_inc` on the root process with no re-assignment to 0 between them, and on any process, the acknowledgment cannot be sent while the previous or the next broadcast is in progress on other processes. □

The corollary of the lemma is that acknowledgment exchanges cannot be interleaved with broadcasts (only local operations can be), and therefore 1) there is no deadlock and 2) consecutive broadcasts cannot interleave.

3.3 Fine-Grain Measurements

There are important concerns we needed to pay attention to when updating SKaMPI for making fine-grain measurements.

Algorithm 5: Timing outside.

```
t1 ← wtime();
for i ← 0 to iterations by 1 do
    shmem_putmem(...);
    shmem_quiet();
ttime ← wtime() − t1;
return ttime/iterations;
```

Algorithm 6: Timing inside.

```
ttime ← 0;
for i ← 0 to iterations by 1 do
    t1 ← wtime();
    shmem_putmem(...);
    shmem_quiet();
    ttime ←
      ttime + wtime() − t1;
return ttime/iterations;
```

Measurement Disturbance. The timing function in SKaMPI (a call to PAPI's timing routine) takes a time of the same order of magnitude or, in some cases, higher that the time taken by some of the functions we are measuring. Hence, we want to minimize the number of calls to the timing function during a measurement. We observed very significant differences between the times obtained using Algorithm 6 and Algorithm 5. A lot of calls to the timing function, which, if using an external function such as PAPI, we might not be able to inline, is causing very significant disturbance to the measurement.

Algorithm 7: Timing `shmem_quiet`.

```
ttime ← 0;
for i ← 0 to iterations by 1 do
    shmem_putmem(...);
    t1 ← wtime();
    shmem_quiet();
    ttime ← ttime + wtime() − t1;
return ttime/iterations;
```

Algorithm 8: Subtraction method.

```
tpost = get_post_time();
t1 ← wtime();
for i ← 0 to iterations by 1 do
    shmem_putmem(...);
    shmem_quiet();
ttime ← wtime() − t1;
return ttime/iterations − tpost;
```

Separating Calls. Some functions we are measuring can be called only in the context of another function. For instance, if we want to measure the time spent waiting for a non-blocking communication to complete, we need to post a non-blocking communication before. We cannot post a set of non-blocking communications and call `shmem_quiet` in a loop, because it waits for completion of all the outstanding non-blocking communications at the same time. Therefore, each `shmem_quiet` must correspond to a previously posted non-blocking communication. However, we cannot isolate it on our measurement such as described by Algorithm 7, for the reasons presented in the previous paragraph. Therefore, we are initializing the measurement by measuring the time taken by the routine that posts the non-blocking communication, measuring the whole loop, and subtracting the post time from the result (Algorithm 8).

Stability. The aforementioned methods rely on subtracting values measured during the initialization of the measurement. Therefore, the experimental conditions must remain stable through the measurement. For instance, we noticed instabilities on machines that were being used by multiple users at the same time, while the measurements were quite stable on nodes used in exclusive mode. Moreover, SKaMPI calls each measuring function multiple times and keeps calling them until the standard deviation between measurements is small enough. However, we found significant improvement in the stability between experiments when each measurement function was, itself, performing a significant number of measurements and returning their mean.

Busy Wait. In order to avoid voluntary context switches, we are not using a `sleep` to wait while the communication is progressing in the background. Instead, we are performing a computation operation that takes the same time, but does not involve the operating system. Our approach is to increment a variable in a loop and we avoid compiler optimization by inserting an call to an empty assembly instruction (`asm("")`) in the loop.

4 Experimental Evaluation

We used our extended SKaMPI on the Summit supercomputer, which features 4 608 two-socket IBM POWER9 nodes, 6 Nvidia V100 GPUs per node and 512 GB of DDR4 plus 96 GB of HBM2 per node. The network is a Mellanox EDR 100G InfiniBand non-blocking fat tree. We used the provided IBM Spectrum MPI and OpenSHMEM library version 10.3.1.02rtm0 and the IBM XL compiler V16.1.1. The input files used to run these experiments are available along with the SKaMPI source file. The remainder of this section discusses selected outcomes from the full set of SKaMPI-OpenSHMEM results.

4.1 Loop Measurement Granularity

In Sect. 3.3 we mentioned the importance of how loops are measured. We compared the time returned by the functions that measure a non-blocking put (`shmem_put` immediately followed by `shmem_quiet`, `shmem_put` and `shmem_quiet` measured separately). We can see that iteration-level measurement introduce a very significant latency, which is not visible for longer measurements that are not latency-bound (higher buffer sizes).

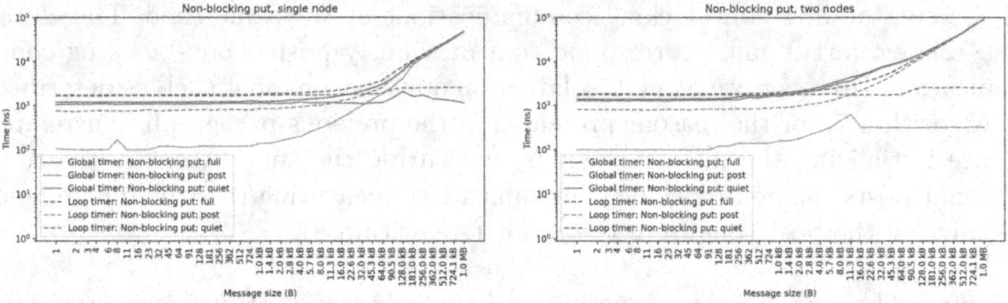

(a) Single node. (b) Two nodes.

Fig. 4. Measurement granularity: iteration vs global loop timer, on the elements of a non-blocking put.

Similarity, we compared these time measurement strategies on the measurement of the overlap capabilities of non-blocking communications. Iteration-level measurement uses four calls to the timing routines in each iteration of the measurement loop: before and after posting the non-blocking communication, and before and after calling `shmem_quiet` to wait for its completion. The global loop measurement times the whole loop and subtracts the time assumed to be taken by the computation used to (try to) overlap the computation. As discussed in Sect. 3.3, it relies on the hypothesis that this time will be stable throughout the measurement. However, as we can see Fig. 5, the latency introduced by the iteration-level measurement strategy is such that the numbers returned by this method are too far from reality for small messages.

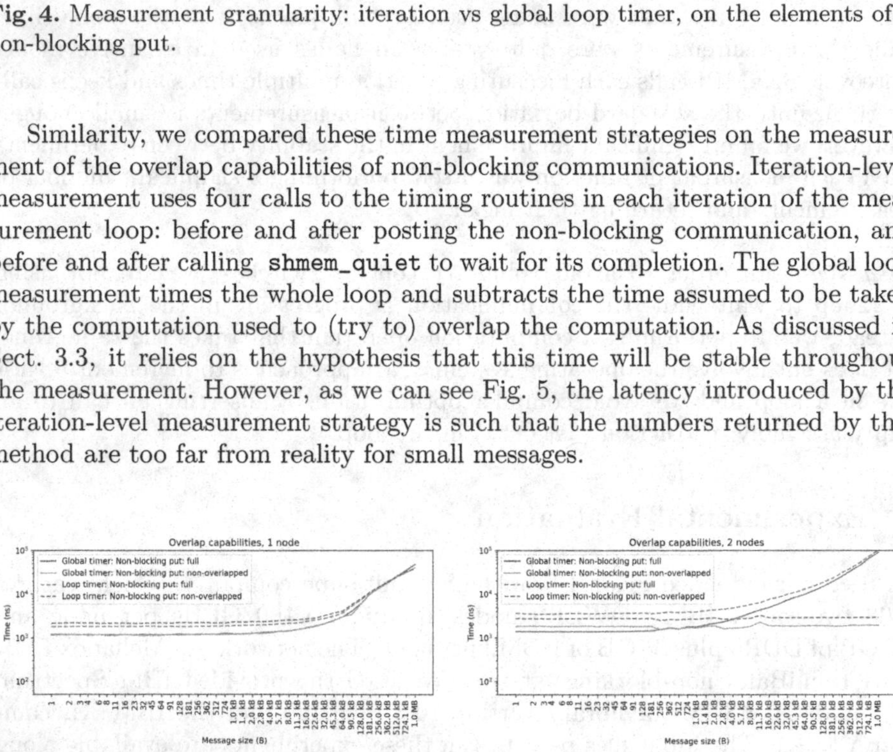

(a) Single node. (b) Two nodes.

Fig. 5. Measurement granularity: iteration vs global loop timer, on the overlap capabilities of a non-blocking put.

Consequently, the results presented in this section were measured using our global timer approach (as described in Sect. 3.3). The results are shown in the figures. It can be seen that the global timer measurements produced smaller and more reliable values versus iteration timers.

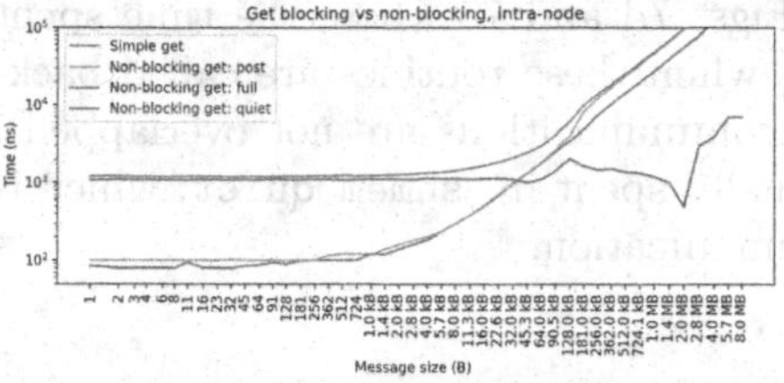

(a) Get, intra-node

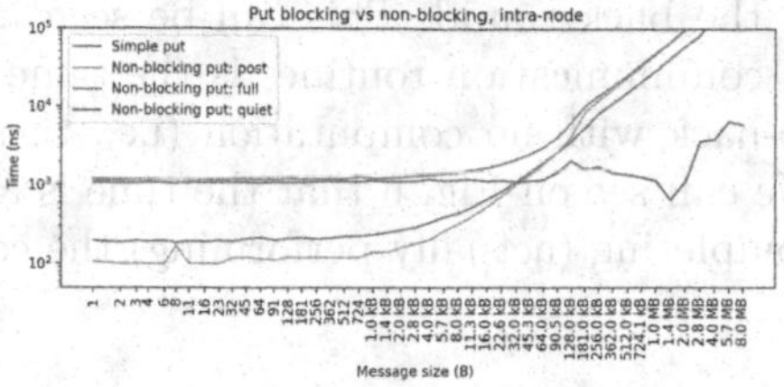

(b) Put, intra-node

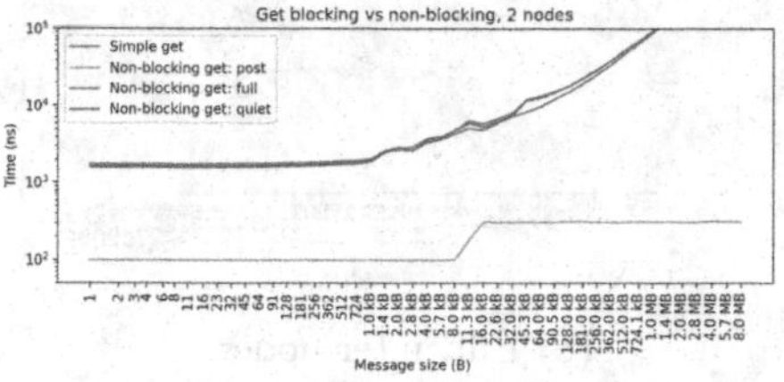

(c) Get, inter-node

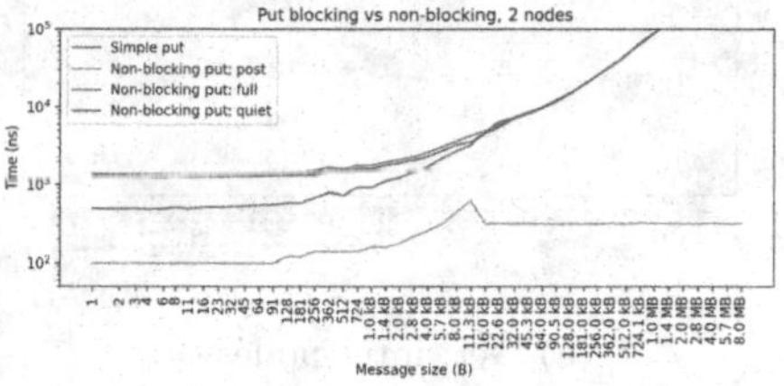

(d) Put, inter-node

Fig. 6. Point-to-point communication performance breakdown.

4.2 Point-to-Point Communications: Blocking vs Non-blocking

We measured the performance difference between a blocking communication and a non-blocking communication, and the time it takes to wait for completion of the communication. For instance, Fig. 6 shows the communication performance on a single node and between two nodes. We can see that blocking communications have a smaller latency than a non-blocking communication followed by a `shmem_quiet` that waits for its completion. We can also see the breakdown between how much time is spent posting the non-blocking communication and how much is spent waiting for its completion.

4.3 Point-to-Point Communications: Overlap Capabilities

We can also use SKaMPI to measure the overlapping capabilities of the OpenSHMEM library, as described in Sect. 3.1. Figure 7 shows how much time is spent in a complete non-blocking operation (`shmem_put` or `shmem_get` immediately followed by `shmem_quiet`) and how much is spent in these operations separated by some computation. We can see on Figs. 7b and 7a that, since the interconnection network used on the Summit machine can make the communication progress in the background, it achieves good overlap between communication and computation. The time spent in communication routines is constant (called "non-overlapped") on the figure, corresponding to the time spent in the communication routines. On the other hand, intra-node communications cannot progress in the background. This can be seen in Figs. 7d and 7c where the time spent in communication routines is the same as when these routines are called back-to-back with no computation (i.e., these communications are not overlapped). We can see on Fig, 6 that the time is actually spent in `shmem_quiet`, which is completing (actually performing) the communication.

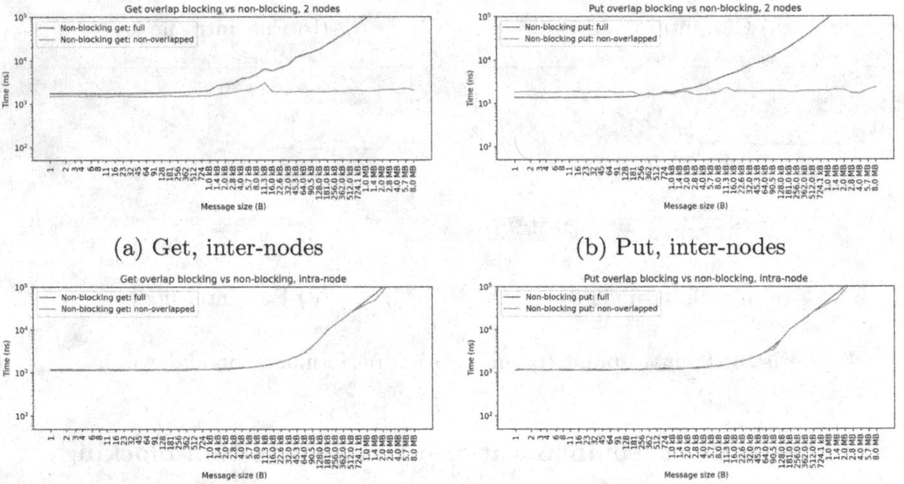

(a) Get, inter-nodes (b) Put, inter-nodes

(c) Get, intra-node (d) Put, intra-nodes

Fig. 7. Overlap capabilities of point-to-point communications.

4.4 Collective Communications: Broadcast

It is interesting to observe the differences in experimental results for the various measurement algorithms. In particular, we expect the *in round* approach to give a smaller value, since consecutive broadcasts can establish a pipeline depending on the communication topology used by the broadcast. We also see on Fig. 8 that the broadcast separated by barriers can give smaller measurement values. As explained in Sect. 4.4, we expect this observation can be explained by the final barrier being faster on the last processes to finish (see Fig. 2).

The other algorithms give very similar results. As discussed in Sect. 3.2, the synchronized broadcast can be less reliable because of time drifts and less significant statistically speaking, since we are measuring broadcasts one by one. Moreover, the SK algorithm with consecutive broadcasts separated by a sleep is likely to be more relevant, although here it gives similar results.

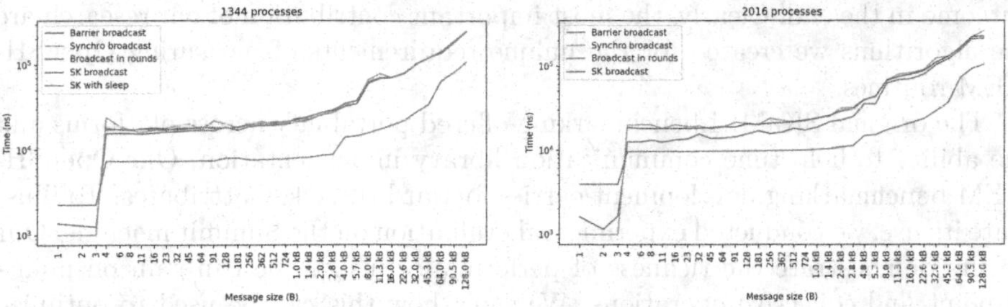

(a) 1 344 processes. (b) 2 016 processes.

Fig. 8. Comparing times returned by the broadcast measurement algorithms.

4.5 Locks

OpenSHMEM provide global locking functions. Our measurement of the time taken by these functions takes into account whether the lock is already taken, who is requesting it, and so on. Some of these measurements and their scalability are shown Fig. 9.

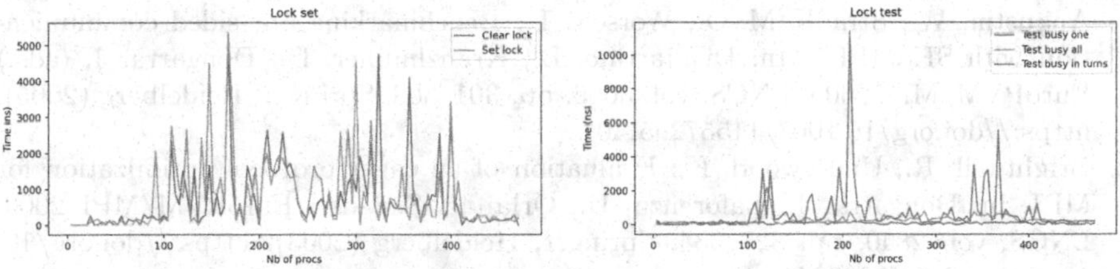

(a) Acquisition and release. (b) Test.

Fig. 9. Global lock functions.

5 Conclusion and Perspectives

Our research work delivers a portable benchmarking framework for OpenSHMEM, in the spirit of the successful SKaMPI benchmarking system for MPI. While the communication libraries are distinct from one another, the benchmarking methodology practiced in SKaMPI is more general and very relevant to our OpenSHMEM benchmarking objectives. Indeed, we made the important decision to work within the SKaMPI benchmarking infrastructure and implement OpenSHMEM-specific functionality, thereby delivering a more robust outcome in the end. Clearly, the most important contribution of our research are the algorithms we created for the unique requirements of measuring OpenSHMEM routines.

The original SKaMPI benchmarking offered portability across platforms and the ability to help tune communication library implementation. Our OpenSHMEM benchmarking development carries forward these key attributes. To illustrate its use, we conducted experimental evaluation on the Summit machine. Our results demonstrate the richness of performance insight we can gain on point-to-point and collective operations. We show how this can be used to optimize certain implementation parameters.

The increasing complexity of HPC environments will further complicate abilities to measure their performance. A well-defined benchmarking methodology can serve as the core for evaluating multiple communication libraries. That perspective is well-supported based on our experience. It is reasonable to expect that the approach we followed of specializing SKaMPI's infrastructure for OpenSHMEM would work well with other communication models and libraries.

SKaMPI-OpenSHMEM can be downloaded from GitHub at the following address: https://github.com/coti/SKaMPI.

References

1. Augustin, W., Straub, M.-O., Worsch, T.: Benchmarking one-sided communication with SKaMPI 5. In: Di Martino, B., Kranzlmüller, D., Dongarra, J. (eds.) EuroPVM/MPI 2005. LNCS, vol. 3666, pp. 301–308. Springer, Heidelberg (2005). https://doi.org/10.1007/11557265_40
2. Brightwell, R., Underwood, K.: Evaluation of an eager protocol optimization for MPI. In: Dongarra, J., Laforenza, D., Orlando, S. (eds.) EuroPVM/MPI 2003. LNCS, vol. 2840, pp. 327–334. Springer, Heidelberg (2003). https://doi.org/10.1007/978-3-540-39924-7_46
3. Culler, D., et al.: LogP: towards a realistic model of parallel computation. In: Proceedings of the Fourth ACM SIGPLAN Symposium on Principles and Practice of Parallel Programming, pp. 1–12 (1993)
4. Geimer, M., Wolf, F., Wylie, B.J., Ábrahám, E., Becker, D., Mohr, B.: The Scalasca performance toolset architecture. Concurr. Comput. Pract. Exp. **22**(6), 702–719 (2010)
5. Ghosh, S., Hammond, J.: OpenSHMEM over MPI-3. Technical report, Argonne National Lab. (ANL), Argonne (2014)
6. Hey, T., Lancaster, D.: The development of Parkbench and performance prediction. Int. J. High Perform. Comput. Appl. **14**(3), 205–215 (2000)
7. Hoefler, T., Schneider, T., Lumsdaine, A.: Accurately measuring overhead, communication time and progression of blocking and nonblocking collective operations at massive scale. Int. J. Parallel Emerg. Distrib. Syst. **25**(4), 241–258 (2010)
8. Hunold, S., Carpen-Amarie, A.: MPI benchmarking revisited: Experimental design and reproducibility. arXiv preprint arXiv:1505.07734 (2015)
9. Hunold, S., Carpen-Amarie, A.: On the impact of synchronizing clocks and processes on benchmarking MPI collectives. In: Proceedings of the 22nd European MPI Users' Group Meeting, pp. 1–10 (2015)

10. Hunold, S., Carpen-Amarie, A.: Autotuning MPI collectives using performance guidelines. In: Proceedings of the International Conference on High Performance Computing in Asia-Pacific Region, pp. 64–74 (2018)
11. Knüpfer, A., et al.: Score-P: a joint performance measurement run-time infrastructure for Periscope, Scalasca, TAU, and Vampir. In: Tools for High Performance Computing 2011, pp. 79–91. Springer, Berlin (2012). https://doi.org/10.1007/978-3-642-31476-6_7
12. Lastovetsky, A., Rychkov, V., O'Flynn, M.: MPIBlib: benchmarking MPI communications for parallel computing on homogeneous and heterogeneous clusters. In: Lastovetsky, A., Kechadi, T., Dongarra, J. (eds.) EuroPVM/MPI 2008. LNCS, vol. 5205, pp. 227–238. Springer, Heidelberg (2008). https://doi.org/10.1007/978-3-540-87475-1_32
13. Luo, X., et al.: HAN: a hierarchical AutotuNed collective communication framework. In: 2020 IEEE International Conference on Cluster Computing (CLUSTER), pp. 23–34. IEEE (2020)
14. Mucci, P.J., London, K., Thurman, J.: The MPBench Report. University of Tenessee, Computer Science (1998)
15. Rabenseifner, R., Koniges, A.E., Livermore, L.: The parallel communication and I/O bandwidth benchmarks: b_eff and b_eff_io. In: Proceedings of 43rd Cray User Group Conference, Indian Wells, California, USA. Citeseer (2001)
16. Reinders, J.: VTune Performance Analyzer Essentials. Intel Press, Hillsboro (2005)
17. Reussner, R., Hunzelmann, G.: Achieving *performance portability* with *SKaMPI* for high-performance MPI programs. In: Alexandrov, V.N., Dongarra, J.J., Juliano, B.A., Renner, R.S., Tan, C.J.K. (eds.) ICCS 2001. LNCS, vol. 2074, pp. 841–850. Springer, Heidelberg (2001). https://doi.org/10.1007/3-540-45718-6_89
18. Reussner, R., Sanders, P., Prechelt, L., Müller, M.: SKaMPI: a detailed, accurate mpi benchmark. In: Alexandrov, V., Dongarra, J. (eds.) EuroPVM/MPI 1998. LNCS, vol. 1497, pp. 52–59. Springer, Heidelberg (1998). https://doi.org/10.1007/BFb0056559
19. Shamis, P., et al.: UCX: an open source framework for HPC network APIs and beyond. In: 2015 IEEE 23rd Annual Symposium on High-Performance Interconnects, pp. 40–43. IEEE (2015)
20. Shende, S.S., Malony, A.D.: The TAU parallel performance system. Int. J. High Perform. Comput. Appl. **20**(2), 287–311 (2006)
21. Si, M., Balaji, P., Rafenetti, K.J., Zhou, H., Iwasaki, S.: OSHMPI: open SHMEM Implementation over MPI (2021). https://doi.org/10.11578/dc.20210319.1, https://www.osti.gov//servlets/purl/1771788
22. de Supinski, B., Karonis, N.: Accurately measuring MPI broadcasts in a computational grid. In: Proceedings of the Eighth International Symposium on High Performance Distributed Computing (Cat. No.99TH8469), pp. 29–37 (1999). https://doi.org/10.1109/HPDC.1999.805279
23. Träff, J.L., Gropp, W., Thakur, R.: Self-consistent MPI Performance Requirements. In: Cappello, F., Herault, T., Dongarra, J. (eds.) EuroPVM/MPI 2007. LNCS, vol. 4757, pp. 36–45. Springer, Heidelberg (2007). https://doi.org/10.1007/978-3-540-75416-9_12
24. Trahay, F., Rue, F., Faverge, M., Ishikawa, Y., Namyst, R., Dongarra, J.: EZTrace: a generic framework for performance analysis. In: 2011 11th IEEE/ACM International Symposium on Cluster, Cloud and Grid Computing, pp. 618–619. IEEE (2011)

25. Worsch, T., Reussner, R., Augustin, W.: On benchmarking collective MPI operations. In: Kranzlmüller, D., Volkert, J., Kacsuk, P., Dongarra, J. (eds.) EuroPVM/MPI 2002. LNCS, vol. 2474, pp. 271–279. Springer, Heidelberg (2002). https://doi.org/10.1007/3-540-45825-5_43
26. Worsch, T., Reussner, R., Augustin, W.: Benchmarking collective operations with SKaMPI. In: Krause, E., Jäger, W. (eds.) High Performance Computing in Science and Engineering 2002, pp. 491–502. Springer, Berlin (2003). https://doi.org/10.1007/978-3-642-59354-3_39

A Tools Information Interface for OpenSHMEM

Md. Wasi-ur-Rahman[1(✉)], David Ozog[2], and Kieran Holland[1]

[1] Intel Corporation, Austin, TX, USA
md.rahman@intel.com
[2] Intel Corporation, Hudson, MA, USA

Abstract. The Partitioned Global Address Space (PGAS) programming model, OpenSHMEM, is getting more traction as a useful method for parallel programming on future-generation platforms. However, very few works have explored on the enabling of external tools to analyze and control performance behavior of OpenSHMEM runtimes. While the OpenSHMEM standard recently introduced the profiling interface allowing tools to collect and monitor performance, it still does not define a mechanism through which an implementation can expose internal performance knobs and metrics to the end users. To write OpenSHMEM programs that perform efficiently in a uniform manner across different platforms, it is necessary to understand and control these internal performance metrics. Early work reveals that OpenSHMEM performance variables can provide insights that are crucial to performance debugging, analysis, and optimization. In this paper, we propose a generic tools information interface with flexible and portable variable representation and a set of APIs that provide users the capability to analyze and control the performance behavior. The goal of this paper is to establish the usefulness and feasibility of such an API that users can leverage to better understand the internal details of the runtime.

1 Introduction

Efficient one-sided communication in Partitioned Global Address Space (PGAS) programming models is becoming more popular to provide high performance memory access solutions as the next-generation compute platforms are employing deep memory hierarchies within and across nodes. Similar to Unified Parallel C (UPC) [15] and the MPI Remote Memory Access (RMA) [11], OpenSHMEM [12] provides the one-sided communication interface over high-performance interconnects. With complex memory hierarchies in next-generation systems, it is increasingly getting important to understand the internal performance details of the operations and also being able to control and tune the operations on different environments.

OpenSHMEM 1.5 [12] has introduced the profiling interface which provides an easy-to-use flexible model for tool developers to interface their tools into OpenSHMEM implementations. This provides a mechanism for the profiling tools to intercept the OpenSHMEM calls and collect performance data in a black-box approach. However, understanding the internal implementation details and controlling the performance behavior through runtime parameters can be more useful for flexibility and performance portability reasons. MPI 3.0 [3] introduced the tools information interface (`MPI_T`) that

S. Poole et al. (Eds.): OpenSHMEM 2021, LNCS 13159, pp. 81–91, 2022.
https://doi.org/10.1007/978-3-031-04888-3_5

defines a set of control and performance variables with APIs to access and use them. This interface provides tool developers ways to understand and control the performance behavior of the underlying implementation. Such interface and flexibility for OpenSHMEM users have so far been elusive.

In this paper, we propose an interface similar to `MPI_T`, to introduce the OpenSHMEM control and performance variables and APIs that define the usage semantics. We refer to this interface as `shmem_t`. We categorize the OpenSHMEM performance-critical information, represent them through performance and control variables, and propose generic APIs that can be used to access them. We define a simple easy-to-use variable representation to ensure minimal programming effort from the tool developers.

The rest of the paper is organized as follows. We discuss existing MPI approach and other related studies on `MPI_T` in Sect. 2. Section 3 provides a summary on earlier research work that shows the benefits of performance variables in OpenSHMEM. Section 4 presents our proposed interface and we provide some example usages in Sect. 5. We conclude in Sect. 6 with future goals.

2 Related Work

MPI introduced the tools information interface for developers and users on MPI-3.0 standard [3]. With MPI tools interface (MPI_T) support, MPI implementers can expose implementation details through performance and control variables and events. MPI_T allows the implementers to choose the variables and events that they wish to expose to the users and provide necessary routines to query and find out the number and details of variables that are supported. MPI_T also provides APIs to retrieve variable description and to read and reset these variables in appropriate cases. An example tool utilizing MPI_T is shown in Listing 1. To minimize space, we highlight the key MPI_T APIs being used and skip detailed error checking, variable declarations, and API arguments.

In this example tool, it is shown that MPI_T defines separate initialization and finalization routines to ensure separate usage from the MPI communication APIs. It also uses a string representation of the variables that allows the user to choose from the list of available variables supported by the underlying implementation using string comparison. MPI_T then allocates a separate handle to generalize the binding of a variable to an MPI object. It uses the handle to read from or write to the variables. At the end, the handle is freed and MPI_T is finalized.

Most of the current major MPI implementations support MPI_T and provide access to control and performance variables through this interface. We investigated MPI implementations as shown in Table 1 to survey the number of variables supported in each of them and observed presence of variables in all of these implementations. We found the presence of performance variables in the open-source implementations, such as MPICH [4], OpenMPI* [8], and MVAPICH2* [7].

Several existing tools utilize MPI_T to collect and control performance through the underlying variables implemented. For example, TAU [9] is a profiling and tracing toolkit that supports MPI_T to collect performance variables' data from the runtime. Caliper [10] is another example of a library that provides performance profiling capabilities into the applications and uses various tool developers' utilities such as MPI_T. Gyan [5] and VarList [6] are other example tools that utilize MPI_T.

Listing 1. An example program in C utilizing MPI_T to read a control variable

```
int main(int argc, char* argv[]) {
  ...
  char desired_var_name[30] = "MPI_T_EAGER_THRESHOLD";

  /* Initialize MPI_T */
  err = MPI_T_init_thread(MPI_THREAD_SINGLE, &ts);

  /* Get the number of control variables supported */
  err = MPI_T_cvar_get_num(&num);

  /* Find the variable using name */
  for (i = 0; i < num; i++) {
    err = MPI_T_cvar_get_info(i, name, ...);
    if (err == MPI_SUCCESS && strcmp(name, desired_var_name) == 0) {
      desired_index = i;
      break;
    }
  }

  /* Allocate handle */
  err = MPI_T_cvar_handle_alloc(index, &comm, &handle, &count);

  /* Read the variable using allocated handle */
  err = MPI_T_cvar_read(handle, val);

  /* Free handle and finalize */
  err = MPI_T_cvar_handle_free(&handle);
  err = MPI_T_finalize();
}
```

Table 1. Support for MPI_T control and performance variables

MPI implementation	MPI_T support	Control variables	Performance variables
MPICH 3.3.2 [4]	✓	265	10
Intel® MPI (2019.6.166) [2]	✓	569	0
OpenMPI* 4.1.0 [8]	✓	1215	20
Cray-MPICH* 7.7.10 [1]	✓	109	0
MVAPICH2* 2.3.6 [7]	✓	105	566

OpenSHMEM introduced a profiling interface (`pshmem`) in OpenSHMEM 1.5. Similar to the MPI profiling interface (`PMPI`), `pshmem` allows the profiling tools to intercept the OpenSHMEM calls by the user application program and information can be collected before and after this call to formulate profiling data. A tools information interface will allow the programmers to directly gain access to control and in some cases, observe the performance of internal operations in the runtime.

3 OpenSHMEM Performance Variables

In this section, we discuss the prior work on OpenSHMEM performance variables. In [13], a set of OpenSHMEM performance counters with example APIs have been proposed that expose communication details for OpenSHMEM Remote Memory Access (RMA) operations. These information were used to influence application performance

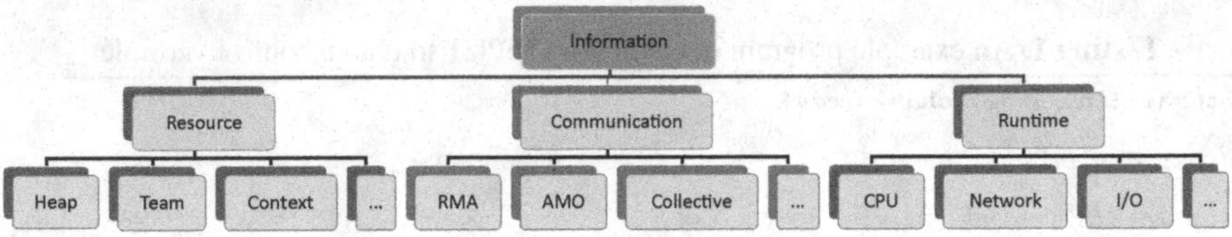

Fig. 1. Example OpenSHMEM information categories for performance and control variables

optimization and to present insightful characteristics of application behavior such as communication pattern, load balance, operation overlap, etc. The examples presented in [13] prove that a tools information interface exposing the communication intrinsics can be useful for performance optimization, tuning, and debugging purposes. This work also investigates on the performance overhead of using these APIs for performance variables on an implementation with Sandia OpenSHMEM [14]. While overhead exists, it largely depends on the frequency of accessing these APIs and [13] shows that a reasonable amount of data can be collected with negligible performance overhead.

While performance variables in OpenSHMEM communication operations reveal the details of data transfer routines, they do not expose the structures and usage of library and system resources that would be extremely useful for OpenSHMEM tool developers. For example, the symmetric heap space usage can provide details of the memory space being used for the symmetric data objects; a specific collective algorithm being used can show the reasons behind observed performance on a scaled network; the process to core mapping in the runtime can be used to avoid over-subscription of system resources, and so on. In general, all of these control and performance data can be broadly categorized into three types - resources, operations, and runtime data.

Figure 1 presents this example of information categories that we will expose through our proposed design choices in Sect. 4. In general, the OpenSHMEM library resources can be further categorized into software resources such as symmetric heap, context, team, etc. OpenSHMEM operations can be divided into RMA, Atomic Memory Operations (AMO), Collective operations, etc. The runtime information can be categorized into system resource information from CPU, network, and I/O usages. While this generic categorization is applicable for most OpenSHMEM implementations, further categorization is possible and depends on specific implementation choices.

4 Design of a Tools Information Interface

In Sect. 2, Listing 1 shows the basic building blocks of a tools information interface that are essential to be used by a tool developer. While this provides a simple interface to users, some aspects of the design choices can be made more flexible to allow efficient implementation for both the library and the tool itself. In this section, we discuss some of these design areas while we propose a tools information interface for OpenSHMEM, `shmem_t`.

Listing 2 lists the proposed APIs for `shmem_t`. All of the APIs have the prefix `shmem_t` to differentiate with the current standard APIs. We define a separate set of initialization and finalization routines than the current specification definition for communication. This will allow the interface to be used independently when desired. The

Listing 2. Proposed APIs in C for OpenSHMEM tools interface

```
/* Initialize and finalize routines */
void shmem_t_init_thread(int requested, int *provided);
void shmem_t_finalize(void);

/* Summary of variable routines */
void shmem_t_var_get_num(int type, int *num);
void shmem_t_var_avail(int type, void **list_vars);

/* Allocate and free handle routines */
void shmem_t_var_handle_alloc(shmem_t_handle_config *handle_config,
                              shmem_t_var_handle *handle);
void shmem_t_var_handle_free(shmem_t_var_handle handle);

/* Read and reset routines */
int shmem_t_var_reset(shmem_t_var_handle handle);
int shmem_t_var_read(shmem_t_var_handle handle, void *buf);
int shmem_t_var_write(shmem_t_var_handle handle, const void *buf);
int shmem_t_var_list_read(shmem_t_var_handle *handles, void **buf);

/* Get variable routines */
int shmem_t_get_var(int var_type, int operation, int bind,
                    int var_scope, int var_class, uint64_t *var);
```

shmem_t_init_thread and shmem_t_finalize routines have the same function signature as the default initialize and finalize routines and will follow the same behavior for out-of-order executions of the default ones. The major purpose of these routines is to initialize and allocate any resources for variables in addition to the default OpenSHMEM initialize and finalize operations. The requested argument denotes the thread level that is requested by the user and provided is returned from the implementation denoting the actual thread level support provided. The shmem_t_finalize routine takes no argument and finalizes the tools interface by freeing up the resources.

The next two APIs in Listing 2 provide summary information of the variables supported by the underlying implementation. The shmem_t_var_get_num API takes the variable type as an argument and returns the total number of variables of the requested type supported. The two types of variables that are supported by the interface are control and performance variables. More details on the variable types are discussed in Sect. 4.1. The shmem_t_var_avail API also takes the variable type argument and returns the corresponding variables of the requested type as an array of variable objects. The implementation can define the data structure for representing its variables and return a list of those objects, or it can choose to return a list of variables represented by basic data types.

Before using the shmem_t variables, users should create a handle for the variable through which the variable will be bound to an OpenSHMEM object (e.g., PE, team, context). The allocation and deallocation of handle of type, shmem_t_var_handle, are done using the following two APIs in Listing 2. For allocation, a pointer to the configuration object of type shmem_t_handle_config is passed as an argument, which provides the necessary information of the object bound to as well as keeps the option of adding future extensions to configurations (e.g., session objects that allow multiple tools to use the interface simultaneously). The proposed structure for shmem_t_handle_config is shown in Listing 3. Further explanation on the variable

Listing 3. Example structure type for handle configuration

```
typedef struct {
   /* Bit representation of the variable */
   uint64_t var;
   /* Reference handle to the object the variable is bound to; */
   /* NULL for generic variables not bound to any object       */
   void *shmem_obj_handle;
} shmem_t_handle_config;
```

representation is given in Sect. 4.1. After the usage of the handle, it is freed using the `shmem_t_var_handle_free` routine.

With the allocated handle, users can read or reset the variables that they would like. This is achieved using the next four APIs presented in Listing 2. To reset a variable to its original default value, `shmem_t_var_reset` is used. The `shmem_t_var_write` is used to write a value to a variable. Before writing a value to a variable, an implementation should check whether the variable can be updated. The APIs `shmem_t_var_read` and `shmem_t_var_list_read` are used to read contents of a variable and a list of variables, respectively. All of these four APIs take the allocated handle as argument to get the associated variable. On return, the APIs provide an integer value indicating the success or failure of the operation.

OpenSHMEM tool developers may also like to get a unique identifier of a variable, which can be achieved using the last API is Listing 2. OpenSHMEM variable identifiers are constructed using different properties of the variables and further discussed in Sect. 4.1. The `shmem_t_get_var` API takes the properties as input arguments and returns the identifier as an unsigned 64-bit integer output argument. The return value of the function represents whether the corresponding variable is supported, and in case of failure, it returns -1.

4.1 `shmem_t` Variables

We design the OpenSHMEM tools interface variables based on the categories of information that are presented in Fig. 1. Each of the boxes in the bottom layer of Fig. 1 represents a set of OpenSHMEM objects or entities in the underlying implementation that are available to the user through OpenSHMEM APIs, but are not directly accessible to extract any internal information. While these objects represent the broad categories of information, each of them can be sub-divided into more categories for which further information can be collected and provided to the user (e.g., RMA information can be sub-divided to Puts and Gets, blocking and non-blocking, etc.). Furthermore, an implementation can also define its own categories of information objects beyond the generic ones presented in Fig. 1.

We design the `shmem_t` variables with respect to the properties of these information objects in an OpenSHMEM implementation. Unlike a string and an array index based representation of the variables in `MPI_T`, a `shmem_t` variable is represented by a unique 64-bit unsigned integer constructed from values of different properties of the variable. Different sets of the bits in the identifier represent a specific property of the variable. An implementation can choose the ordering and mapping of the properties to specific

Table 2. Example `shmem_t` variable properties with minimum number of bits

Property	Examples	Minimum bits	Possible options
Variable type	CVAR, PVAR	2	4
Variable class	Counter, Aggregate	4	16
Binding to	Contexts, Teams	4	16
Associated operation	Put, Fetch-AMO	12	4,096
Variable scope	Completed, Pending	10	1,024
Other (unused)	Implementation defined	32	Over 4 billion

values. We propose the following properties to represent a variable: *type*, *class*, *associated operation*, *binding to* an OpenSHMEM object, and *variable scope*. While the values for these properties are implementation specific, a defined minimum number of bits for each of them will make the implementation flexible and portable. An example of the minimum number of bits assigned for each of these properties from the 64-bit unsigned integer identifier is shown in Table 2.

Variable type defines whether the variable is a performance or a control variable. To keep scope for future additional variable types, we propose to keep 2 bits to represent this property. *Variable class* defines the basic semantic and possible datatype of the variable, similar to the MPI performance variable classes. Examples include counter, size, state, aggregate, etc. A counter type variable can represent the number of put operations completed, whereas an aggregate type variable provides the total number of bytes transferred for put operations. We propose to have at least 4 bits assigned to represent this property. The *bind-to* property indicates which OpenSHMEM object a variable is bound to. For example, a variable can be bound to a context (providing information pertaining to the specific context in a PE) or to the PE itself. We keep at least 4 bits to represent this property. The *associated OpenSHMEM operation* and the *variable scope* are the two properties that can hold many possible values and we assign at least 12 and 10 bits for these properties, respectively, to allow enough options for the current OpenSHMEM standard and future extensions. While implementations can choose to use more bits for each of these properties, they can also define implementation specific custom properties by utilizing the unused 32 bits (over 4 billion options) from the 64-bit integer.

Apart from the robustness and ease-of-use benefits of the proposed variable representation, there are additional advantages over the string representation in `MPI_T`. If an OpenSHMEM implementation chooses to expose their variable's bit mapping and ordering to their users, it will require little programming effort from the users to form the variables using bitwise operations before accessing the variables. We provide some examples in Sect. 5 to illustrate these use-cases.

5 Example Tool Usage

In this section, we provide some example codes to demonstrate the usage of our proposed `shmem_t`. In the first example, shown in Listing 4, we keep the usage similar to the current `MPI_T` usage shown in Sect. 2. Using this example, tool developers can

Listing 4. Example C program utilizing tools interface to read a performance variable

```
static void *perf_collector(void *arg) {
  ...
  /* Collect the number of performance variables supported */
  shmem_t_var_get_num(&num_pvars, SHMEM_T_VAR_TYPE_P);

  /* Get the list of performance variables supported */
  shmem_t_var *pvar_list = malloc(num_pvars * sizeof(shmem_t_var));
  shmem_t_var_avail(&pvar_list, SHMEM_T_VAR_TYPE_P);

  int desired_pvar_operation = SHMEM_T_VAR_CAT_RMA_PUT;
  int desired_pvar_binding = SHMEM_T_VAR_BIND_CTX;
  int desired_pvar_scope = SHMEM_T_VAR_OP_PENDING;
  int desired_pvar_class = SHMEM_T_VAR_CLASS_COUNTER;
  int desired_pvar_index = -1;

  /* Search for the desired variable in the list */
  for (i = 0; i < num_pvars; i++) {
    if (pvar_list[i].operation == desired_pvar_operation &&
        pvar_list[i].binding == desired_pvar_binding &&
        pvar_list[i].scope == desired_pvar_scope &&
        pvar_list[i].class == desired_pvar_class) {
      desired_pvar_index = i;
    }
  }

  /* If no such variable available, exit */
  if (desired_pvar_index == -1) {
    fprintf(.., "No_support");
    return;
  }

  /* Allocate handle and reset */
  uint64_t pvar = pvar_list[desired_pvar_index].var_id;
  shmem_t_handle_config conf;
  conf.var = pvar;
  shmem_t_var_handle_alloc(&conf, &handle);
  shmem_t_var_reset(handle);

  /* Read the variable and store data */
  while (running) {
    shmem_t_var_read(handle, &curr_val);
    store_data(curr_time, curr_val);
  }

  /* Free handle */
  shmem_t_var_handle_free(&handle);
}

int main(int argc, char *argv[]) {
  /* Initialize shmem_t */
  shmem_t_init_thread(SHMEM_THREAD_MULTIPLE, &provided);

  /* Launch the collector thread */
  pthread_create(&thread, NULL, perf_collector, &args);
  ...
  /* Finalize shmem_t */
  shmem_t_finalize();
  return 0;
}
```

enable OpenSHMEM performance and control variables with minimal code changes compared to that for MPI_T variables.

Listing 5. Example of using shmem_t_get_var in C to get the variable

```
...
int desired_pvar_operation = SHMEM_T_VAR_CAT_RMA_PUT;
int desired_pvar_binding = SHMEM_T_VAR_BIND_CTX;
int desired_pvar_scope = SHMEM_T_VAR_OP_PENDING;
int desired_pvar_class = SHMEM_T_VAR_CLASS_COUNTER;
uint64_t pvar;

/* Get the variable identifier; If not supported, -1 is returned */
int pvar_supported = shmem_t_get_var(SHMEM_T_VAR_TYPE_P, desired_pvar_operation,
                                     desired_pvar_binding, desired_pvar_scope,
                                     desired_pvar_class, &pvar);

/* If no such variable available, exit */
if (pvar_supported == -1) {
  fprintf(.., "No␣support");
  return;
}

/* Allocate handle and reset */
shmem_t_handle_config conf;
conf.var = pvar;
shmem_t_var_handle_alloc(&conf, &handle);

...
```

In the example shown in Listing 4, we show how a performance data collector can interface with shmem_t and collect data from a variable defined within the implementation. To keep the code concise, we have highlighted the portion where the shmem_t APIs are being used and skipped details such as basic error checking, declaration of variables, etc. In this example, the `main` function in the program launches the collector thread after initializing the tools interface. The collector thread starts with querying the interface to get the number of supported variables and retrieves the list of variables from the OpenSHMEM library. It then searches for the variable in the list to get the desired variable identifier (`var_id`). If the implementation does not support this variable, the thread exits and returns. In case of success, it allocates a handle for the variable and then resets and reads the variable. After collecting the data for some duration, it deallocates the handle and returns.

With our proposed APIs, the tool developers can also simply retrieve the desired variable using the `shmem_t_get_var` API. This would allow a much simpler use-case for tools to find out whether the variable is supported in the underlying implementation and thus can be used. Listing 5 shows the corresponding part of the code where this API can be used to retrieve the variable.

The OpenSHMEM implementation can define its own bit representation of the variables and may choose to provide the representation and the valid values to the users so that users can access the variables by constructing the variable identifiers themselves. Listing 6 shows such example usage where the tool developers can use bitwise OR operations to construct the identifier and then use it accordingly.

Listing 6. Example of retrieving variable using bitwise operation

```
...
int desired_pvar_operation = SHMEM_T_VAR_CAT_RMA_PUT;
int desired_pvar_binding = SHMEM_T_VAR_BIND_CTX;
int desired_pvar_scope = SHMEM_T_VAR_OP_PENDING;
int desired_pvar_class = SHMEM_T_VAR_CLASS_COUNTER;

/* Bit organization of the variables */
/* Bits 0 - 3    :    variable class */
/* Bits 4 - 13   :    variable scope */
/* Bits 14 - 25  :         operation */
/* Bits 26 - 29  :           binding */
/* Bits 30 - 31  :     variable type */
/* Bits 32 - 63  :            unused */
uint64_t pvar = desired_pvar_class | (desired_pvar_scope << 4) |
                (desired_pvar_operation << 14) |
                (desired_pvar_binding << 26) |
                (SHMEM_T_VAR_TYPE_P << 30);

/* Allocate handle and reset */
shmem_t_handle_config conf;
conf.var = pvar;
shmem_t_var_handle_alloc(&conf, &handle);
...
```

With the bit representation made available to the user, implementations can also define special values to identify a group of variables and provide additional APIs to enable or access them. As an example, an implementation can define a special value of the bits to identify all the RMA variables and APIs can support read or write to the group of variables, instead of a single variable.

6 Conclusion

This paper conceptualizes the tools information interface for OpenSHMEM and proposes an API structure that tool developers can use for controlling, tuning, and debugging applications for correctness and performance. While we propose an API similar to the state-of-the-art usages in other programming models, we design the variables in a way that they can be utilized in a more flexible manner. We plan to implement our proposed model in an open-source OpenSHMEM implementation, Sandia OpenSHMEM [14], and to explore other opportunities to extend and improve the usages with respect to tools.

References

1. Cray-MPICH. https://docs.nersc.gov/development/programming-models/mpi/mpich/
2. Intel® MPI Library. https://software.intel.com/content/www/us/en/develop/tools/oneapi/components/mpi-library.html
3. MPI: A Message Passing Interface Standard Version 3.0. https://www.mpi-forum.org/docs/mpi-3.0/mpi30-report.pdf
4. MPICH: High Performance Portable MPI. https://www.mpich.org/
5. MPI_T: Gyan. https://computing.llnl.gov/projects/mpi_t/gyan
6. MPI_T: VarList. https://computing.llnl.gov/projects/mpi_t/varlist

7. MVAPICH: MPI over InfiniBand, Omni-Path, Ethernet/iWARP, and RoCE. https://mvapich.cse.ohio-state.edu/
8. OpenMPI: Open Source High Performance Computing. https://www.open-mpi.org/
9. TAU Performance System. https://www.cs.uoregon.edu/research/tau/home.php
10. Boehme, D., et al.: Caliper: performance introspection for HPC software stacks. In: SC 2016: Proceedings of the International Conference for High Performance Computing, Networking, Storage and Analysis, pp. 550–560 (2016). https://doi.org/10.1109/SC.2016.46
11. MPI Forum: MPI: A message-passing interface standard version 3.1. Technical report, University of Tennessee, Knoxville, June 2015
12. OpenSHMEM application programming interface, version 1.5, June 2020. http://www.openshmem.org
13. Rahman, M.W., Ozog, D., Dinan, J.: Lightweight instrumentation and analysis using openshmem performance counters. In: Pophale, S., Imam, N., Aderholdt, F., Gorentla Venkata, M. (eds.) OpenSHMEM 2018. LNCS, vol. 11283, pp. 180–201. Springer, Cham (2019). https://doi.org/10.1007/978-3-030-04918-8_12
14. Sandia OpenSHMEM (2018). https://github.com/Sandia-OpenSHMEM/SOS
15. UPC Consortium: UPC language and library specifications, v1.3. Technical report, LBNL-6623E, Lawrence Berkeley National Lab, November 2013

CircusTent: A Tool for Measuring the Performance of Atomic Memory Operations on Emerging Architectures

Brody Williams[1(✉)], John D. Leidel[2], Xi Wang[3], David Donofrio[2], and Yong Chen[1]

[1] Texas Tech University, Lubbock, TX, USA
{brody.williams,yong.chen}@ttu.edu
[2] Tactical Computing Laboratories, Muenster, TX, USA
{jleidel,ddonofrio}@tactcomplabs.com
[3] RISC-V International Open Source Laboratory, Shenzhen, China
xi.w@rioslab.org

Abstract. Endeavors to engineer the next generation of exascale platforms have resulted in a fundamental shift in system architectures. Orthogonal to what was once considered conventional wisdom, high performance systems designed today are characterized by heterogeneous architectures wherein distinct components are carefully combined in order to optimize system performance and energy efficiency. One unintended consequence of this new paradigm is an increasingly complex memory hierarchy that frequently spans multiple devices and may be composed of disparate memory types. Unfortunately, the effect on performance of this new memory model is not well understood. Moreover, a quantifiable, system-agnostic methodology capable of assessing the performance of the diverse memory subsystems within emerging architectures has yet to be introduced. The CircusTent benchmark suite has been introduced to fill this void by measuring system performance with respect to atomic memory operations using established parallel programming models. However, a detailed description and evaluation of CircusTent in a distributed memory environment, critical to both current and future system architectures, has yet to be produced. In this work, we rectify this shortcoming by introducing CircusTent implementations based on the OpenSHMEM and MPI programming models and evaluating these implementations across a variety of platforms. We then detail our conclusions and characterize our observations regarding the effect of different system interconnects, memory hierarchies, and instruction set architectures on system performance.

Keywords: Benchmark · Atomic memory operations · OpenSHMEM · MPI · Performance

1 Introduction

Modern high performance system architectures are becoming increasingly heterogeneous. Galvanized by the end of Moore's Law and Dennard Scaling, as well as

S. Poole et al. (Eds.): OpenSHMEM 2021, LNCS 13159, pp. 92–110, 2022.
https://doi.org/10.1007/978-3-031-04888-3_6

inherent limitations to multicore scaling [11], system architects have been forced to adopt a new strategy in order to continue realizing improvements to system performance. At the heart of this new paradigm is the principle of hardware/software codesign. Herein, the concurrent design of hardware and software inform one another, often towards the optimization of a particular class of problem. Devices such as general-purpose graphics processing units, tensor processing units [16], and data processing units/smartNICs [5,22] represent prominent designs derived from this philosophy. As we move into the exascale era and beyond, it is widely accepted that only by integrating these workload optimized components into existing high performance computing infrastructures can we continue to enhance system capabilities and simultaneously strive to improve energy efficiency.

As such, the ability to measure the performance of these emerging heterogeneous architectures is critical. Regrettably, the introduction of widely dissimilar components into otherwise conventional architectures complicates efforts to conduct such measurements. One such impediment can be attributed to the increasingly complex memory hierarchies present in heterogeneous systems. In addition to traditional multilevel processor caches and DDR-based memory, these systems also typically feature some number of separate memory pools directly coupled to their constituent devices. Moreover, recent advances in memory technology have resulted in a diversification of memory types. The development of 3D stacked memory technologies such as high-bandwidth memory [17] and the hybrid memory cube [15] have provided a mechanism for improving memory bandwidth. In contrast, non-volatile random access memory devices have proven effective at alleviating I/O related bottlenecks [8] and have already inspired extensions to existing programming models [13]. The effect of multiple discrete memory pools, which, along with a system's main memory, may be composed of novel memory types, on overall system behavior is not well understood or quantified.

The CircusTent benchmark suite has been proposed as a tool for measuring the performance of memory subsystems on both conventional and advanced architectures. CircusTent utilizes atomic memory operations (AMOs), which, while crucial in parallel execution environments, also represent a bottleneck for memory hierarchies, in order to measure the performance of a target system. Implemented upon well-established parallel programming models, CircusTent provides a generalized methodology that remains agnostic of any system specific requirements. In our previous work [32], we introduced the CircusTent benchmark suite and performed an experimental analysis of shared memory systems using our OpenMP backend. Orthogonally, in this work we explore the performance of atomic memory operations in the distributed memory environments that are necessitated by problems driving the design of emerging architectures.

The remainder of this work is organized as follows. Section 2 provides a primer on atomic memory operations in distributed memory systems as well background information on the CircusTent benchmark suite. Section 3 introduces the design and implementation of CircusTent upon prominent distributed memory parallel programming models. In Sect. 4, we conduct an evaluation of our OpenSHMEM and MPI CircusTent backends using several diverse platforms. Section 5 briefly introduces related work. Section 6 summarizes our findings and observations related to CircusTent in the context of distributed memory architectures. Finally, Sect. 7 concludes this study with a discussion of planned future work.

2 Background

2.1 Atomic Operations in Distributed Memory

Analogous to shared memory environments, atomic memory operations in distributed memory systems represent a bottleneck to overall performance. CircusTent seeks to provide a portable methodology for measuring the performance of atomic operations on these systems. However, a thorough understanding of the behavior of these operations is also necessary in order alleviate shortcomings and improve performance when designing future platforms.

The behavior of a given atomic operation, as implemented in distributed memory programming models such as OpenSHMEM and MPI, is dependent upon the physical proximity of the executing process and the target memory location. If the process and the memory location in question are co-located, the atomic operation can be translated into its ISA-level analog for execution. However, if the referenced memory location is physically decoupled from the process, the implementation of this "remote atomic" is more complex.

Broadly, remote atomic operations may be implemented in either hardware or software, with the former being highly preferable for improved performance. The ability of a system to perform hardware-based atomic memory operations is determined by the remote direct memory access (RDMA) capabilities of its network interconnect. Modern high speed interconnects such as the InfiniBand and Cray Aries architectures include support for RDMA-based remote atomic operations. More conventional Ethernet-based networks may also incorporate RDMA support through utilization of adapters that support the RDMA over Converged Ethernet (RoCE) or iWARP protocols.

RDMA-based remote atomic operations are performed through coordination of the NICs[1] on both ends of the operation as demonstrated in Figure 1. When a remote atomic operation is encountered during execution, the executing process first sends a signal to its NIC to begin fulfillment of the request (1). The NIC attached to this process then builds a request encapsulating the atomic operation to be performed, the target remote memory location, and associated metadata which is transmitted across the interconnect to the NIC responsible for

[1] In this work, we use the generic term "NIC" to refer to network adapters in both Ethernet and Cray Aries networks as well as InfiniBand HCAs.

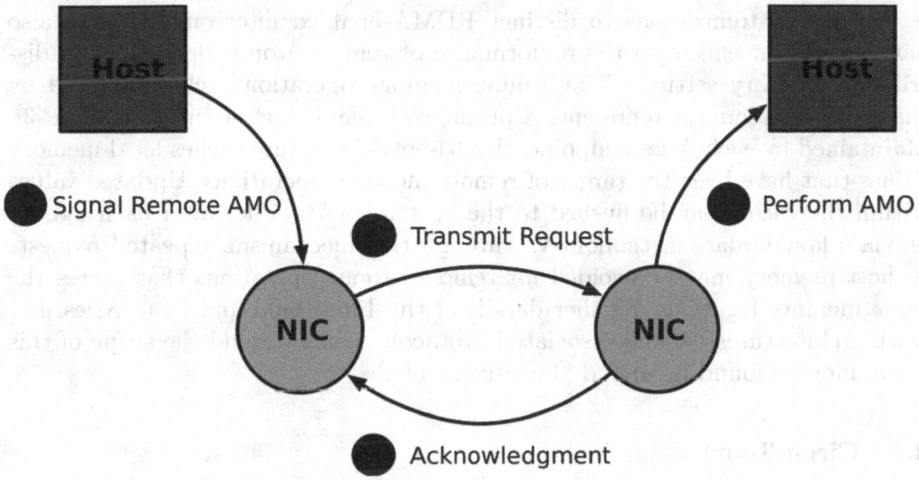

Fig. 1. Demonstration of RDMA-enabled remote atomic operation

the memory location (2). Once this request is received, the recipient NIC performs the solicited read-modify-write atomic operation on the target memory location (3). After the atomic operation is complete, the receiving NIC constructs a response acknowledging the operation completion which it forwards to the original requesting NIC (4). For *Compare-and-Swap* and *Fetch-and-Op* atomic operations, the original value located at the targeted memory location is returned inside this response. Thus, from the perspective of the original process, the atomic memory operation is considered complete only after the corresponding response is received.

As a result of this behavior, wherein the actual atomic operation is performed by the target side NIC, atomicity of remote atomic operations with respect to other memory operations within local memory is not guaranteed. Some interconnects, such as InifiniBand, provide within their specification the option for individual hardware implementations to guarantee atomicity between atomic operations executed by different NICs and/or ports [4]. However, since this behavior is not standardized, distributed memory programming models do not adopt such assurances.

It should be noted that a given interconnect may only support a subset of the remote atomic operations offered by higher level APIs in hardware. For example, InifiniBand hardware implements only 64-bit Compare-and-Swap and Fetch-and-Add atomic operations [4]. Other operations are supported through a combination of these mechanics or via active messages, but may incur associated overheads. In contrast to InfiniBand, the Aries interconnect supports a richer set of atomic operations in both 32-bit and 64-bit variations [24]. In the absence of hardware support, software based implementations of atomic operations may be utilized as a fallback [26].

Unique customizations to distinct RDMA-enabled interconnects may also have significant effects on the performance of remote atomic operations in distributed memory settings. The atomic memory operation cache employed by the Aries interconnect represents a prime example of such a customization [3]. Maintained by each Aries endpoint, this 64-entry structure caches local memory values that have been the target of remote memory operations. Updated values within the cache may be flushed to the host memory either after each update or via a lazy update methodology. Through this mechanism, repeated requests to host memory may be avoided for remote atomic operations that access the same memory locations. Further details of the InfiniBand and Cray Aries network architectures, as well associated protocols, while beyond the scope of this work, may be found in [4] and [3], respectively.

2.2 CircusTent

As noted in Sect. 1, CircusTent is designed to remain independent of any specific hardware or software constraints. Instead, CircusTent is based on an easily extensible, modular design that is built around ubiquitous parallel programming models. Therefore, the performance of any architecture of interest may be benchmarked using CircusTent as long the system in question implements one or more of these models in some form. Moreover, this philosophy also enables the user to leverage the presence of system specific optimizations in order to more accurately gauge expected system performance. In conjunction with CircusTent's generalized performance metric, the result is a benchmark suite which is broadly applicable and whose results are directly comparable.

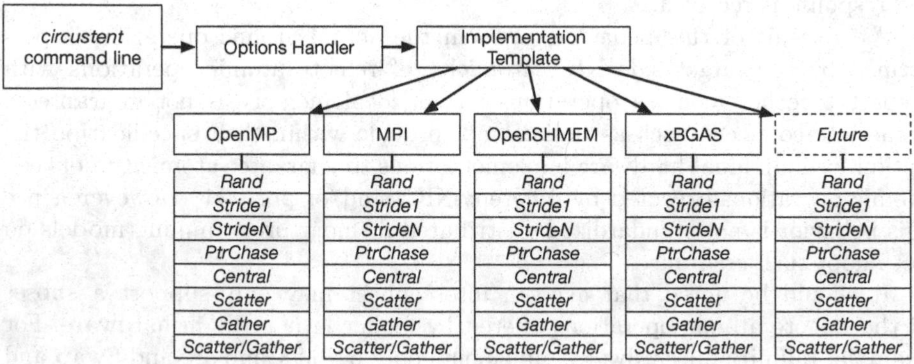

Fig. 2. CircusTent architecture

CircusTent is implemented in a mixture of ANSI C and C++ and architected around an abstraction of two independent modules. The structure of the CircusTent architecture is shown in Fig. 2. The first component of CircusTent is the frontend. The frontend module defines the template imposed on underlying programming model implementations and is responsible for parsing command line options. Positioned directly below the universal frontend are interchangeable backend modules that encapsulate distinct implementations of the CircusTent benchmark suite based on prominent parallel programming models. Currently, CircusTent supports backend implementations for the Pthreads, OpenMP, MPI [12], OpenSHMEM [6,27], and xBGAS [18,30] programming models. Each implementation is, in turn, composed of eight benchmark kernels that emulate common memory access patterns in high performance computing applications. The Stride-1 and Stride-N kernels replicate sequential access patterns as well those defined by a regular, user-defined unit stride, respectively. In contrast, the Random Access kernel accesses memory locations in an unpredictable manner. The Pointer Chasing kernel demonstrates a memory access pattern common to applications that utilize linked data structures. The Central kernel measures performance in the presence of high memory hotspotting. Finally, the Scatter, Gather, and Scatter/Gather kernels utilize a combination of sequential and indexed memory accesses to replicate the common patterns of the same name. Each kernel may be executed using either atomic *Add* or *Compare and Swap* primitives. For a more detailed description of the individual benchmark kernels, we refer the reader to our previous work [32]. As a result of its modular design, CircusTent is intrinsically extensible such that support for new programming paradigms may be added with minimum overhead. Further, additional benchmark kernels and/or atomic primitives may be incorporated through modification of the frontend template.

3 CircusTent for Distributed Memory

CircusTent currently provides backend implementations built upon the OpenSHMEM, MPI RMA, and xBGAS programming models for evaluating the performance of system architectures with respect to distributed memory hierarchies. In this section, we provide a brief overview of the OpenSHMEM and MPI RMA implementations by utilizing the Scatter/Gather (SG) kernel, which is the most complex of the eight CircusTent benchmark kernels, as an illustrative example. We compare the design of these backends targeting distributed memory environments with their OpenMP analog as described in [32]. Moreover, we also emphasize distinctions between the OpenSHMEM and MPI RMA implementations necessitated by the differing semantics of the programming models themselves. Note that the xBGAS programming model is designed to mirror that of OpenSHMEM. Differences that exist between the two paradigms do so at the microarchitectural level. As such, a separate discussion of the xBGAS backend is not included as part of this work.

3.1 OpenSHMEM

```
void SHMEM_SG_ADD(uint64_t *restrict ARRAY, uint64_t *restrict IDX,
                  int *restrict TARGET, uint64_t iters){

  uint64_t i = 0, start = 0, src = 0, dest = 0, val = 0;

  for(i=0; i<iters; i++){
    src  =(uint64_t)(shmem_long_atomic_fetch_add((long *)(&IDX[i]),
                                                  (long)(0x00ull),
                                                  TARGET[i]));
    dest =(uint64_t)(shmem_long_atomic_fetch_add((long *)(&IDX[i+1]),
                                                  (long)(0x00ull),
                                                  TARGET[i]));
    val  =(uint64_t)(shmem_long_atomic_fetch_add((long *)(&ARRAY[src]),
                                                  (long)(0x01ull),
                                                  TARGET[i]));
    start=(uint64_t)(shmem_long_atomic_fetch_add((long *)(&ARRAY[dest]),
                                                  (long)(val),
                                                  TARGET[i]));
  }
}
```

Listing 1. OpenSHMEM SG Kernel Code

The OpenSHMEM implementation of the Scatter/Gather kernel is shown in Listing 1. In many ways, the structure of this kernel is similar to that of its OpenMP analog. Herein, `ARRAY` represents an array of randomized 64-bit values. Similarly, `IDX` points to an array whose values correspond to random indices within `ARRAY`. In contrast however, both `ARRAY` and `IDX` are now allocated in the symmetric heap in order to make their respective memory locations remotely accessible. The addition of the local `TARGET` array, which contains a random OpenSHMEM processing element (PE) identifier for each kernel loop iteration, represents another difference between the OpenSHMEM and OpenMP Scatter/-Gather implementations. Utilizing the arguments detailed above, the OpenSH-MEM Scatter/Gather kernel replicates its eponymous memory access pattern in a distributed memory environment through the use of four atomic operations. First, a `src` value representing an index within `ARRAY` is set using the return value from an atomic operation on the target remote `IDX` array. A subsequent atomic operation retrieves a `dest` value in the same manner. Using `src` obtained in the first step, a data value, represented by `val`, is gathered using a third atomic operation. Finally, `val` is scattered to the location denoted by `dest` to finish the given kernel iteration. Although Listing 1 demonstrates the Scatter/Gather kernel using the *Fetch-And-Add* atomic operation, which is directly analogous to *Add* in our OpenMP implementation, a *Compare-And-Swap* variation is also provided. Notably, the PGAS semantics of the OpenSHMEM model, which, for fetching atomic operations, require no synchronization beyond the atomic operation calls themselves, map particularly well to the CircusTent Scatter/Gather kernel.

3.2 MPI RMA

As demonstrated by Listing 2, the MPI RMA Scatter/Gather kernel is considerably more complex than its OpenSHMEM counterpart. For the most part, this is due to the semantics of the MPI RMA model itself. CircusTent performs remote memory accesses to randomized memory locations across all active PEs during execution. As such, local memory segments associated with a given PE that are designated for remote access must be exposed to all other PEs during kernel execution. Moreover, the results of each atomic operation at the target memory locations must be immediately visible to all other PEs after the operation is complete. In order to accommodate these requirements, the CircusTent MPI implementation utilizes the MPI passive target synchronization model. This model, which most closely emulates the one-sided remote memory access semantics of PGAS programming models, also enables better performance as compared to the active synchronization model. In this implementation, `ARRAY`, `IDX`, and `TARGET` are all allocated in a PE's local memory, but otherwise behave as described for the OpenSHMEM Scatter/Gather implementation. The two additional arguments, `AWin` and `IWin`, define the windows of "exposed" memory for the `ARRAY` and `IDX` data values, respectively. The procedure utilized by the MPI implementation of the Scatter/Gather kernel itself is highly reminiscent of the OpenSHMEM variation, but with one critical difference. In contrast to the OpenSHMEM *Fetch-And-Add* atomic operation previously described, MPI atomic operations are not blocking operations. Therefore, in order to ensure correctness and consistency, an `MPI_Win_flush` call is necessary between each atomic operation. This extra synchronization operation ensures that the result of each atomic operation is visible to both the calling and target processes before proceeding. Consistent with the OpenSHMEM Scatter/Gather kernel shown above, Listing 2 utilizes *MPI_Fetch_and_Op* (in conjunction with MPI_SUM) to formulate a *Fetch-And-Add* atomic operation. Again, a *Compare-And-Swap* based MPI implementation is also included in CircusTent.

```
void MPI_SG_ADD(uint64_t *restrict ARRAY, uint64_t *restrict IDX,
                int *restrict TARGET, uint64_t iters,
                MPI_Win AWin, MPI_Win IWin){

  uint64_t i = 0, start = 0, src = 0, dest = 0, val = 0,
              zero = 0x00ull, one = 0x01ull;

  MPI_Win_lock_all(0, AWin);
  MPI_Win_lock_all(0, IWin);

  for( i=0; i<iters; i++ ){
    MPI_Fetch_and_op((unsigned long *)(&zero),(unsigned long *)(&src),
                     MPI_UNSIGNED_LONG,TARGET[i],
                     ((&IDX[i])-(&IDX[0])),MPI_SUM,IWin);
    MPI_Win_flush(TARGET[i], IWin);

    MPI_Fetch_and_op((unsigned long *)(&zero),(unsigned long *)(&dest),
                     MPI_UNSIGNED_LONG,TARGET[i],
                     ((&IDX[i+1])-(&IDX[0])),MPI_SUM,IWin);
    MPI_Win_flush(TARGET[i], IWin);

    MPI_Fetch_and_op((unsigned long *)(&one),(unsigned long *)(&val),
                     MPI_UNSIGNED_LONG,TARGET[i],
                     ((&ARRAY[src])-(&ARRAY[0])),MPI_SUM,AWin);
    MPI_Win_flush(TARGET[i], AWin);

    MPI_Fetch_and_op((unsigned long *)(&val),(unsigned long *)(&start),
                     MPI_UNSIGNED_LONG,TARGET[i],
                     ((&ARRAY[dest])-(&ARRAY[0])),MPI_SUM,AWin);
    MPI_Win_flush(TARGET[i], AWin);
  }
  MPI_Win_unlock_all(AWin);
  MPI_Win_unlock_all(IWin);
}
```

Listing 2. MPI RMA SG Kernel Code

4 Evaluation

4.1 Methodology

In this section, we conduct a series of experiments using the CircusTent OpenSHMEM and MPI RMA backend implementations in order to evaluate the viability of our benchmark suite as a tool for measuring the performance of heterogeneous memory hierarchies in distributed memory environments. We utilize a small set of diverse evaluation platforms to better illuminate the effect of distinct system components on overall performance. On each of our evaluation platforms, we conduct trials of all eight CircusTent benchmark kernel using 2–7 nodes. Further, for each node configuration we vary the number of coresident PEs from 1–16. Across each of our conducted trials, a static size of 2 GiB was used for the `ARRAY` data structure on each PE. Similarly, a static stride size of 9 was used for all STRIDE-N tests. For each benchmark kernel, 100,000 iterations were performed by each PE. Due to space considerations, we present only a subset of these results in this work. For the same reason, and because the results did not significantly vary, we detail only the results gathered using the *Fetch-And-Add* atomic operation. In order to standardize performance comparisons across platforms, we utilize CircusTent's portable **G**iga **A**tomic **M**emory Operations per **S**econd metric as shown in Eq. 1. Herein, *AMOs_Per_Iter* represents the number of atomic memory operations utilized by each kernel during a given loop iteration. While this value varies across kernels, it remains fixed across backend implementations.

$$GAMs = \frac{(PEs \times Iters \times AMOs\_Per\_Iter)/1e^9}{time} \tag{1}$$

4.2 Platforms

We utilize four distinct platforms throughout our evaluation of CircusTent for distributed memory systems. In conjunction, these systems provide a varied cross section of architectures and, in particular, system interconnects for conducting our investigation. Two of these systems, Trinitite and Capulin, are Cray systems hosted by Los Alamos National Laboratory that utilize the Aries interconnect. The former features conventional server class Xeon processors while the latter employs Cavium ThunderX2 processors. Our third platform, Texas Tech University's Nocona system, utilizes Xeon processors similar to Trinitite, but implements an InfiniBand interconnect. Finally, Tactical Computing Labratory's Pennywise cluster represents a more traditional commodity class system utilizing an Ethernet based network that does not employ RDMA-enabled NICs. In an attempt to focus our investigation on the hardware aspects of our platforms, we uniformly utilized OpenMPI and OSHMEM, respectively, for our MPI and OpenSHMEM implementations. Moreover, utilization of the Modular Component Architecture (MCA) employed by these implementations enabled fine-grained control of diverse transports across platforms and ensured proper configuration. Each OpenMPI/OSHMEM installation was built upon UCX v1.10.1 [25] regardless of platform. A detailed specification of each evaluation platform's configuration is given by Table 1.

Table 1. Evaluation platform characteristics

	Trinitite	Capulin	Nocona	Pennywise
ISA	x86_64	ARMv8.1	x86_64	x86_64
CPU	2× Intel Xeon E5-2698 v3 16 cores/socket, 2 threads/core	2× Cavium ThunderX2 9975, 28 cores/socket, 4 threads/core	2× AMD EPYC 7702, 64 cores/socket, 1 thread/core	2× Intel Xeon E5-2650, 8 cores/socket, 2 threads/core
Cache configuration	L1 d/i: 32 KiB, L2: 256 KiB, L3: 40 MiB	L1 d/i: 32 KiB, L2: 256 KiB, L3: 32 MiB	L1 d/i: 32 KiB, L2: 512 KiB, L3: 16 MiB	L1 d/i: 32 KiB, L2: 256 KiB, L3: 20 MiB
Memory	128 GiB	256 GiB	512 GiB	64 GiB
Interconnect	Cray Aries Topology: Dragonfly	Cray Aries Topology: Dragonfly	InfiniBand HDR 200G Topology: Fat Tree	1Gbps Ethernet Topology: Fat Tree
Operating system	CLE SLES 15.1	CLE SLES 15.1	CentOS 8.1	Ubuntu 18.04
Compiler	GCC 10.2.0	GCC 10.2.0	GCC 10.2.0	GCC 7.3.0
MPI implementation	OMPI 3.1.6	OMPI 3.1.6	OMPI 4.1.1	OMPI 4.1.0
OpenSHMEM implementation	OSHMEM 3.1.6	OSHMEM 3.1.6	OSHMEM 4.1.1	OSHMEM 4.1.1

4.3 Kernel Scalability

The performance of both conventional high performance platforms, as well as the increasingly heterogeneous platforms of the future, is inherently to coupled to the system architecture's ability to effectively scale out. As such, the ability to measure the performance of atomic memory operations as physical memory resources become increasingly distributed is critical. We apply CircusTent to this use case to investigate the scalability of different memory access patterns across not only platforms, but also distinct programming models, as the number of nodes is increased. Figure 3 demonstrates the effect on performance of monotonously increasing the number of distinct nodes executing each benchmark kernel. The number of PEs across trials is kept constant at 16 PEs per node.

Multiple trends are immediately apparent upon examination. Notably, the performance of each individual kernel remains fairly consistent relative to both platform and programming model. Moreover, the GAMs performance of the benchmark kernels increases in an approximately consistent manner alongside the number of participating nodes. Herein, the kernels that exhibit regular memory access patterns, such as STRIDE-1, demonstrate the highest performance. In contrast, the Random Access kernel performs most poorly among the CircusTent kernels. Notably, the CircusTent OpenSHMEM implementation demonstrates higher performance than its MPI analog with respect to platform and memory access kernel.

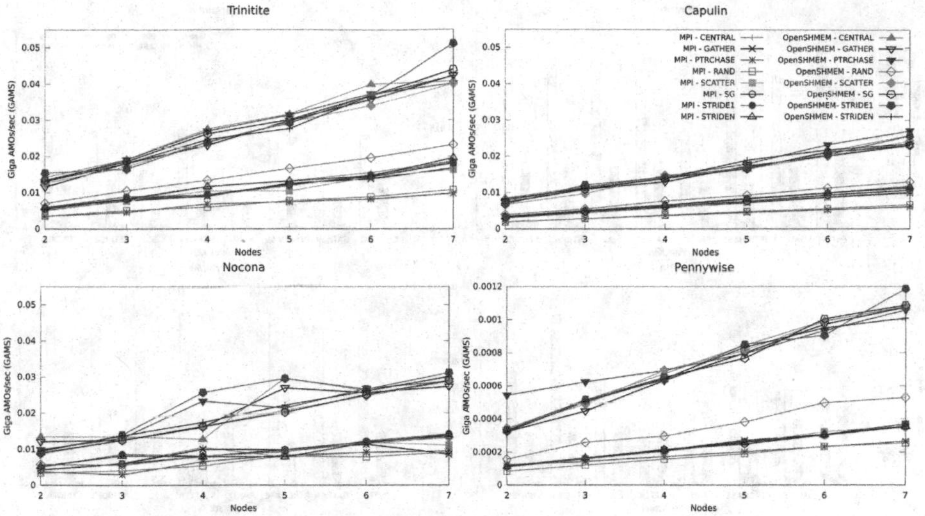

Fig. 3. Kernel scalability across platform/model

4.4 Shared Memory Optimizations

Orthogonal to the use case detailed above, CircusTent can also be employed to explore the effect of co-located resources on performance when utilizing programming models that support physically distributed memory. For this experiment, we fix the number of nodes participating in kernel execution at four. Instead, we conduct trials of each benchmark kernel using our OpenSHMEM and MPI RMA implementations and vary the number of PEs executing on each node. We gather results for both 1 PE per node and 16 PEs per node to perform our analysis.

As shown in Fig. 4, results from this experiment differ in several ways. Most apparent is the considerable performance gain shown by both implementations when scaling from 1 PE per node to 16 PEs per node. This behavior, demonstrated across platforms and benchmark kernels, fits well with what one might expect. In line with the results shown above, the OpenSHMEM implementation demonstrates superior intranode performance in comparison to the MPI RMA backend. Also notable is some interesting behavior with respect to the kernels themselves. Unsurprisingly, the irregular memory access patterns of the Random Access kernel again demonstrate the poorest performance across platforms. Perhaps more unexpectedly, only the Nocona platform demonstrates appreciably higher performance for the Stride-1 trials in comparison to other kernels.

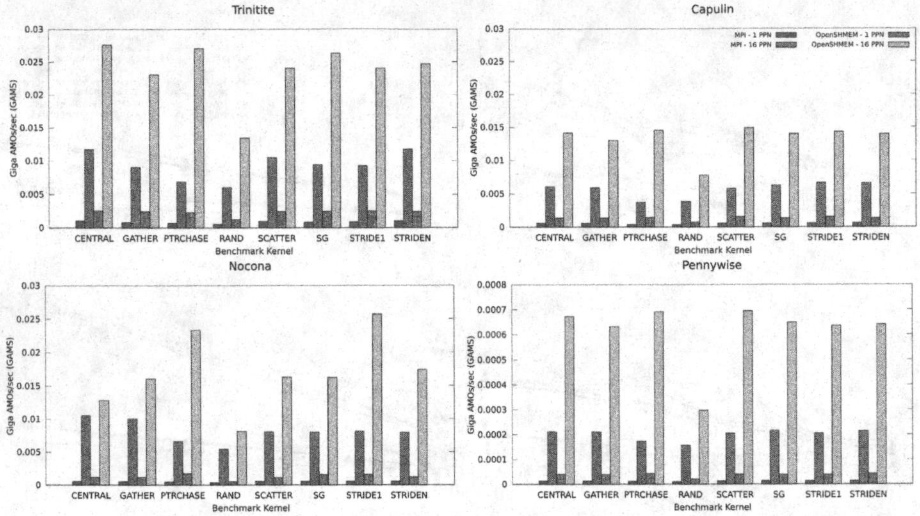

Fig. 4. Effect of physically shared memory across platform/model

4.5 Observations

Several general observations can made based on the results of our evaluation. First and foremost, the impact of the network interconnect on the performance of atomic memory operations in distributed memory environments is paramount. The roughly comparable performance of the Trinitite, Capulin, and Nocona systems, each of which utilizes a high speed, RDMA-enabled interconnect, testify to this fact. In contrast, the Pennywise cluster, which employs a Ethernet network limited to more conventional communication protocols, performed up to two orders of magnitude more poorly.

It also seems that the atomic memory operation cache employed by the Aries interconnect may offer significant benefits for remote atomic operation performance. This is demonstrated by the fact that, despite the similar processors employed by Trinitite and Nocona, Trinitite typically showcases higher GAMs performance. This is particularly true as the number of nodes is increased and for regular memory access patterns.

Although the interconnect is critical to the performance of atomic memory operations in distributed memory environments, the effect of the node architecture itself cannot be discounted. Assuming the Aries interconnect enables higher performance for similar architectures as noted above, the fact that Nocona performs comparably, or in some cases exceeds the performance of Capulin, lends credence to this conclusion.

5 Related Work

A significant number of previous studies have been devoted to improving our understanding of the behavior and performance of memory subsystems. We classify works particularly relevant to CircusTent into those associated with atomic memory operations, and those introducing novel memory benchmarks, as detailed below.

5.1 Atomic Memory Operations

In perhaps the most exhaustive study to date, David et al. conducted an investigation of synchronization that spanned multiple hardware and software methodologies [10]. Notably, as part of this study, the authors performed experiments using atomic memory operations analogous to the CircusTent CENTRAL kernel in a shared memory environment. Herein, they conclude that the performance of these operations varies depending on the socket and cache configurations of the underlying platforms. In [23], Schweizer et al. develop a methodology for analyzing the latency and bandwidth of atomic operations. In particular, they study the effects of different cache coherency states and complex memory hierarchies on these operations. As part of their evaluation, they show that, contrary to popular belief, all of the tested atomic operations exhibit comparable performance in terms of latency and bandwidth. Hoseini et al. also study the properties of atomic operations in physically shared memory systems [14]. For their investigation, they monitor accesses to shared cache lines in conditions that simulate both high and low levels of contention. Finally, the Bale project [1], which explores parallel programming methodologies in conjunction with communication aggregation mechanisms, includes several applications, such as histogram and indexgather, that employ atomic operations.

The studies enumerated above provide useful insights into the behavior and performance of atomic memory operations. However, most employ an approach specific to the architecture under test and/or target only shared memory environments. In contrast, CircusTent provides a portable methodology for measuring the performance of atomic memory operations in both shared and distributed memory scenarios.

5.2 Memory Benchmarks

Several benchmark suites have been proposed for measuring the performance of memory hierarchies in heterogeneous architectures. The Rodinia benchmark suite [7] is composed of a variety of applications and kernels parallelized using OpenMP and CUDA. As such, it is well-suited to its original target of benchmarking multicore CPU and GPU enabled platforms. In a similar vein, MP-STREAM [20] adapts the conventional STREAM benchmark, an exemplar for measuring memory bandwidth, to a variety of heterogeneous devices via an OpenCL-based implementation. Spatter is a memory benchmark developed by Lavin et al. [19] designed to measure an architecture's performance with respect to indexed memory access patterns such as scatter and gather operations. CircusTent also integrates kernels that replicate these memory access patterns, but does so using atomic operations in lieu of traditional loads and stores. The Hopscotch benchmark suite [2], which incorporates kernels replicating a variety of memory access patterns, provides a powerful tool for benchmarking memory systems. Moreover, it is also tunable, and can be used to emulate read-only, write-only, or mixed access workloads. Regrettably, the benchmarks detailed above do not employ distributed memory programming models. As such, they are limited to measuring physically isolated memory spaces.

In contrast, a number of benchmark suites have been widely adopted for measuring the performance of distributed memory systems. The majority of these solutions, such as those from The Ohio State University [29] and Sandia National Laboratories [31], examine performance as the intersection of a system's memory hierarchy and network interconnect. Metrics such as latency and bandwidth are standard in these suites. Most often, however, they do not explicitly incorporate different memory access patterns nor utilize atomic operations. Benchmarks that do incorporate atomic operations do not measure their performance in high contention scenarios in the same manner as CircusTent. The OpenSHMEM benchmark suite from Oak Ridge National Laboratory [21] is something of an exception to this generalization. Although this suite does, to some degree, incorporate these elements, it does so in the context of larger applications rather than small micro-kernels. A final interesting benchmark of note is Apex-Map [28], which examines global data accesses using the MPI, OpenSHMEM, and UPC programming models. One of the most novel aspects of Apex-Map is its ability to model performance for a variety of applications based on provided spatial and temporal locality parameters.

Each of the benchmark suites listed above are imminently useful and, in many cases, widely recognized standards for benchmarking heterogeneous architectures. However, they do not explicitly stress memory hierarchies with respect to atomic memory operations, which represent a point of contention regardless of architecture. To the best of our knowledge, CircusTent is the first portable benchmark suite for both shared and distributed memory architectures that measures memory performance using read-modify-write atomic operations. As such, we believe CircusTent will prove a useful supplement to existing solutions and further enable comprehensive analyses of existing and emerging platforms.

6 Conclusion

Motivated to meet the needs of the exascale era and beyond, the landscape of high performance system architectures is rapidly changing. Marked by the adoption of increasingly heterogeneous systems composed of novel device types, this shift has introduced a new set of challenges. Among these challenges is the difficulty associated with measuring the performance of these diverse platforms in a standardized, portable manner. The open source CircusTent benchmark suite has been proposed to help meet this need by measuring the performance of memory hierarchies within heterogeneous architectures through the use of atomic memory operations.

In this work, we introduced CircusTent backend implementations based on the prominent OpenSHMEM and MPI RMA programming models. We next detailed some of the semantic differences between these two distributed memory paradigms and discussed the resulting consequences on each model's respective implementation. In order to evaluate the viability of CircusTent for distributed memory systems, we conducted a series of experiments using both implementations across a set of distinctive platforms. Utilizing the results of these experiments, we then highlighted the effects of shared memory optimizations, varied interconnects, and the programming models themselves on system performance. Based upon these observations, we believe that CircusTent will prove to be a useful tool for measuring the capabilities of distributed memory hierarchies within emerging heterogeneous system architectures. We will continue to refine and improve the CircusTent benchmark suite in the hope of increasing its usefulness to the community at large.

7 Future Work

This study, in conjunction with our previous work [32], has introduced the CircusTent benchmark suite as a tool for measuring the performance of heterogeneous memory hierarchies. Herein, we have demonstrated CircusTent implementations targeting both shared and distributed memory systems and evaluated them across a variety of platforms. Nevertheless, multiple avenues exist for improving the viability of the CircusTent benchmark suite moving forward. Although we have constructed CircusTent backends around the OpenSHMEM, MPI, and xBGAS programming models, numerous other distributed paradigms exist. In order improve the generalizability of CircusTent, we will pursue development of implementations based on other PGAS models such as Chapel, UPC, and Coarray Fortran. Moreover, while we have targeted general-purpose shared and distributed memory models, we have neglected to include more specialized backends designed for accelerator-style devices. Adding support for programming models such as OpenACC, CUDA, and OpenCL will help rectify this shortcoming.

Beyond increasing the generalizability of CircusTent, several interesting research topics also bear further exploration. As noted in Sect. 2.1, software based remote atomic operations must often be utilized in lieu of more optimized hardware based solutions. However, the performance penalties of such solutions across distinct interconnects is unclear. Adding support for additional atomic primitives, including those not supported in hardware, would enable a quantifiable investigation of these penalties. Similarly detailed in Sect. 2.1, network adapters play a critical role in the execution of remote atomic operations. As such, the increasing adoption of DPU/SmartNIC devices stands to make a significant impact on the future of high performance system architectures. Given its unique methodology, CircusTent is well-suited to evolve in order to assist this transition and the design of associated interfaces such as OpenSNAPI [9].

Acknowledgments. The authors would like to thank Los Alamos National Laboratory for use of the Trinitite and Capulin systems during the evaluation of this work. This study is authorized for unlimited release under LA-UR-21-28928.

References

1. Bale project repository (2020). https://github.com/jdevinney/bale
2. Ahmed, A., Skadron, K.: Hopscotch: a micro-benchmark suite for memory performance evaluation. In: Proceedings of the International Symposium on Memory Systems, MEMSYS 2019, pp. 167–172. Association for Computing Machinery, New York (2019). https://doi.org/10.1145/3357526.3357574
3. Alverson, B., Froese, E., Kaplan, L., Roweth, D.: Cray XC series network. Cray Inc., White Paper WP-Aries01-1112 (2012)
4. InfiniBand Trade Association: Infiniband architecture specification volume 1 release 1.3. http://www.infinibandta.org/content/pages.php?pg=technology_download
5. Broadcom: Stingray PS250 SmartNIC product brief. https://docs.broadcom.com/doc/PS250-PB
6. Chapman, B., et al.: Introducing OpenSHMEM: SHMEM for the PGAS community. In: Proceedings of the Fourth Conference on Partitioned Global Address Space Programming Model, PGAS 2010. Association for Computing Machinery, New York (2010). https://doi.org/10.1145/2020373.2020375
7. Che, S., et al.: Rodinia: a benchmark suite for heterogeneous computing. In: 2009 IEEE International Symposium on Workload Characterization (IISWC), pp. 44–54 (2009). https://doi.org/10.1109/IISWC.2009.5306797
8. Chen, R., Shao, Z., Li, T.: Bridging the I/O performance gap for big data workloads: a new NVDIMM-based approach. In: 2016 49th Annual IEEE/ACM International Symposium on Microarchitecture (MICRO), pp. 1–12 (2016). https://doi.org/10.1109/MICRO.2016.7783712
9. UCF Consortium: OpenSNAPI project homepage. https://www.ucfconsortium.org/projects/opensnapi/
10. David, T., Guerraoui, R., Trigonakis, V.: Everything you always wanted to know about synchronization but were afraid to ask. In: Proceedings of the Twenty-Fourth ACM Symposium on Operating Systems Principles, SOSP 2013, pp. 33–48. Association for Computing Machinery, New York (2013). https://doi.org/10.1145/2517349.2522714
11. Esmaeilzadeh, H., Blem, E., St. Amant, R., Sankaralingam, K., Burger, D.: Dark silicon and the end of multicore scaling. In: Proceedings of the 38th Annual International Symposium on Computer Architecture, ISCA 2011, pp. 365–376. Association for Computing Machinery, New York (2011). https://doi.org/10.1145/2000064.2000108
12. MPI Forum: MPI: A Message-Passing Interface Standard Version 3.0. Chapter author for Collective Communication, Process Topologies, and One Sided Communications (2012)
13. Grodowitz, M., Shamis, P., Poole, S.: OpenSHMEM I/O extensions for fine-grained access to persistent memory storage. In: Nichols, J., Verastegui, B., Maccabe, A.B., Hernandez, O., Parete-Koon, S., Ahearn, T. (eds.) SMC 2020. CCIS, vol. 1315, pp. 318–333. Springer, Cham (2020). https://doi.org/10.1007/978-3-030-63393-6_21

14. Hoseini, F., Atalar, A., Tsigas, P.: Modeling the performance of atomic primitives on modern architectures. In: Proceedings of the 48th International Conference on Parallel Processing, ICPP 2019. Association for Computing Machinery, New York (2019). https://doi.org/10.1145/3337821.3337901
15. Jeddeloh, J., Keeth, B.: Hybrid memory cube new dram architecture increases density and performance. In: 2012 Symposium on VLSI Technology (VLSIT), pp. 87–88 (2012). https://doi.org/10.1109/VLSIT.2012.6242474
16. Jouppi, N.P., et al.: In-datacenter performance analysis of a tensor processing unit. In: Proceedings of the 44th Annual International Symposium on Computer Architecture, ISCA 2017, pp. 1–12. Association for Computing Machinery, New York (2017). https://doi.org/10.1145/3079856.3080246
17. Jun, H., et al.: HBM (high bandwidth memory) dram technology and architecture. In: 2017 IEEE International Memory Workshop (IMW), pp. 1–4 (2017). https://doi.org/10.1109/IMW.2017.7939084
18. Labs, T.C.: RISC-V extended addressing architecture extension specification codenamed: xBGAS. https://github.com/tactcomplabs/xbgas-archspec
19. Lavin, P., Young, J., Riedy, J., Vuduc, R., Vose, A., Ernst, D.: Spatter: a tool for evaluating gather/scatter performance (2018)
20. Nabi, S.W., Vanderbauwhede, W.: MP-STREAM: a memory performance benchmark for design space exploration on heterogeneous HPC devices. In: 2018 IEEE International Parallel and Distributed Processing Symposium Workshops (IPDPSW), pp. 194–197 (2018). https://doi.org/10.1109/IPDPSW.2018.00036
21. Naughton, T., Aderholdt, F., Baker, M., Pophale, S., Gorentla Venkata, M., Imam, N.: Oak ridge OpenSHMEM benchmark suite. In: Pophale, S., Imam, N., Aderholdt, F., Gorentla Venkata, M. (eds.) OpenSHMEM 2018. LNCS, vol. 11283, pp. 202–216. Springer, Cham (2019). https://doi.org/10.1007/978-3-030-04918-8_13
22. NVIDIA: Bluefield-2 data sheet. https://www.nvidia.com/content/dam/en-zz/Solutions/Data-Center/documents/datasheet-nvidia-bluefield-2-dpu.pdf
23. Schweizer, H., Besta, M., Hoefler, T.: Evaluating the cost of atomic operations on modern architectures. In: 2015 International Conference on Parallel Architecture and Compilation PACT, pp. 445–456. IEEE (2015)
24. Seager, K., Choi, S.-E., Dinan, J., Pritchard, H., Sur, S.: Design and implementation of OpenSHMEM using OFI on the aries interconnect. In: Gorentla Venkata, M., Imam, N., Pophale, S., Mintz, T.M. (eds.) OpenSHMEM 2016. LNCS, vol. 10007, pp. 97–113. Springer, Cham (2016). https://doi.org/10.1007/978-3-319-50995-2_7
25. Shamis, P., et al.: UCX: an open source framework for HPC network APIS and beyond. In: 2015 IEEE 23rd Annual Symposium on High-Performance Interconnects, pp. 40–43. IEEE (2015)
26. Shamis, P., et al.: Development and extension of atomic memory operations in OpenSHMEM. In: Proceedings of the 8th International Conference on Partitioned Global Address Space Programming Models, PGAS 2014. Association for Computing Machinery, New York (2014). https://doi.org/10.1145/2676870.2676891
27. OSS Solutions: OpenSHMEM 1.4 specification. http://www.openshmem.org/site/sites/default/site_files/OpenSHMEM-1.4.pdf
28. Strohmaier, E., Shan, H.: Apex-map: a global data access benchmark to analyze HPC systems and parallel programming paradigms. In: SC 2005: Proceedings of the 2005 ACM/IEEE Conference on Supercomputing, p. 49 (2005). https://doi.org/10.1109/SC.2005.13
29. TOS University: OSU micro-benchmarks. https://mvapich.cse.ohio-state.edu/benchmarks/

30. Wang, X., et al.: xBGAS: a global address space extension on RISC-V for high performance computing. In: 2021 IEEE International Parallel and Distributed Processing Symposium (IPDPS), pp. 454–463 (2021). https://doi.org/10.1109/IPDPS49936.2021.00054
31. Weeks, H., Dosanjh, M.G.F., Bridges, P.G., Grant, R.E.: SHMEM-MT: a benchmark suite for assessing multi-threaded SHMEM performance. In: Gorentla Venkata, M., Imam, N., Pophale, S., Mintz, T.M. (eds.) OpenSHMEM 2016. LNCS, vol. 10007, pp. 227–231. Springer, Cham (2016). https://doi.org/10.1007/978-3-319-50995-2_16
32. Williams, B., Leidel, J., Wang, X., Donofrio, D., Chen, Y.: CircusTent: a benchmark suite for atomic memory operations. In: The International Symposium on Memory Systems, MEMSYS 2020, pp. 144–157. Association for Computing Machinery, New York (2020). https://doi.org/10.1145/3422575.3422789

SHMEM-ML: Leveraging OpenSHMEM and Apache Arrow for Scalable, Composable Machine Learning

Max Grossman[1(✉)], Steve Poole[2], Howard Pritchard[2], and Vivek Sarkar[1]

[1] Georgia Institute of Technology, Atlanta, GA, USA
max.grossman@gatech.edu
[2] Los Alamos National Laboratory, Los Alamos, NM, USA

Abstract. SHMEM-ML is a domain specific library for distributed array computations and machine learning model training & inference. Like other projects at the intersection of machine learning and HPC (e.g. dask, Arkouda, Legate Numpy), SHMEM-ML aims to leverage the performance of the HPC software stack to accelerate machine learning workflows. However, it differs in a number of ways.

First, SHMEM-ML targets the full machine learning workflow, not just model training. It supports a general purpose nd-array abstraction commonly used in Python machine learning applications, and efficiently distributes transformation and manipulation of this ndarray across the full system.

Second, SHMEM-ML uses OpenSHMEM as its underlying communication layer, enabling high performance networking across hundreds or thousands of distributed processes. While most past work in high performance machine learning has leveraged HPC message passing communication models as a way to efficiently exchange model gradient updates, SHMEM-ML's focus on the full machine learning lifecycle means that a more flexible and adaptable communication model is needed to support both fine and coarse grain communication.

Third, SHMEM-ML works to interoperate with the broader Python machine learning software ecosystem. While some frameworks aim to rebuild that ecosystem from scratch on top of the HPC software stack, SHMEM-ML is built on top of Apache Arrow, an in-memory standard for data formatting and data exchange between libraries. This enables SHMEM-ML to share data with other libraries without creating copies of data.

This paper describes the design, implementation, and evaluation of SHMEM-ML – demonstrating a general purpose system for data transformation and manipulation while achieving up to a 38× speedup in distributed training performance relative to the industry standard Horovod framework without a regression in model metrics.

Keywords: OpenSHMEM · ML · Machine · Learning · Scalable · Composable · Python · Ecosystem · Data · Science

S. Poole et al. (Eds.): OpenSHMEM 2021, LNCS 13159, pp. 111–125, 2022.
https://doi.org/10.1007/978-3-031-04888-3_7

1 Motivation

Data science and machine learning techniques have found broad applications, from proxy modeling in scientific applications to consumer recommendation engines to autonomous vehicles.

Most DS/ML frameworks are written to maximize programmability and portability, sacrificing performance. For example, most are written for Python, an extremely flexible but also interpreted programming language with high overheads. Pandas, a popular Python library for data scientists, mostly follows a copy-on-write semantic for mutating large n-dimensional arrays. This can lead to massive memory consumption on moderately-sized datasets. While this trade-off makes sense for small-scale projects, this causes problems for even simple data processing, exploration, and visualization workflows on the large-scale datasets that are common place today.

As a result, several efforts have explored taking well-known techniques and frameworks from the HPC community and applying them to DS/ML frameworks to yield both productive and high performance domain specific libraries/languages. These past works generally fall in to two buckets: (1) efforts to transparently use HPC frameworks underneath existing, industry-standard DS/ML frameworks, or (2) effort to replace existing DS/ML frameworks with new ones built with HPC technologies from the start.

1.1 Related Work: Using HPC Frameworks Under Existing DS/ML Frameworks

For example, in [11] the authors used OpenSHMEM [7] to accelerate distributed Caffe training jobs of the LeNet Solver network by replacing the existing MPI-based gradient exchange with equivalent OpenSHMEM operations. While this yielded a 30% improvement in training time over the existing implementation, this application of HPC technologies ignores the rest of the data science workflow. Projects like this one focus on a relatively small segment of the data science workflow (in this case, model gradient updates). Additionally, given that these optimizations are generally done at the lowest level of the data science software stack, they may miss optimizations that are only possible when higher level semantics are exposed.

1.2 Related Work: Novel HPC DS/ML Frameworks

On the other hand, there are several recent projects that aim to offer an all new data science software stack built on top of HPC technologies.

Legate Numpy [2] aims to offer a numpy-like [6] interface for multi-dimensional array processing on top of a high performance, distributed programming model called Legion [3]. Legate exposes a SPMD interface in Python, and a bridge to arrays stored in Legion (called logical regions) that allows for Python programmers to interact with Legion arrays in a similar manner to how they would interact with a Numpy array. While the programming model will be familiar, the authors call out that only a "a subset of the full NumPy API" is currently supported. To our knowledge, there would also be no straightforward way to use Legate arrays with other Python libraries (e.g. Tensorflow, scikit-learn).

Arkouda [5] is another example of a high performance data science framework, in this case built on top of Chapel [4]. It aims to offer "distributed arrays with parallel primitives", a "familiar interactive interface", and "smooth integration with mature HPC code". In the case of Arkouda, the high level architecture is a Chapel-based cluster communicating with a Jupyter/Python client. In this way, the user can run their analyses in an easy-to-use and familiar Python environment most of the time but still ship larger kernels to a massive, distributed environment when needed (while accepting that the functionality supported in that larger environment is also more limited).

In both the case of Arkouda and Legate, we can see some challenges with these approaches. While Legate tries to offer a familiar programming model and Arkouda supports single-threaded Python execution on the client, both approaches essentially ignore the existing and massive DS/ML Python ecosystem of libraries and tools that users may expect to have access to (even in an HPC, distributed environment).

1.3 Contributions

SHMEM-ML is a new distributed nd-array and distributed inference/training machine learning system built on top of OpenSHMEM, exposing productive C++ & Python APIs, and leveraging Apache Arrow to support integration with the broader Python ecosystem. SHMEM-ML is available open source at https://github.com/agrippa/shmem_ml.

The remainder of this paper is structured as follows. Section 2 will cover the high level programming model and APIs of SHMEM-ML, as well as walk through some simple examples of SHMEM-ML's usage. Section 3 will describe its implementation in detail. Section 4 will walk through some illustrative performance benchmarks, and Sect. 5 will wrap up with some discussion and conclusions.

2 Programming Model

2.1 Distributed SHMEM-ML Arrays

SHMEM-ML exposes C++ and Python APIs for:

1. Distributed nd-array creation, manipulation, and destruction.
2. Distributed training and inference of machine learning models, applied to SHMEM-ML's distributed nd-array abstractions.

Creating and mutating distributed SHMEM-ML arrays can be done concisely in both C++ and Python. Table 1 includes a few example SHMEM-ML APIs.

The full SHMEM-ML C++ and Python APIs is too long to be included inline, but in general SHMEM-ML arrays support:

Table 1. Example SHMEM-ML routines for creating, accessing, and manipulating SHMEM-ML arrays in C++ and Python.

Operation	C++	Python
Create a 1D array of length N initialized to zero	`ShmemML1D<float> arr(N, 0.0);`	`PyShmemML1DD(N)`
Create a 2D array of size MxN initialized to zero	`ShmemML2D<float> arr(M, N, 0.0);`	`PyShmemML2DD(M, N)`
Apply a function to each element of an array	`arr.apply_ip([] ... );`	`arr.apply(lambda ...)`
Access a single local or remote element	`arr.get(i);`	`arr.get(i)`

- Allocation of distributed one- and two-dimensional arrays of primitive types and arbitrary size, up to the limits of the machine being used.
- Applying custom functions element-wise.
- Getting or setting elements.
- Clearing arrays to a specified value.
- Atomically updating local or remote array elements.
- Global reductions across the entire array (e.g. sum reduction).
- Saving and restoring of arrays to disk.

2.2 SHMEM-ML Arrays with Third Party Python Libraries

Additionally, today SHMEM-ML arrays integrate with commonly used Python data science libraries, including numpy, scikit-learn [8], and keras [12]. Section 3 includes more details on the implementation of this integration. For example, you can use a numpy random number generation API to populate data in a distributed SHMEM-ML array:

```
from PyShmemML import rand
vec = rand(vec)
```

Under the covers, the above code snippet uses the `numpy.random.rand` interface to implement random number generation.

It is also possible to train and apply scikit-learn models on SHMEM-ML distributed arrays. In the example below, `Xtrain`, `Ytrain`, `Xvalid`, and `predictions` are all distributed SHMEM-ML arrays.

```
from PyShmemML import SGDRegressor
clf = SGDRegressor(max_iter=niters)

clf.fit(Xtrain, Ytrain)
predictions = clf.predict(Xvalid)
```

The same can be done with Keras:

```
from tensorflow import keras
from PyShmemML import Sequential

clf = Sequential()
clf.add(tensorflow.keras.Input(shape=(5,)))
clf.add(tensorflow.keras.layers.Dense(3, activation='relu'))
clf.add(tensorflow.keras.layers.Dense(1, activation='relu'))
opt = keras.optimizers.SGD(learning_rate=0.01)

clf.compile(optimizer=opt, loss='mse')

clf.fit(Xtrain, Ytrain, epochs=niters)
predictions = clf.predict(Xvalid)
```

The structure of the code above will be very familiar to any existing Python data scientists. However, behind the scenes the data and workload is being distributed across an OpenSHMEM-based cluster. At the same time, we are leveraging all of the existing software in the Python data science ecosystem by relying on third party libraries like scikit-learn and keras for algorithms like forward propagation, backward propagation, gradient calculation, optimizers, etc.

2.3 Client-Server vs. SPMD

One of the main differences between how data scientists and HPC programmers interact with high performance clusters today is in the fundamental parallelism model exposed to them. Most data scientists are familiar with a client-server style model, in which a single Python notebook or shell distributes work to a large cluster. This is also the approach taken in Arkouda. However, most HPC programmers are more familiar with SPMD-style programming as it generally offers better scalability by removing the bottleneck of distributing work from a single client. This is the approach taken by Legate.

While it is safe to assume that SPMD-style programming will be more scalable for most use cases, it is also important to meet data scientists where they are comfortable. As a result, SHMEM-ML supports both a client-server style interface and an SPMD-style interface.

By default, SHMEM-ML in Python runs in SPMD mode with each process executing the same Python program in parallel. Processes have access to a `PyShmemML.pe()` function to fetch their unique OpenSHMEM PE ID, and `PyShmemML.npes()` to fetch the number of running OpenSHMEM PEs.

To run in client-server mode, rather than launching the Python program using the `python` interpreter (e.g. `python foo.py`), the programmer uses a SHMEM-ML wrapper called `shmem_ml_client_server` (e.g. shmem_ml_client_server foo.py). Then, the SHMEM-ML program will be run with a single process distributing work to the entire cluster.

In this way, users in both the data science and HPC communities can choose the programming abstractions they are most comfortable with. In the case of Arkouda and Legate, each programming system dictated whether the programmer worked in client-server or SPMD mode.

3 Implementation

SHMEM-ML is built on top of a number of open source or third party software packages. This section offers a brief overview of the fundamental building blocks of SHMEM-ML, as well as how they are put together to support distributed arrays and integration with the broader Python ecosystem.

At a high level, SHMEM-ML uses:

- Apache Arrow [1] for in-memory data storage and zero-copy data exchange with third party Python libraries.
- OpenSHMEM [7] for distributed job creation, inter-process communication, and inter-process coordination.
- Tensorflow, Keras, scikit-learn, numpy and other Python data science libraries for the implementation of more algorithmically complex data science functionality such as training and inference of deep neural networks.

3.1 Background: OpenSHMEM

The OpenSHMEM library provides a single program, multiple data (SPMD) execution model in which N instances of the program are executed in parallel. Each instance is referred to as a processing element (PE) and is identified by its integer ID in the range from 0 to $N - 1$. PEs exchange information through one-sided *get* (read) and *put* (write) operations that access remotely accessible *symmetric objects*. Symmetric objects are objects that are present at all PEs and they are referenced using the local address to the given object. By default, all objects within the data segment of the application are exposed as symmetric; additional symmetric objects are allocated through OpenSHMEM API routines. OpenSHMEM's communication model is unordered by default. Point-to-point ordering is established through *fence* operations, remote completion is established through *quiet* operations, and global ordering is established through *barrier* operations.

3.2 Background: Apache Arrow

Apache Arrow is an open community effort to define a universal in-memory data format for n-dimensional arrays. Arrow's aim is to enable zero-copy, efficient data exchange between different libraries regardless of language and without each library having to provide explicit support for every other library. Apache Arrow defines a number of commonly used objects and functionalities, including one-dimensional arrays, two-dimensional tables, and file I/O.

3.3 Background: Scikit-Learn, Tensorflow, and Horovod

scikit-learn and Tensorflow/Keras are industry standard libraries for training and applying data-driven or machine learned models. Scikit-learn focuses on providing classes for more classical and statistically-derived machine learning models (e.g. linear regressors, support vector machines, random forests, gaussian mixtures). Tensorflow/Keras focus on more recent developments in deep learning models, making it simple and straightforward to create deeply layered models with a variety of built-in layer types supported (e.g. Dense, Convolutional, Pooling, Recurrent, Normalization). Custom layer types can also be added by programmers. While Keras was started as an independent framework for training deep learning models, it was eventually merged into Tensorflow in 2017 as an alternative API.

While scikit-learn does not support distributed training today, Tensorflow/Keras offer a number of options. The most commonly used framework for distributed training of Keras models is Horovod [9] which uses an efficient ring-allreduce method to distributed gradient updates while sitting on top of high performance communication libraries (e.g. MPI) when supported. The introduction of Horovod to the Tensorflow/Keras communities drastically improved the scalability and productivity of distributed training.

3.4 ND-Array Implementation

Today, SHMEM-ML distributed arrays are limited to being either one- or two-dimensional – in the future, this restriction could be lifted. In either case, the core data backing a SHMEM-ML array is an Apache Arrow data structure allocated on the OpenSHMEM symmetric heap. In the case of a one-dimensional array, we use Arrow's `FixedSizeBinaryArray` class which allows us to allocate a contiguous array of elements, each containing `sizeof(T)` bytes. In the case of two-dimensional SHMEM-ML arrays, we use Arrow's `Table` class to store columns of Arrow `Arrays`.

To have the backing allocations for Arrow's `Table` and `Array` classes allocated in the OpenSHMEM symmetric heap, we have also implemented a custom Arrow `MemoryPool` that supports `Allocate`, `Reallocate`, and `Free` functions that operate on memory regions in the symmetric heap. This custom memory pool is passed to the Arrow runtime when constructing a new `Array` or `Table`, and in turn the Arrow runtime calls it when memory is needed.

One-dimensional SHMEM-ML arrays are distributed in chunks across the available OpenSHMEM PEs, and two-dimensional arrays are chunked across rows. Today, the type of distribution and chunk size is chosen for the programmer – future work could extend this to support different data distributions (e.g. cyclic). SHMEM-ML also supports what we call "replicated" arrays. When allocated with a size `N`, they allocate `N` elements on every PE (rather than distributing them across PEs). In general, replicated arrays are useful when a programmer wants to update the local copy and then perform some type of a global sync of every PE's local updates (e.g. a global sum of all local values).

SHMEM-ML arrays include functions for looking up basic information on a distributed array, including the number of elements in the array, which PE stores a given element based on its index, and the starting/ending indices of elements stored on the local PE.

SHMEM-ML arrays also support a number of getter and setter APIs. For example, one-dimensional arrays support both getting and setting elements in the array using either global indices into the entire distributed array or local indices into the local chunk of the array. Some example one-dimensional APIs are included below. Under the covers, all remote operations are performed using OpenSHMEM APIs (e.g. `shmem_putmem` or `shmem_getmem`).

```
// A remote get based on the global index in the distributed array
inline T get(int64_t global_index);

// A remote set based on the global index in the distributed array
inline void set(int64_t global_index, T val);
```

The getter and setter methods above are not atomic (i.e. if two PEs try to set the same global index, the result is undefined). As a result, SHMEM-ML also supports atomic operations on elements of arrays. There are two implementations of atomic operations in SHMEM-ML: OpenSHMEM-based and message-based. OpenSHMEM-based atomic operations are directly implemented using OpenSHMEM atomics APIS (e.g. `shmem_longlong_atomic_fetch_add`. Message-based atomics are packaged up by the SHMEM-ML runtime as a small packet encoding the operation to be performed and sent in batches to the target PE through asynchronous mailboxes. In the cases of workloads performing large numbers of atomic operations, this approach increases latency of individual operations but can also drastically improve throughput. On the receiving side of an atomic message, updates are simply done using memory reads and writes – this means that the two types of atomics in SHMEM-ML are not atomic with respect to each other. Additionally, because message-based atomics are asynchronous an additional `sync` call is needed on the array in question to ensure all outstanding atomics have been sent and processed. Some example atomics APIs are included below.

```
// Perform an atomic compare-and-swap at the designated element.
// Return the previous value at that location.
T atomic_cas(int64_t global_index, T expected, T update_to);

// Perform an atomic compare-and-swap at the designated element,
// using the message-based atomics implementation.
void atomic_cas_msg(int64_t global_index, T expected, T update_to);

// Wait for all pending message-based atomics to complete on the
// target array.
void sync();
```

Finally, SHMEM-ML arrays also support global reductions performed on their contained elements (e.g. max reduction, sum reduction). In general, a local result is computed sequentially and then an OpenSHMEM reduction is performed to compute the global result based on each PE's local result. Some example reduction array APIs are shown below.

```
T max(T min_val);
T sum(T zero_val);
```

3.5 Client-Server Implementation

Section 2 described the difference between SPMD and client-server execution from the user's perspective. All that was needed to switch to a client-server architecture for SHMEM-ML was to use a special `shmem_ml_client_server` executable when launching your distributed Python program, rather than the standard `python` interpreter.

Under the covers, this custom executable does the following:

1. Initializes OpenSHMEM and the Python runtime (if we are running client-server mode from Python, and not from C++).
2. Sets a flag on each OpenSHMEM PE to indicate which are servers/workers, and which is the client. In general, we select PE 0 as the client.
3. Symmetrically allocates what we call a command mailbox on every PE. This is the only mechanism by which the client PE issues work to worker/server PEs. Every time a distributed operation occurs on the client PE (e.g. distributed array allocation, a distributed `apply`, a global reduction), coordination messages are sent from the client PE to all server PEs informing them of the distributed operation to be performed.
4. All PEs that are servers then enter a command loop, waiting on new incoming commands from the client and then performing the requested operations.
5. The client PE then launches the provided Python program using `PyRun_SimpleFileExFlags`. When it completes, it sends all servers a command to indicate that the program has completed and a collective `shmem_finalize` occurs.

Naturally, client-server mode faces some intrinsic scalability bottlenecks that SPMD mode does not. However, for programmers that are less familiar with an HPC-style programming environment it offers a more comfortable on-ramp to using SHMEM-ML.

3.6 Integration with Scikit-Learn and Tensorflow/Keras

SHMEM-ML's use of Apache Arrow enables zero-copy data exchange between SHMEM-ML and other Arrow-based libraries, including numpy, Pandas, scikit-learn, and Tensorflow. However, integrating into their workflows (particularly for model training) does require some added logic.

Supporting executing numpy functions on SHMEM-ML arrays is relatively straightforward. All SHMEM-ML arrays expose functions for (1) getting the local Arrow arrays backing them (`get_local_arrow_array`), and (2) updating their contents from another Arrow array (`update_from_arrow`). Arrow arrays can then be converted to or from numpy arrays, which can be passed to numpy's routines.

Model inference workloads are also relatively simple, and generally consist of applying a model element-wise to an input SHMEM-ML array after it has been converted to a numpy array via Apache Arrow. Below is a simplified example of the glue code between SHMEM-ML arrays and scikit-learn models for model inference.

```
def predict(self, x):
    # Convert the local chunk of our SHMEM-ML array to a Pandas
    # Dataframe using Apache Arrow
    x_arr = x.get_local_arrow_table().to_pandas(
            zero_copy_only=True, split_blocks=True)

    # Run the trained scikit-learn model on our local chunk,
    # producing a new numpy array as output
    pred = self.model.predict(x_arr)

    # Allocate a new distributed SHMEM-ML array to store the
    # result of the inference
    dist_pred = PyShmemML1DD(x.M())

    # Update the contents of dist_pred with the output of the model
    dist_pred.update_from_arrow(pyarrow.array(pred))

    # Return the new SHMEM-ML array containing the predictions
    return dist_pred
```

However, model training workloads require more extensive glue code between SHMEM-ML arrays and scikit-learn/Tensorflow models. In particular, because the models themselves are responsible for updating their weights but are not aware that they are being trained in parallel (i.e. that there are updates occurring on remote PEs to remote copies of the model), SHMEM-ML must (1) take over the iterative training process, (2) manage inter-process gradient exchange between iterations, and (3) rely on models' incremental training APIs to support iteration-by-iteration training updates. This is in contrast with how models are generally trained, by passing in the full training dataset and training for a large number of iterations.

However, this process is relatively uniform across frameworks. Indeed, the SHMEM-ML code base uses a single model training function to perform distributed training of both scikit-learn and Tensorflow models – with some model-specific logic plugged in (e.g. to fetch the weights from a given model type). A simplified version of that training function is shown below. Note that this implementation is likely making some assumptions about the type of model and type of optimizer being used for training, such that an averaging of weights on each iteration will yield convergence. While this approach has been tested for stochastic gradient descent optimizers, it may need customization for different types of model optimization.

```
def _training_driver(model, x_arr, y_arr, epochs, **custom_args):
    dist_weights_grad = PyReplicatedShmemML1DD(...)

    for it in range(epochs):

        # Rely on the model supporting incremental training
        model._fit_one_epoch(x_arr, y_arr, **custom_args)

        # Fetch the model's new weights as an arrow array, and
        # convert it to a distributed, replicated SHMEM-ML array
        arrow_weights = pyarrow.array(model._copy_weights())
        dist_weights_grad.update_from_arrow(arrow_weights)

        # Perform a sum reduction across all PEs on the model
        # weights following this iteration's updates
        dist_weights_grad.reduce_all_sum()

        # Extract a local numpy array containing the summed
        # weights, and normalize the new weights by number of
        # PEs (taking the mean of model weights across all PEs)
        all_weights_grads = dist_weights_grad \
                .get_local_arrow_array() \
                .to_numpy(zero_copy_only=True) / npes()

        # Update the model itself with the new average of all
        # model updates across all PEs
        model._update_weights(all_weights_grads)
```

4 Performance Evaluation

In this section, we will compare the performance and accuracy of models trained on scikit-learn, Tensorflow, and SHMEM-ML. All results were collected on the TACC Frontera machine's primary compute system [10]. Each node of Frontera includes a dual-socket Intel Xeon Platinum 8280 "Cascade Lake" CPU with 56 cores per node. Each node also includes 192 GB of DDR4 system memory. Nodes are connected by a Mellanox Infiniband HDR-100 interconnect.

SHMEM-ML was built using OSSS-UCX OpenSHMEM and Apache Arrow built from source code as of October 2020. GCC 9.1.0 was used. Tensorflow v2.1.0, scikit-learn 0.23.2, and Horovod 0.21.1 were used in this evaluation.

To evaluate SHMEM-ML's performance when training a scikit-learn model, we will compare the performance of training a scikit-learn linear regression model in a single-threaded Python process to distributed training in SHMEM-ML using both client-server and SPMD modes.

To evaluate SHMEM-ML's performance when training a Tensorflow model, we will compare between (1) Tensorflow single-node, (2) Tensorflow multi-node using Horovod, (3) SHMEM-ML SPMD, and (4) SHMEM-ML client-server.

4.1 Scikit-Learn

The source code for model training in both the SHMEM-ML and scikit-learn implementations of this benchmark are identical:

```
clf = SGDRegressor(max_iter=50)
clf.fit(X, Y);
predictions = clf.predict(X)
```

We use a synthetic dataset with 5 million samples and 5 32-bit floating point features per sample for the purposes of benchmarking.

Table 2 includes wall times for training on a single node for scikit-learn and SHMEM-ML. Note that running SHMEM-ML on a single node implies running one PE per core, and so the SHMEM-ML numbers are with 56-way parallelism. As expected, that added parallelization yields large speedups for SHMEM-ML in client-server and SPMD mode relative to scikit-learn (37.3× and 45.3×, respectively) with SPMD achieving slightly higher throughput. The sublinear speedup on a single node for even the SPMD version can be attributed to coordination and communication overheads required to exchange gradient updates between PEs on each iteration of training. This is commonly the largest challenge to training scalability, and a source of future work for SHMEM-ML (e.g. by leveraging more efficient communication patterns, similar to Horovod).

Table 2. Training performance running SHMEM-ML and scikit-learn on a single node

Framework	Training (s)	Training speedup
Single-threaded scikit-learn	509.83	1.0×
Client-server SHMEM-ML on one node	13.67	37.3×
SPMD SHMEM-ML on one node	11.26	45.3×

Figure 1 shows the execution time of SHMEM-ML's scaling while training the SGDRegressor model. We can observe the throughput benefits of SPMD mode, though both modes of execution fail to scale beyond 1,792 PEs (32 nodes).

4.2 Tensorflow

Like scikit-learn, the source code for the SHMEM-ML and Tensorflow implementations of this benchmark are identical:

```
clf = Sequential()
clf.add(tensorflow.keras.Input(shape=(nfeatures,)))
clf.add(tensorflow.keras.layers.Dense(1, activation='relu'))

opt = keras.optimizers.SGD(learning_rate=0.005)
clf.compile(optimizer=opt, loss='mse')
```

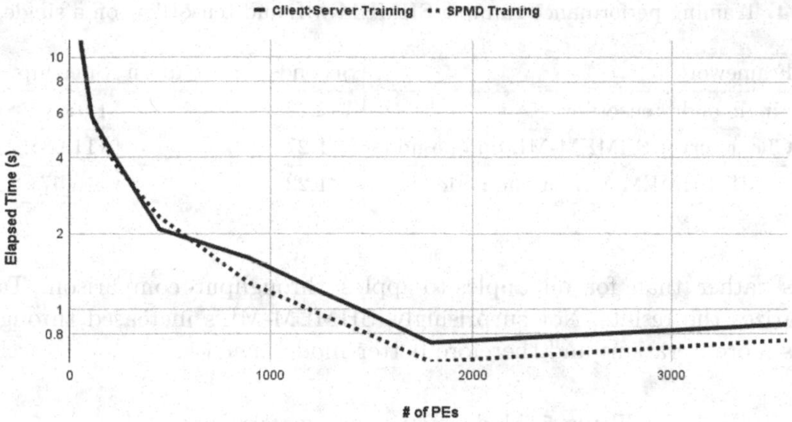

Fig. 1. SHMEM-ML execution time in client-server and SPMD modes for training. Note the log scale Y axis.

```
clf.fit(X, Y, epochs=niters, batch_size=128)
pred = clf.predict(X)
```

Like with scikit-learn, we use a synthetic dataset with 5 million samples and 5 32-bit floating point features per sample for the purposes of benchmarking.

There are additional hyperparameters in training of deep learning models which did not have to be considered in the scikit-learn comparison. In particular, we increase both the number of iterations/epochs in the distributed case and the batch size per iteration to yield better convergence. In general, the following tables and figures will report performance per iteration to ensure an apples-to-apples comparison. Table 3 describes the full set of hyperparameters tuned for our local and distributed jobs.

Table 3. Per framework hyperparameters

Framework	Iterations	Batch size
Single node tensorflow	40	32
Multi node tensorflow	5	128
Multi node SHMEM-ML	400	128

Table 4 includes wall times for training on a single node for Tensorflow and SHMEM-ML. Again, the parallelism added by SHMEM-ML yields large speedups in both client-server and SPMD mode relative to Tensorflow (111.98× and 116.57×, respectively). Numbers are not reported for Horovod+Tensorflow, as an OOM was encountered with only a single node.

Additionally, we ran experiments to compare the accuracy of the models produced by each framework – attempting to optimize hyperparameters for model

Table 4. Training performance running SHMEM-ML and tensorflow on a single node

Framework	Seconds per iteration	Speedup
Single node tensorflow	142.22	1.0×
Client-server SHMEM-ML on one node	1.27	111.98×
SPMD SHMEM-ML on one node	1.22	116.57×

metrics rather than for an apples-to-apples throughput comparison. Table 5 summarizes the results. Not surprisingly, SHMEM-ML's increased throughput enables more iterations and therefore better model metrics.

Table 5. Model metrics and performance

	Tensorflow	Horovod	SHMEM-ML
Iterations	40	130	500
Batch size	32	128	128
# Nodes	1	32	32
Total wall time	5899.15	2334.89	61.21
Seconds per iter.	147.48	17.96	0.12
RMSE	4.504500E−08	5.000000E−06	9.676908E−23

Finally, Fig. 2 shows the elapsed time per iteration of SHMEM-ML out to 32 nodes. While Horovod fails with an out of memory error below 16 nodes, its execution time per iteration at 16 and 32 nodes is much higher than SHMEM-ML. At 16 nodes, Horovod takes 65.65 s per iteration while SHMEM-ML SPMD takes 0.15 s per iteration. At 32 nodes, Horovod takes 14.13 s and SHMEM-ML SPMD takes 0.09 s.

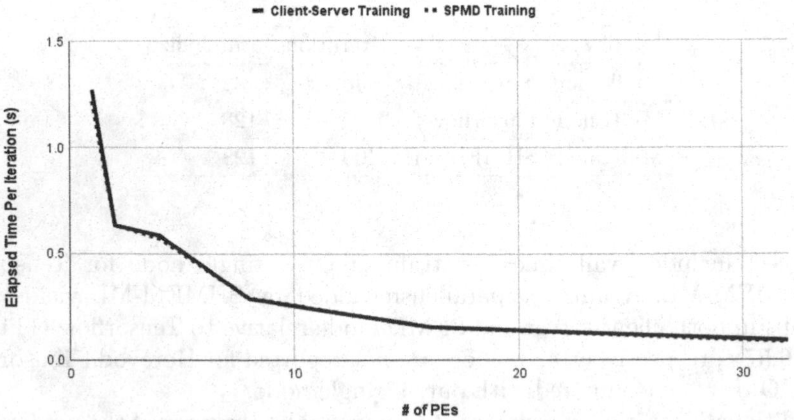

Fig. 2. SHMEM-ML execution time per iteration for training

5 Conclusions

SHMEM-ML leverages OpenSHMEM to accelerate data science and machine learning workflows. By focusing on a scalable distributed array data structure and composability with the existing Python data science ecosystem, SHMEM-ML aims to enable scalable end-to-end data science workflows – including data loading, data manipulation, model training, and model inference.

Acknowledgement. This research is part of the Frontera computing project at the Texas Advanced Computing Center. Frontera is made possible by National Science Foundation award OAC-1818253. This publication has been approved for public, unlimited distribution by Los Alamos National Laboratory, with document number LA-UR-21-29037.

References

1. Apache Arrow. https://arrow.apache.org/
2. Bauer, M., Garland, M.: Legate NumPY: accelerated and distributed array computing. In: Proceedings of the International Conference for High Performance Computing, Networking, Storage and Analysis, pp. 1–23 (2019)
3. Bauer, M., Treichler, S., Slaughter, E., Aiken, A.: Legion: expressing locality and independence with logical regions. In: SC 2012: Proceedings of the International Conference on High Performance Computing, Networking, Storage and Analysis, pp. 1–11. IEEE (2012)
4. Chamberlain, B.L., Callahan, D., Zima, H.P.: Parallel programmability and the chapel language. Int. J. High Perform. Comput. App. **21**(3), 291–312 (2007)
5. Merrill, M., Reus, W., Neumann, T.: Arkouda: interactive data exploration backed by chapel. In: Proceedings of the ACM SIGPLAN 6th on Chapel Implementers and Users Workshop, pp. 28–28 (2019)
6. NumPy. https://numpy.org/
7. OpenSHMEM application programming interface, version 1.5 (2020). http://www.openshmem.org
8. Scikit-Learn. https://scikit-learn.org/stable/
9. Sergeev, A., Del Balso, M.: Horovod: fast and easy distributed deep learning in tensorflow. arXiv preprint arXiv:1802.05799 (2018)
10. TACC Frontera. https://www.tacc.utexas.edu/systems/frontera
11. Taylor, G., Ozog, D., Wasi-ur Rahman, M., Dinan, J.: Scalable machine learning with openshmem
12. Tensorflow Keras. https://www.tensorflow.org/api_docs/python/tf/keras

Programming Models and Extensions

OpenSHMEM Active Message Extension for Task-Based Programming

Wenbin Lu(✉), Tony Curtis, and Barbara Chapman

Institute for Advanced Computational Science, Stony Brook University, Stony Brook, USA
{wenbin.lu,anthony.curtis,barbara.chapman}@stonybrook.edu

Abstract. As a lightweight library-based Partitioned Global Address Space (PGAS) programming model, OpenSHMEM provides efficient one-sided and collective communications and is receiving more attention in recent years. However, task-based programming models are getting bigger traction in scientific computing communities. Application developers are attracted by their ability to achieve better load balance in the face of ever-growing application complexity, and the increasing on-node parallelism in modern high-performance computing machines. Although communication contexts provide threads with first-class access to the network in the OpenSHMEM+X model, OpenSHMEM still has very limited ability to perform advanced operations found in other task-based models. For example, compared to the remote procedure call (RPC) mechanism in the UPC++ programming model, more work is required if the signal/wait routines are used to achieve similar remote task launching operations. In this paper, we introduce a lightweight active message (AM) extension to OpenSHMEM that is designed to perform short, non-blocking remote function invocations. This extension aims to bring some benefits of task-based programming to OpenSHMEM without making it a full-blown heavyweight tasking system with a sophisticated scheduler. We study the performance of this active message extension by running micro-benchmarks, and by evaluating its computation efficiency at different task granularities using the TaskBench framework.

Keywords: PGAS · OpenSHMEM · Active message · Tasking

1 Introduction

The increasing complexity of software and hardware in the exascale era calls for more adaptive and dynamic programming models. In recent years we are seeing a surge of new programming models that break away from the traditional SPMD-way of expressing parallelism and embrace the flexibility and scalability provided by dynamic execution of operations, mostly in the form of tasks or a variant of active messages [8]. In today's diverse and heterogeneous HPC systems, an application using HPX [11], an active global address space programming model, was able to achieve a much higher parallel efficiency at scale than MPI [6].

S. Poole et al. (Eds.): OpenSHMEM 2021, LNCS 13159, pp. 129–143, 2022.
https://doi.org/10.1007/978-3-031-04888-3_8

Many members in the family of partitioned global address space (PGAS) programming models already have some way to launch functions remotely: Coarray Fortran [20], GASNetEX [3]/UPC++ [1], and Chapel [4] are among the most prominent ones. Their ability to insert operations into another process's execution flow is a simpler, sometimes more scalable, way to realize tasks and their dependencies than using distributed signal variables. As of OpenSHMEM 1.5 [15], a similar feature is not available, and we believe it is affecting OpenSHMEM's adoption in the supercomputing community.

In this paper, we propose a lightweight active message extension for OpenSHMEM that is designed to support a basic form of task-based programming without feeling out-of-place when mixed with other parts of the model. It enables efficient remote invocation of pre-defined message handler functions across Processing Elements (PEs). Our work provides a basis for the inclusion of this important feature, and we hope to spark discussion in the OpenSHMEM community on this topic.

This paper is organized as follows: Sect. 2 discusses the background of this work. Section 3 describes the proposed API extension and its implementation. Section 4 provides a preliminary evaluation of the work and Sect. 5 gives a conclusion and talks about future work.

2 Background

2.1 Task-Based Programming and Active Messages

Task-based programming is the practice of expressing parallelism in terms of small units of computation called tasks. Two tasks can be executed independently or have an order imposed on them in the form of task dependency. The directed acyclic graph (DAG) constructed with task dependencies is expressive enough for the majority of HPC applications, while still can be mapped and executed on supercomputers. Due to its ability to express sophisticated workflows in an organized manner and expose more opportunities for load balancing, task-based programming is playing an increasingly prominent role in the exascale era.

Active messages [8] enable one process to schedule a function (AM handler) invocation on a remote process, using a pre-registered AM handler ID and a set of handler arguments (AM payload) contained in the scheduling request. AM and its derivatives have become building blocks of many HPC programming models and machine learning frameworks for performing distributed control flow (e.g. work assignments, load balancing). While a simple AM implementation lacks the central/distributed task scheduler found in fully-fledged tasking frameworks, it still can be used to construct tasks and dependencies between them. The developer needs to implement an application-specific scheduler to decide when and where to send AM requests, but this might be preferable for some applications.

2.2 OpenSHMEM

OpenSHMEM [5] is an SPMD programming model that implements the PGAS memory model. It is library-based and uses one-sided remote memory access (RMA) as its main method for doing point-to-point communication and synchronizations between its processes/PEs. Due to its elegant and implementer-friendly design, it has been well-received in both academia and commercial products like NVSHMEM [14].

However, when compared to other members of the PGAS family, OpenSHMEM lacks advanced features that could help developers achieve scalability and portability in the face of the exploding complexity of the modern HPC ecosystem. The recent addition of teams [17] and contexts [7] are solid steps towards this direction and have been shown to improve application performance [13], but data movement is still the main focus.

Currently, if the developers want to have a task-like workflow in an OpenSHMEM application, the entire DAG of tasks must be hard-coded into the application, with every task spawning operation and dependency realized through a dedicated signal variable and a wait operation. This approach not only loses the flexibility of task-based programming but also requires heroic effort and is very error-prone. Moreover, inputs and outputs of the tasks must be placed on the symmetric heap and passed using PUTs or GETs even if they are single integers/floating-point numbers, which further increases complexity and reduces scalability.

The active message extension proposed in this paper could bridge the gap between OpenSHMEM and other programming models on handling control flow on the distributed-memory level. Instead of using signals to trigger task execution and notify the availability of execution results of tasks, parent tasks can inject tasks into any PE's execution flow and the children tasks can invoke AM handlers on the parent task's PE to fetch computation results, or simply send the results as the AM payload if the sizes are within the limits. If designed with care, the AM extension will blend nicely with the rest of the OpenSHMEM specification and does not introduce unnecessary overhead to other OpenSHMEM operations.

2.3 Related Work

An AM extension for OpenSHMEM has been proposed before [10], in which a set of APIs is presented to initiate, progress, and perform active message operations between PEs. Their GASNet-based implementation features opportunistic execution of incoming active messages using a background polling thread. The potential risk of data race on internal data structures and other progression issues leads to the need of banning the invocation of most OpenSHMEM routines from the AM handler, as well as a dedicated mutex interface for handler safety. The main difference between their design and ours is that: we allow the use of simple point-to-point communication routines including sending AMs from the handler, give the user total control of where the handler gets executed, and let the user handle thread-safety using whatever mechanism they see fit. As a result, our design does not require SHMEM_THREAD_MULTIPLE when not requested by the application and is much more flexible in what can be done inside the handler.

MPI, being the most popular distributed-memory programming model for HPC, also has had a few attempts to retrofit it with active message capabilities. The MPI-Interoperable Generalized Active Messages [24] is the most complete one, which is similar to the MPI_Op of MPI-3's RMA accumulate operation but is extended with user-defined operations and a data streaming-like interface. Compared to our design, their API is extremely complex and requires more effort to use. Another attempt at MPI AM is presented in [21] and has achieved good performance. However, the work focused on implementing an active message mechanism using MPI RMA and did not design a general-purpose API interface for it.

Active message-like functionalities can be found in many other programming models. UPC++'s RPC mechanism supports automatic serialization and provides future objects that can be waited on to obtain the RPC's return value. Charm++ [12] features location-agnostic method invocations on a unified view of all the distributed C++ objects, with its runtime performs automatic object migration and load balancing behind the scene. Legion [2] implements a mapper layer that controls the placement of the tasks instead of having to specify on which process each task should run in the application's main workflow. These advanced features are too heavy-weight for both the OpenSHMEM specification and its implementations.

3 Design and Implementation

This section describes the design of our OpenSHMEM active message extension and the rationale behind it. The extension's implementation is also discussed to demonstrate how we are able to allow the use of simple point-to-point communication operations from within the AM handlers.

3.1 OpenSHMEM Active Message API Extension

The type and macro definitions for the AM handler are shown in Listing 1.1. The size of the active message payload is limited by the implementation-defined macro SHMEMX_AM_PAYLOAD_MAX_SIZE, typically this will be a few kilobytes. We decide to add this restriction to avoid introducing the rendezvous protocol to handle large payload sizes. Since OpenSHMEM focuses on fast one-sided communication operations, an active message interface with MPI-like request objects and/or callbacks deviates too far away from OpenSHMEM's communication semantics. If the user needs to transfer a large amount of data with an AM request, our design allows invoking PUTs/GETs from within the AM handler so it should not be a problem.

Active message handlers must be registered on the destination PE before the initiator PE can schedule its execution. The handlers must have the same

```
// Maximum active message payload size.
#define SHMEMX_AM_PAYLOAD_MAX_SIZE

// Active message handler signature.
typedef void (*shmemx_am_handler_t)(void*  payload,
                                    size_t length,
                                    void*  args_r,
                                    void*  args_p,
                                    int    source_pe)

  [IN] payload     Active message payload
  [IN] length      Size of the payload
  [IN] args_r      Registration-time user arguments
  [IN] args_p      Polling-time user arguments
  [IN] source_pe   PE number of the initiator of this AM
```

Listing 1.1. Proposed OpenSHMEM Active Message API type definitions

function type defined by `shmemx_am_handler_t`, and its definition must be visible to the compiler/linker when the application is compiled. When a handler is invoked by the destination PE, the payload and its size, a pointer provided by the user when the handler was registered, a pointer passed to the polling routine that invoked this handler, and the PE number of the source of the AM request are passed as function arguments. Once the handler returns, the payload buffer is freed.

One of the main advantages of our design is the ability to call OpenSHMEM routines from the AM handler. Point-to-point communication operations like PUT/GET/atomic operations are all supported, as well as `shmem_fence` and `shmem_quiet`, and even send AM requests using the API in Listing 1.2. Usage of collective communications, distributed locking routines, symmetric heap management routines, and contexts & teams routines inside the handlers are still forbidden. Additionally, the user can make `libc` and other external function calls inside the AM handler, but we strongly discourage performing any potentially blocking operation in the handler, as doing so could prevent timely handling of other AM requests or even cause deadlocks. Our proposed API is inter-operable with shared-memory tasking frameworks, so long-running computations or system calls like I/O can be handled by offloading them to other threads.

Listing 1.2 defines the API extension that will be used to register, send and progress OpenSHMEM active messages. A PE can call `shmemx_am_set_handler` to register an AM handler and receive an integer as the ID of the registered handler, this ID will be used by an initiator PE to send an AM request that invokes this handler. The registration routine is not a collective call and the application is not required to have the same handler-to-ID mapping across all PEs. A pointer to local arguments can be registered along with the handler, and it will be passed as the third argument (`args_r`) to the handler for every AM request of this ID.

```
// Set & reset active message handler.
void shmemx_am_set_handler(shmemx_am_handler_t handler,
                           void*                args_r,
                           int*                 id)
  [IN]  handler   Active message handler (NULL to reset)
  [IN]  args_r    User-defined local arguments
  [OUT] id        Active message ID

// Send an active message.
void shmemx_am_send_nbi(int    id,
                        void*  payload,
                        size_t length,
                        int    pe)
  [IN] id         Active message ID
  [IN] payload    Payload to send
  [IN] length     Size of the payload
  [IN] pe         PE number of the remote PE

// Non-blocking poll of incoming active messages.
int shmemx_am_poll(void* args_p)
  [IN]     args_p User-defined local arguments
  [RETURN] Non-zero if any AM was processed, zero otherwise.

// Blocking wait on incoming active messages.
void shmemx_am_wait(void* args_p)
  [IN] args_p     User-defined local arguments
```

Listing 1.2. Proposed OpenSHMEM Active Message API routines

To send an AM request, the initiator PE should pass the ID, the payload and its size, and the PE number of the destination to the `shmemx_am_send_nbi` routine. Safe reuse of the payload buffer is not guaranteed when the non-blocking send routine returns and so the user should use the `shmem_quiet` routine to wait for the completion of all outbound AM requests, as the AM requests are sent through the default context `SHMEM_CTX_DEFAULT`. We do not provide any guarantee of the ordering of consecutive AM requests, as well as the atomicity of the execution of the handlers.

For the progression and completion of active message requests, we provide the `shmemx_am_poll` and `shmemx_am_wait` pair of routines. The `shmemx_am_poll` routine checks for arrived AM requests, it returns 0 immediately if no pending requests could be found, or a non-zero number if it was able to execute one or more AM requests. Alternatively, if the application calls the `shmemx_am_wait` routine and it could not find pending AM requests, it blocks the execution, enters a passive polling mode until an AM request arrives. Both routines could pass another pointer to user-defined arguments as the fourth argument (`args_p`) to the handler, so the handler can have easy access to the calling context.

```
// Active message handler definition
void am_handler(void* payload,
                size_t length,
                void* args_r,
                void* args_p,
                int src_pe)
{
  database_t* db          = args_r;
  scheduler_ctx_t* ctx = args_p;
  int payload_index       = db->store(payload, length,
     src_pe);
  ctx->insert_task(payload_index);
}

// Initiating PE of the AM request
shmemx_am_send_nbi(am_id, payload, length, pe_id);
shmem_quiet();

// Destination PE
shmemx_am_set_handler(am_handler, &database, &am_id);

while (!scheduler_ctx.done()) {
  shmemx_am_wait(&scheduler_ctx);
  int got_new_am;
  do {
    got_new_am = shmemx_am_poll(&scheduler_ctx);
  } while (got_new_am != 0);
}
```

Listing 1.3. Sample Usage of the Proposed OpenSHMEM Active Message API

The two polling routines can be combined in a fashion that is similar to the adaptive spinlocks: wait is used to put the thread to "sleep" while waiting for incoming AM requests to reduce resource usage; after wake-up, we perform busy non-blocking polling with the other routine until it returns 0, then go back to the blocking wait.

We deliberately choose to not have a background polling thread because we want the developers to have precise control over when and where the AM handlers are executed. This decision is crucial for inter-operating with OpenMP tasks: OpenMP does not provide an "entry" to its task scheduler for inserting new tasks on the fly, the user must write `#pragma omp task` inside the AM handler and make sure the handler is executed by an OpenMP-managed thread to inject a new task into a parallel region.

An example showing how the proposed API extension could be used to insert a task into a hypothetical shared-memory tasking system is presented in Listing 1.3. The active message handler stores the payload and the ID of the initiator PE into a database on the destination PE. Then the handler inserts a task into the task scheduling context that processed this AM request, so the shared-memory tasking framework can pick it up later and process the corresponding entry in the payload database. The initiator sends the AM request using an `am_id` that is the same as the one returned by the `shmemx_am_set_handler` routine on the destination PE and flushes the default context so the payload buffer can be reused. On the destination PE, we use the wait-and-poll combo to receive AM requests and insert tasks to the current scheduling context, until the work is done.

The example above can also be viewed as a child task sending its execution results to the parent task, or as a parent task sends a unit of work to one of its children for execution. This approach could be extended to execute a dynamic DAG of tasks that changes based on run-time information. Task migration through our active message extension is more flexible and maintainable than allocating one signal variable for each edge in the DAG and perform manual task queue management.

3.2 Implementation

Our implementation is based on the reference implementation of OpenSHMEM, OSSS-UCX [16]. This implementation uses UCX [22] as its communication substrate, which provides unified low overhead access to various vendor-specific communication protocols like InfiniBand Verbs and Cray uGNI. UCX provides a simple active message interface that works as follows: AM handlers are registered on UCP workers, AM requests are sent through UCP endpoints which represent pairs of "linked" workers, and calling the `ucp_worker_progress` routine on the destination process executes incoming active messages. The UCX AM handlers are invoked from the progress context, so trying to perform nested progression by calling `ucp_worker_progress` from within the handler is not allowed, thus prohibiting the handler from tracking the completion of various non-blocking operations. Constraints like this are common in similar frameworks to prevent deadlocks and other issues, with GASNet being another notable example.

Figure 1 shows how a PE processes an incoming AM request and sends another one from the AM handler. Rectangular boxes represent the execution contexts of different UCP workers and AM handlers, and the outermost rounded boxes represent the execution context of the OpenSHMEM runtime library. The `shmemx_am_send_nbi` routine sends the AM request and the accompanying payload to a dedicated UCP worker (`AM_worker`) on the destination PE, along with some metadata, using the UCX AM mechanism and an internal UCX AM handler. When the destination PE calls `shmemx_am_poll`, the OpenSHMEM runtime calls `ucp_worker_progress` on the `AM_worker` to process incoming AM requests. The UCX AM handler simply stores the pointer to the payload and returns `UCS_INPROGRESS` so that the UCX runtime does not deallocate the payload when the handler returns. Then, the OpenSHMEM runtime calls the requested OpenSHMEM AM handler using the ID assigned during registration. Any communication request initiated from the OpenSHMEM AM handler goes through

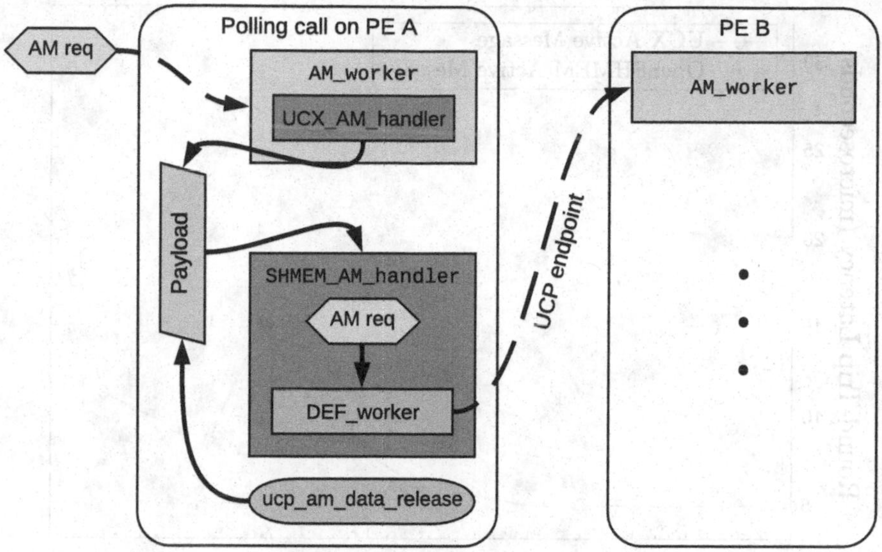

Fig. 1. OpenSHMEM active message implementation in OSSS-UCX.

the worker (`DEF_worker`) that handles the default context to avoid accidentally invoking another incoming AM request. Finally, when the OpenSHMEM AM handler finishes execution, `ucp_am_data_release` is called on the payload buffer to return it to UCX.

This design adds some overhead when compared to UCX active messages, but the two-worker approach enables chaining of AM requests and avoids execution of AM handlers in unexpected places (e.g. quiet, barriers) if the default worker is also used to process incoming active messages.

Advanced features like active message completion notification, automatically return data from the handler to the initiating PE and aggregated active message queues are have been considered for inclusion. These features could be very useful for many applications, but they will increase the complexity of the API and its implementation significantly, so we have decided to not support them in this work. The resulting API is still capable of being used as a task-based programming model and is inter-operable with a shared-memory tasking framework.

4 Performance Evaluation

We perform a preliminary evaluation of the performance of our implementation using two point-to-point micro-benchmarks and the TaskBench [23] framework. The performance numbers presented below were obtained on a cluster equipped with Fujitsu A64FX FX700 CPUs and NVIDIA Mellanox ConnectX-6 100 GB/s network cards. On the software side, the machine is running CentOS 8.1.1911 AArch64, Linux 4.18.0, MOFED 5.0-2.1.8.0, UCX 1.10.1, and GCC 10.3.0. For all MPI results, we use OpenMPI 4.1.1 linked to the same version of UCX.

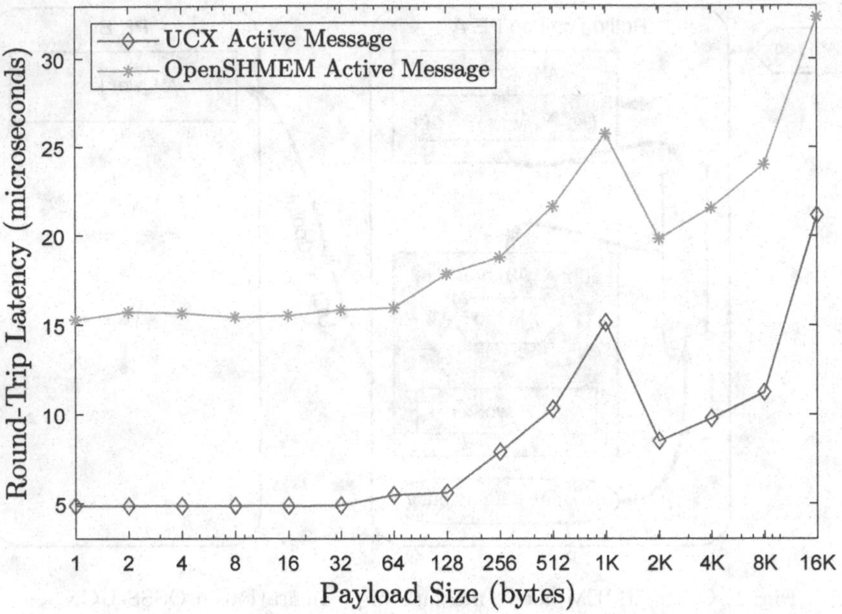

Fig. 2. Active message inter-node round-trip latency results (UCX protocol switching threshold = 1KiB).

4.1 Latency and Throughput

The classic ping-pong micro-benchmark is a good way to measure the latency of communication operations. A pair of PEs exchange active messages of a certain payload size between two nodes, each side sends one AM request and polls for the other side's AM request to arrive before moving on to the next iteration. We compared the round-trip latency of our OpenSHMEM AM extension against vanilla UCX AM to see how much overhead is added by the implementation shown in Fig. 1. The handler only sends an AM request to the other PE so this benchmark does not measure unrelated workload.

From Fig. 2, we can see that our implementation adds roughly 10 μs to every round-trip of active messages, so it's 5 μs of overhead per AM request. This overhead is the result of fetching the OpenSHMEM AM handler from the hash table of registered handlers, parsing the AM metadata, and other internal operations. The drop in latency when the payload increases from 1K to 2K is caused by UCX switching its communication protocols. It is worth noting that the two worker approach slightly increases memory usage and slows down the launching of OpenSHMEM applications, but once the application is up and running, the impact should be minimal.

Message throughput benchmark results are shown in Fig. 3, where one PE sends a large amount of AM requests with a trivial handler to the other PE and waits for the completion of all the requests. From the numbers, we can see that

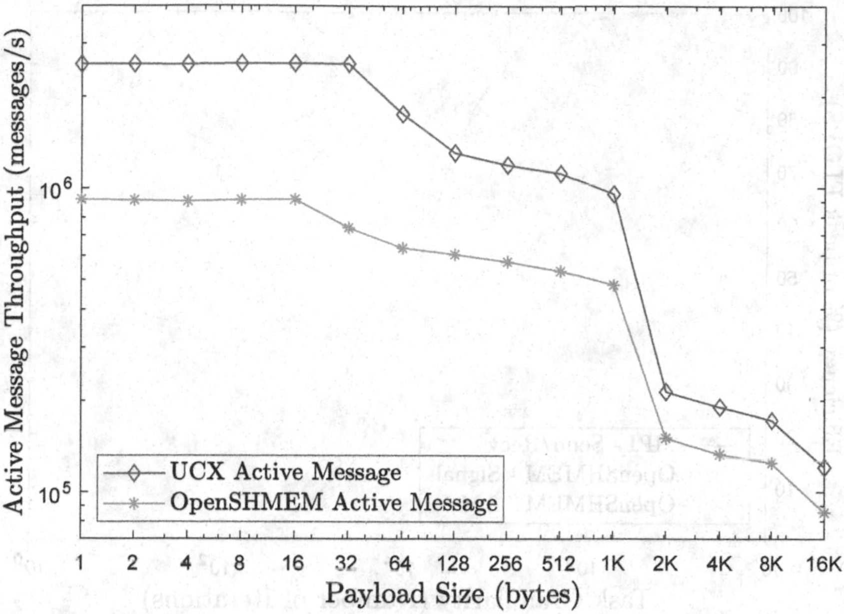

Fig. 3. Active message inter-node throughput results (UCX protocol switching threshold = 1KiB).

the message rate of OpenSHMEM AM is consistently lower than that of vanilla UCX AM, but the difference is within a reasonable range and is expected since the OpenSHMEM runtime library performs extra work. Again, the sudden drop of throughput in both implementations is caused by UCX switching protocols.

4.2 Tasking Framework Efficiency

Measuring the performance of a tasking framework is not easy: micro-benchmark results do not translate well to real-world application performance; it is difficult to create comparable ports of mini-apps and above to different tasking frameworks; even strong and weak scalability results can have different measuring methodologies and interpretations. TaskBench [23] is a new benchmark framework designed to provide a better way to compare different ways to do task-based programming. TaskBench makes the process of creating benchmarks (different DAGs and types of workload) orthogonal to the process of adding a new tasking framework backend, thus enabling the comparison of different programming models on equal grounds. Additionally, minimum effective task granularity (METG) is proposed as a new metric to compare the performance of tasking frameworks. METG is defined as the minimum task granularity that can utilize the hardware effectively for a given combination of hardware and workload, with a user definition of what is effective (usually being the ability to reach a certain percentage of the computer's peak performance). It is based on

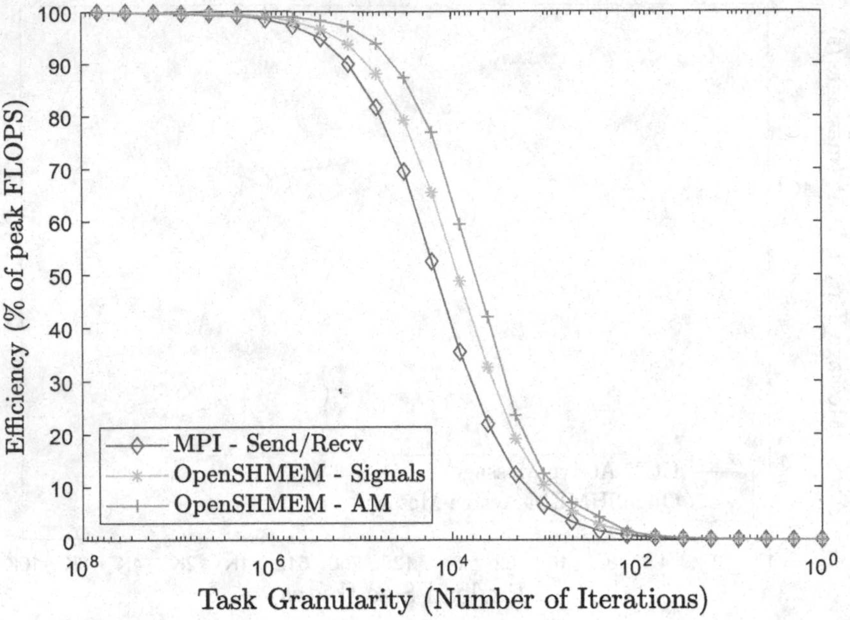

Fig. 4. TaskBench efficiency v.s. task granularity results.

the assumption that application efficiency drops as task granularity decreases, which is generally true due to the high scheduling cost of the execution of a large task DAG.

To compare the METG of our active message extension against OpenSHMEM's signal variable approach and MPI's message-passing approach, we run TaskBench on 8 nodes with 8 PEs/ranks per node (a total of 64 processes). The DAG used here is a 256×256 array of tasks with the all-to-all dependency pattern and 16 bytes of input/output data along the edges. Each task runs a compute-bound kernel with various numbers of iterations of synthetic computations to simulate tasks of different granularities. We use the MPI backend that comes with the TaskBench package, a signal-and-get OpenSHMEM back-end, and an OpenSHMEM active message back-end that uses AM requests to launch tasks and complete dependencies.

The results are presented in Fig. 4. Similar to the original paper's methodology [23], we define the machine's peak performance to be the FLOPS achieved when using a very large task granularity and calculate the efficiency of a particular task granularity by dividing the FLOPS obtained at that granularity by the peak FLOPS. From the achieved percentages of peak FLOPS show in Table 1, we can see that our OpenSHMEM active message backend shows a clear advantage (6%–24%) between task granularities from 2^{10} to 2^{16} iterations. DAGs with longer tasks are compute-bound and DAGs with shorter tasks are latency-bound, so we see similar results for all three backends. Also, from the embolden per-

Table 1. Percentage of peak FLOPS achieved at different task granularities

Task granularity	MPI Send/Recv	OpenSHMEM signals	OpenSHMEM AM
1024	6.503%	10.41%	12.51%
2048	12.35%	19.11%	23.60%
4096	21.91%	32.59%	42.06%
8192	35.49%	48.78%	59.48%
16384	52.48%	65.49%	**76.85%**
32768	69.46%	**79.22%**	87.32%
65536	**81.66%**	88.05%	93.85%

centages in Table 1, we can see that to reach 80% of the peak FLOPS of our test setup, the active message backend only requires about 1/2 of the task size of the signal-and-get backend, and about 1/4 of the task size of the MPI send/receive backend. This shows that our implementation of the proposed extension provides better performance for a wider range of task-based applications than MPI and classic OpenSHMEM.

5 Conclusion and Future Work

In this paper, we present an OpenSHMEM active message extension and its implementation that is designed to support basic task-based programming on its own, and inter-operates well with shared-memory tasking frameworks. Our proposed API is simple and adheres to the look and feel of existing OpenSHMEM routines. The user is given full control of when and where the AM handlers are executed, and the ability to perform selected communication operations from the AM handlers. The two-worker approach used in our UCX-based prototype implementation separates the initialization and completion of AM requests, which is crucial for the flexibility of the AM handler.

The performance of the implementation of the active message extension was evaluated using point-to-point micro-benchmarks and TaskBench. Evaluation results show that our design adds a reasonable amount of overhead when compared to vanilla UCX AM, and it beats both the MPI back-end and a signal-and-get-based OpenSHMEM back-end of TaskBench in minimum effective task granularity. The proposed active message extension narrows the functionality gap between OpenSHMEM and other task-based programming models.

In the future, we plan to explore the feasibility and performance trade-off of adding optional AM completion notifications, as it could further simplify dependency management of the task DAG. We also plan to port mini-apps like Mini-AMR [19] to OpenSHMEM+X where X is a shared-memory tasking model like OpenMP, Intel TBB [18] and Taskflow [9], and evaluate the real-world performance benefits of our active message extension in load-imbalanced applications.

Acknowledgement. This research was funded in part by the United States Department of Defense, and was supported by resources at Los Alamos National Laboratory, operated by Triad National Security, LLC under Contract No. 89233218CNA000001.

The authors would also like to thank Stony Brook Research Computing and Cyberinfrastructure, and the Institute for Advanced Computational Science at Stony Brook University for access to the innovative high-performance Ookami computing system, which was made possible by a $5M National Science Foundation grant (#1927880).

References

1. Bachan, J., et al.: UPC++: a high-performance communication framework for asynchronous computation. In: Proceedings of the 33rd IEEE International Parallel and Distributed Processing Symposium, IPDP. IEEE (2019). https://doi.org/10.25344/S4V88H, https://escholarship.org/uc/item/1gd059hj
2. Bauer, M., Treichler, S., Slaughter, E., Aiken, A.: Legion: expressing locality and independence with logical regions. In: SC 2012: Proceedings of the International Conference on High Performance Computing, Networking, Storage and Analysis, pp. 1–11 (2012). https://doi.org/10.1109/SC.2012.71
3. Bonachea, Dan, Hargrove, Paul H..: GASNet-EX: a high-performance, portable communication library for Exascale. In: Hall, Mary, Sundar, Hari (eds.) LCPC 2018. LNCS, vol. 11882, pp. 138–158. Springer, Cham (2019). https://doi.org/10.1007/978-3-030-34627-0_11
4. Chamberlain, B.L.: Chapel (Cray Inc. HPCS Language). In: Padua, D. (ed.) Encyclopedia of Parallel Computing, pp. 249–256. Springer, Boston (2011). https://doi.org/10.1007/978-0-387-09766-4_5
5. Chapman, B.M., et al.: Introducing openshmem: Shmem for the pgas community. In: PGAS (2010)
6. Daiß, G., et al.: From piz daint to the stars: simulation of stellar mergers using high-level abstractions. In: Proceedings of the International Conference for High Performance Computing, Networking, Storage and Analysis, SC 2019, Association for Computing Machinery, New York (2019). https://doi.org/10.1145/3295500.3356221, https://doi.org/10.1145/3295500.3356221
7. Dinan, J., Flajslik, M.: Contexts: a mechanism for high throughput communication in OpenSHMEM. In: Proceedings of the 8th International Conference on Partitioned Global Address Space Programming Models, pp. 10:1–10:9. ACM, New York (2014). https://doi.org/10.1145/2676870.2676872, http://doi.acm.org/10.1145/2676870.2676872
8. Eicken, T., Culler, D., Goldstein, S., Schauser, K.: Active messages: a mechanism for integrated communication and computation. In: 1992 Proceedings the 19th Annual International Symposium on Computer Architecture, pp. 256–266 (1992). https://doi.org/10.1109/ISCA.1992.753322
9. Huang, T.W., Lin, D.L., Lin, Y., Lin, C.X.: Taskflow: a general-purpose parallel and heterogeneous task programming system. IEEE Trans. Comput. Aided Des. Integr. Circuits Syst. (2021). https://doi.org/10.1109/TCAD.2021.3082507
10. Jana, S., Curtis, T., Khaldi, D., Chapman, B.: Increasing computational asynchrony in OpenSHMEM with active messages. In: Gorentla Venkata, M., Imam, N., Pophale, S., Mintz, T.M. (eds.) OpenSHMEM 2016. LNCS, vol. 10007, pp. 35–51. Springer, Cham (2016). https://doi.org/10.1007/978-3-319-50995-2_3

11. Kaiser, H., et al.: HPX - the C++ standard library for parallelism and concurrency. J. Open Source Softw. **5**(53), 2352 (2020). https://doi.org/10.21105/joss.02352
12. Kale, L.V., Krishnan, S.: Charm++: a portable concurrent object oriented system based on C++. In: Proceedings of the Eighth Annual Conference on Object-Oriented Programming Systems, Languages, and Applications, OOPSLA 1993, pp. 91–108. Association for Computing Machinery, New York (1993). https://doi.org/10.1145/165854.165874
13. Lu, W., Curtis, T., Chapman, B.: Enabling low-overhead communication in multi-threaded OpenSHMEM applications using contexts. In: 2019 IEEE/ACM Parallel Applications Workshop, Alternatives To MPI (PAW-ATM), pp. 47–57 (2019). https://doi.org/10.1109/PAW-ATM49560.2019.00010
14. NVSHMEM. https://developer.nvidia.com/nvshmem
15. OpenSHMEM Application Programming Interface Version 1.4. http://openshmem.org/site/sites/default/site_files/OpenSHMEM-1.4.pdf
16. Open Source Software Solutions (OSSS) OpenSHMEM Implementation on top of OpenUCX (UCX) and PMIx. https://github.com/openshmem-org/osss-ucx
17. Ozog, D., Rahman, M.W.U., Taylor, G., Dinan, J.: Designing, implementing, and evaluating the upcoming OpenSHMEM teams API. In: 2019 IEEE/ACM Parallel Applications Workshop, Alternatives To MPI (PAW-ATM), pp. 37–46 (2019). https://doi.org/10.1109/PAW-ATM49560.2019.00009
18. Pheatt, C.: Intel® threading building blocks. J. Comput. Sci. Coll. **23**(4), 298 (2008)
19. Sasidharan, A., Snir, M.: MiniAMR - a miniapp for adaptive mesh refinement (2016)
20. Scherer, W.N., Adhianto, L., Jin, G., Mellor-Crummey, J., Yang, C.: Hiding latency in Coarray Fortran 2.0. In: Proceedings of the Fourth Conference on Partitioned Global Address Space Programming Model, PGAS 2010. Association for Computing Machinery, New York (2010). https://doi.org/10.1145/2020373.2020387
21. Schuchart, J., Bouteiller, A., Bosilca, G.: Using MPI-3 RMA for active messages. In: 2019 IEEE/ACM Workshop on Exascale MPI (ExaMPI), pp. 47–56 (2019). https://doi.org/10.1109/ExaMPI49596.2019.00011
22. Shamis, P., et al.: UCX: an open source framework for HPC network APIs and beyond. In: 2015 IEEE 23rd Annual Symposium on High-Performance Interconnects, pp. 40–43. IEEE (2015)
23. Slaughter, E., et al.: Task bench: a parameterized benchmark for evaluating parallel runtime performance. In: Proceedings of the International Conference for High Performance Computing, Networking, Storage and Analysis. SC 2020. IEEE Press (2020)
24. Zhao, X., Balaji, P., Gropp, W., Thakur, R.: MPI-interoperable generalized active messages. In: 2013 International Conference on Parallel and Distributed Systems, pp. 200–207 (2013). https://doi.org/10.1109/ICPADS.2013.38

UCX Programming Interface for Remote Function Injection and Invocation

Luis E. Peña[1(✉)], Wenbin Lu[2], Pavel Shamis[1], and Steve Poole[3]

[1] Arm Research, Austin, TX 78735, USA
{Luis.EPena,Pavel.Shamis}@arm.com
[2] Stony Brook University, Stony Brook, NY 11794, USA
Wenbin.Lu@stonybrook.edu
[3] Los Alamos National Laboratory, Los Alamos, NM 87545, USA
swpoole@lanl.gov

Abstract. Network library APIs have historically been developed with the emphasis on data movement, placement, and communication semantics. Many communication semantics are available across a large variety of network libraries, such as send-receive, data streaming, put/get/atomic, RPC, active messages, collective communication, etc. In this work we introduce new compute and data movement APIs that overcome the constraints of the single-program, multiple-data (SPMD) programming model by allowing users to send binary executable code between processing elements. Our proof-of-concept implementation of the API is based on the UCX communication framework and leverages the RDMA network for fast compute migration. We envision the API being used to dispatch user functions from a host CPU to a SmartNIC (DPU), computational storage drive (CSD), or remote servers. In addition, the API can be used by large-scale irregular applications (such as semantic graph analysis), composed of many coordinating tasks operating on a data set so big that it has to be stored on many physical devices. In such cases, it may be more efficient to dynamically choose where code runs as the applications progresses.

Keywords: Active message · Code injection · UCX

1 Introduction

The emergence of distributed heterogeneous systems is driven by the ever increasing demands for performance, energy efficiency, and cost reduction. For example, in the last decade, the HPC community has been driving the adoption of GPU as an accelerator for large-scale distributed systems and applications. Recently, hyperscale service providers have introduced two new types of datacenter infrastructure accelerators: the data processing unit (DPU) and the computational storage drive (CSD). In contrast to GPUs, which have been well-adopted by applications, both DPUs and CSDs are relatively new and have

L. E. Peña and W. Lu—Contributed equally.

S. Poole et al. (Eds.): OpenSHMEM 2021, LNCS 13159, pp. 144–159, 2022.
https://doi.org/10.1007/978-3-031-04888-3_9

very limited adoption. DPUs and CSDs are usually programmable devices that are realized using FPGAs and/or Arm cores. Despite being designed with user programmability in mind, these devices are typically exposed as fixed-function components that provide transparent acceleration for a few popular usages, e.g., embedded Open vSwitch, IPSEC, and compression. As the list of available functionalities are determined by datacenter vendors, applications are not exposed to the programmable elements of DPUs and CSDs, and therefore cannot take advantage of the devices' processing power for application specific purposes.

Developers are also challenged by the rapidly increasing amount of data they have to deal with in their applications. For some applications the type and distribution of the workload is highly dependent on the data and therefore changes dynamically. Since moving data is still orders of magnitude slower than doing computation, ideally we would like to move compute to data to improve locality, not the other way around. Additionally, with new features being added and tested on a daily basis, it could further slow down the development cycle if the application needs to be re-compiled and re-deployed for every feature addition and/or bug fix.

In this work, we aim to overcome the programmability barriers of such devices by introducing the `ifunc` API, an UCX API designed to facilitate the movement of application-defined compute and data. Injected functions (`ifuncs`), taking the form of messages that contain binary code and data, are sent to and invoked by other remote processes via the *Two-Chains* framework [7]. `ifuncs` are similar to active messages in that each message contains data and an action to perform, but their main difference is that `ifuncs` actually contain the code to be executed, while active messages contain only a reference to the function to be called. `ifuncs` provide more versatility because the available functions are no longer fixed and a target system can register new functions during run-time, without having to recompile UCX or the application. Our API breaks the commonly used SPMD model of computation to benefit dynamic, irregular, and data-driven applications on a wider range of heterogeneous devices. The main contribution of this paper is an API and implementation of RDMA-based remote function injection and linking.

The rest of this paper is organized as follows: Sect. 2 provides an overview on *Two-Chains*, the high performance remote linking and messaging framework leveraging the `ifunc` API. This section also discusses some related work on dynamic computation migration. Next, Sect. 3 presents the `ifunc` API, how it could be used, how it is implemented, how it compares to UCX Active Messages (AM), and how it can be secured. In Sect. 4, we describe how we validated our prototype implementation and discuss the initial benchmark results. Finally, Sect. 5 provides our plans to continue to improve the `ifunc` API and *Two-Chains* framework.

2 Background

The `ifunc` API is an evolution of the remote function invocation mechanism of the *Two-Chains* framework. In this section we discuss the *Two-Chains* framework as the background of the work presented in this paper, as well as several related works.

2.1 *Two-Chains*

The original *Two-Chains* framework is presented in [7], which covers implementation details of the framework and how its performance can be improved using existing hardware features.

Two-Chains is an extension of UCX [12], providing packaging, transfer and execution of C functions in a fast and lightweight manner. It aims at an API and a toolchain to enable the migration of compute and data between local and remote CPU, GPU, DPU and CSD processes using UCX communication capabilities. The users write the functions to be injected using a macro-based interface, then use the *Two-Chains* toolchain to compile them into dynamic libraries that can be loaded by the application at runtime. On the source process, the executable code of the to-be-injected function is loaded from the dynamic library, and is packaged with function arguments and a variable-length payload to form a message (referred to as *jams* in the original publication).

Upon receipt of a message containing injected functions, the target system directly executes the C function embedded in the message. This mechanism employs dynamic linking to support calling functions from libraries resident in the target system from the injected functions.

Two-Chains uses one-sided UCX put operations to enable fast delivery and execution of injected functions. The runtime sets up a receiver thread waiting to call the embedded function with minimal latency when a message arrives. For code in the message to execute correctly on the receiver, the *Two-Chains* toolchain statically modifies the assembly to allow runtime linking against symbols on an arbitrary host by redirecting all global offset table (GOT) accesses to an indirection stored in the message. Remote runtime linking allows distributed application updates to sub-processes of the application that alter their execution behavior (without re-starting the process) by loading a library into a process to change the resolution of objects or functions with fixed symbolic names. This way, applications can implement dynamic control and compute with library loading and linking.

2.2 Related Work

There are numerous libraries, frameworks, and runtimes that implement active message semantics that have influenced the development of *Two-Chains* and the `ifunc` API presented in this work. In brief, these projects include GASNet, Snap Microkernel, Charm++, CHAMELEON, and FaRM.

GASNet [4] is a communication library widely used on high-performance computing clusters to implement advanced programming models. In addition to normal data transfer routines, GASNet also provides a series of APIs for registering and invoking active messages. GASNet uses the classical function registration mechanism for identifying active message handlers, while `ifuncs` sends the executable code and does not require actions from the target side. The Snap Microkernel [10] project provides a platform for remote procedure calls in the context of network functionality distribution. Like many of the other computation placement and migration frameworks, it is a heavyweight multifunction entity. Our `ifunc` API has a smaller scope and could be used as a building block as part of such a system. In the datacenter setting, lightweight container launch for Lambda functions is implemented with Firecracker [3]. Another work from Fouladi et al. provides very fast container launch to create highly granular lambda function execution [6]. None of these projects addresses issues like heterogeneity of hardware, since containerization is meant to abstract this. *Two-Chains* can be used as a shim between hardware and higher level libraries.

Charm++ [2] implements distributed C++ objects with a unified logical view of them (not partitioned to processes/ranks from the programmer's perspective), plus the ability to call methods on those objects regardless of their physical location, unlike regular active message where the developer must decide when and where to request function invocations. The Charm++ scheduler works behind the scene to distribute and migrate the objects automatically, based on load distribution and communication patterns. Its programming model runs at a very high level compared to *Two-Chains* and UCX and its runtime system supports lots of advanced features like fault tolerance. The CHAMELEON [9] framework by Klinkenberg et al. uses compiler directives and runtime APIs to encapsulate OpenMP tasks as migratable entities in a reactive workload balancer for irregular applications written in MPI. Unlike CHAMELEON, *Two-Chains* does not contain a load balancer, does not depend on OpenMP or MPI or C++, nor requires explicit task progress if the UCX library uses progress threads. Further, CHAMELEON's remote virtual address resolution process to move tasks between address spaces is a heavyweight exchange of references via MPI Send/Recv for each migration event. Our work could potentially be used as a communication layer to greatly simplify and speed up CHAMELEON, especially since they found in the course of their work that push-oriented compute movement (as we have implemented here) is a better mechanism than work stealing for load balancing since it allows computation-communication overlap.

The FaRM [5] project implements a shared address space programming model that uses the RDMA network for remote object manipulation. *Two-Chains* uses RDMA not only for moving data, it also injects user-defined functions to remote machines using RDMA to provide higher flexibility while avoiding re-compiling the application for functionality changes.

The *Two-Chains* API developed in this paper builds on the semantics of the active message API [13], which combines a data payload with executable code on a receiver. The primary innovation of the *Two-Chains* API relative to classical active message semantics is the ability to send binary function and data payload simultaneously, without requiring the function to be present at runtime compile time.

3 Design and Implementation

In this section, we present the design and implementation of the `ifunc` API, provide an example on the expected usage, and talk about its security implications.

3.1 The ifunc API

```
ucs_status_t
ucp_register_ifunc(ucp_context_h context,
                   const char*   ifunc_name,
                   ucp_ifunc_h*  ifunc_p)

void
ucp_deregister_ifunc(ucp_context_h context,
                     ucp_ifunc_h   ifunc_h)

ucs_status_t
ucp_ifunc_msg_create(ucp_ifunc_h        ifunc_h,
                     void*              source_args,
                     size_t             source_args_size,
                     ucp_ifunc_msg_t*   msg_p)

void
ucp_ifunc_msg_free(ucp_ifunc_msg_t msg)

ucs_status_t
ucp_ifunc_msg_send_nbix(ucp_ep_h           ep,
                        ucp_ifunc_msg_t    msg,
                        uint64_t           remote_addr,
                        ucp_rkey_h         rkey)

ucs_status_t
ucp_poll_ifunc(ucp_context_h context,
               void*         buffer,
               size_t        buffer_size,
               void*         target_args)
```

Listing 1.1. UCP `ifunc` API

To start, the source process calls the `ucp_register_ifunc` function with the `ifunc`'s name *ifunc_name* to register an `ifunc` library. The UCX runtime will search the directory defined by the `UCX_IFUNC_LIB_DIR` environment variable for the dynamic library named *`ifunc_name`*`.so`, and uses `dlopen` and `dlsym` to load the library and the user-provided ifunc library functions defined in Listing 1.2, and finally returns a handler to the registered ifunc. Now ifunc messages can be constructed using the ucp_ifunc_msg_create routine, which accepts user arguments and passes them to the ifunc library routines to prepare the ifunc's payload that will be sent to the target process. Once the ifunc message object is created, it is ready to be written into the target process's memory using the ucp_ifunc_send_nbix routine, which uses the ucp_put_nbi routine to write a continuous buffer into a memory region mapped by ucp_mem_map.

On the target process, the ucp_poll_ifunc routine should be used to wait on a UCP mapped memory region for incoming ifunc messages. This routine returns immediately if it could not find a newly received ifunc message in buffer. If a valid ifunc message is found, the UCX runtime will invoke the code contained in the ifunc message with a pointer to the payload, the size of the payload, and the target_args pointer that points to user-provided arguments on the target process. Currently, in our implementation, the target process does not yet construct a GOT that contains redirections for all the functions used by the ifunc code, instead it uses the ifunc's name contained in the message header to auto-register the specific ifunc dynamic library and uses the local GOT to patch the code shipped within the ifunc message. We plan to add GOT reconstruction functionalities in the future and the target process will not need to register the ifunc library anymore.

```
void
[ifunc_name]_main(void*  payload,
                  size_t payload_size,
                  void*  target_args)

size_t
[ifunc_name]_payload_get_max_size(void*  source_args,
                                  size_t source_args_size)

int
[ifunc_name]_payload_init(void*  payload,
                          size_t payload_size,
                          void*  source_args,
                          size_t source_args_size)
```

Listing 1.2. ifunc library API

A valid ifunc library should define all three routines specified in Listing 1.2. The [ifunc_name]_main launches the execution of the ifunc code; it gets invoked when a ifunc message is received by ucp_poll_ifunc on the target process, with the three arguments described in the previous subsection.

The [ifunc_name]_payload_get_max_size and [ifunc_name]_payload_init routines are both invoked by the ucp_ifunc_msg_create routine on the source process. The first routine is used by the UCX runtime to calculate the maximum size of the payload to be sent within a ifunc message for a given set of source process arguments source_args. Then the UCX runtime will allocate a ifunc message frame with a payload buffer of the requested size, and pass the same source process arguments to the [ifunc_name]_payload_init routine to populate the payload buffer. This way, we eliminate unnecessary memory copies while maintaining the flexibility of the interface.

3.2 Using the API

```
#include <paq8px.h>

size_t paq8px_payload_get_max_size(void *source_args,
                                   size_t source_args_size) {
    return est_output_size(source_args, source_args_size);
}

int paq8px_payload_init(void *payload,
                        size_t payload_size,
                        void *source_args,
                        size_t source_args_size) {
    encode(payload, payload_size,
           source_args, source_args_size);
    return 0;
}

void paq8px_main(void *payload,
                 size_t payload_size,
                 void *target_args) {
    db_handler dbh = target_args;
    decode_insert(dbh, payload, payload_size);
}
```

Listing 1.3. Sample `ifunc` library

Here we provide an example on the expected usage of the `ifunc` API. Suppose the target process manages a database that stores voice recordings. When another process wants to send a record compressed by the **paq8px** algorithm, which is unsupported by the database, it can use the `ifunc` library shown in Listing 1.3 to perform the task. The header file included at the top of the library code contains the implementation of the algorithm, which will be visible to the compiler during compilation. The first two user-provided functions are used to encode and package payload on the source process, while the main function performs payload decoding and database insertion on the target process.

```
/* On the source process */
ucp_ifunc_h ih;
ucp_ifunc_msg_t msg;

ucp_register_ifunc(ucp_ctx, "paq8pv", &ih);
ucp_ifunc_msg_create(ih, record, record_size, &msg);

ucp_ifunc_send_nbix(ep, msg, recv_buffer, rmt_rkey);
ucp_ep_flush_nb(ep); // And wait on completion

ucp_ifunc_msg_free(msg);
```

```
ucp_deregister_ifunc(ucp_ctx, ih);

/* On the target process */
ucs_status_t s;
do {
    s = ucp_poll_ifunc(ucp_ctx, recv_buffer,
                       recv_buffer_size, db_handle);
} while (s != UCS_OK);
```

Listing 1.4. Sample `ifunc` API usage

During run-time, as demonstrated by Listing 1.4, the source process registers the **paq8px** library, constructs an `ifunc` message with the recording as its payload, and sends it to the target process. On the target process, the polling loop calls the `ucp_poll_ifunc` function until it returns `UCX_OK`, which indicates that it has received and executed an `ifunc` message. If the user would like the target process to poll for incoming `ifunc` messages continuously, the `ucs_arch_wait_mem` routine can be used to wait on memory locations that `ifunc` messages are expected to arrive and reduce resource usage.

3.3 ifuncs *versus* UCX Active Messages

Injected functions are inspired by active messages but are different in many aspects. A comparison between *Two-Chains* injected functions and UCX active messages helps the reader know the differences and decide which one to use.

We start by listing the main similarities. `ifuncs` and UCX AMs allow sending payloads of various sizes and launching functions on remote processes. Both accept user-defined arguments when the functions are launched on the target processes, so the functions have access to resources in the local address space. Lastly, both mechanisms require active progression on the target side to process the received messages, in the form of non-blocking polling calls.

The main difference between active messages and injected functions is that, instead of establishing a mapping between registered functions and unique IDs, `ifunc` messages carry the actual binary code of the functions and the functions themselves are identified by a name. This key `ifunc` feature enables a set of `ifunc` benefits over UCX AMs. The first of these benefits is that `ifuncs` can be loaded on-demand during run-time, without recompiling the application; AM handlers are determined at compile time, requiring the application to be stopped and recompiled when AM handlers are added or modified. A related benefit to this one is that, since the function code is sent with each invocation, the code can be modified anytime under the same `ifunc` name. Another *Two-Chains* difference is that `ifuncs` are registered on the source process while AM handlers are registered at the target process; this feature of the `ifunc` API enables the system to dynamically add nodes with no previous knowledge of what functions it might need to execute in the future.

UCX AMs use on-demand internal buffers for receiving messages, while `ifuncs` require the user to allocate special buffers and a consensus about where the target processes expect the messages to arrive. `ifuncs` need special modifications to the assembly code before they can be used, while AM code does not. We expect these limitations to go away as we keep improving the *Two-Chains* framework.

3.4 Implementing the API

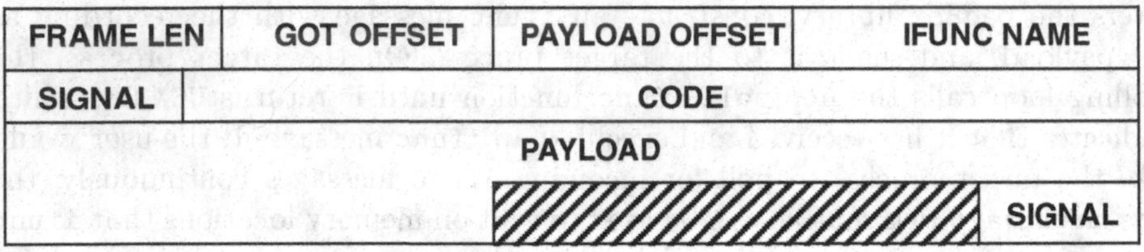

Fig. 1. Structure of an `ifunc` message

Each `ifunc` message, constructed by the `ucp_ifunc_message_create` routine, is composed of a header, a code section, an optional payload section, and a trailer signal, as seen on Fig. 1. If the code section is a direct copy of the `.text` section of the `ifunc` dynamic library, external function calls (e.g. `printf`) and accesses to global variables will not have the correct relocations on the target process, due to Linux's relative addressing and address space layout randomization (ASLR). To fix this issue, we compile the `ifunc` dynamic library with the `-fno-plt` flag to force all relocations to go through the global offset table (GOT), skipping the procedure linkage table (PLT). Then we use a Python script to modify the assembly code so that all references to the GOT will redirect through another table on the target process. A pointer to this alternative table is inserted as a hidden global variable by the script and is shipped with the `ifunc` message as part of the code, and the target process is expected to fill this variable with the address of a reconstructed GOT before invoking the `ifunc`'s main function.

When an `ifunc` message arrives at the target process, the integrity of the header is verified using the header signal, and messages that are ill-formed or too long will be rejected. Then the runtime parses the header to get the total size of the message frame and waits for the trailer signal to arrive, as shown in Fig. 2. In our tests, we use the `WFE` instruction to reduce resource usage when busy-waiting on the trailer signal, without incurring a heavy performance penalty.

Before calling the main function of a fully delivered `ifunc` message, the target process should perform work similar to a dynamic linker: construct a GOT that has all the relocations needed by the `ifunc` code in the correct offsets. This mechanism is not implemented yet. Instead, we assume the same `ifunc` dynamic library is also available on the target process's file system, so the target

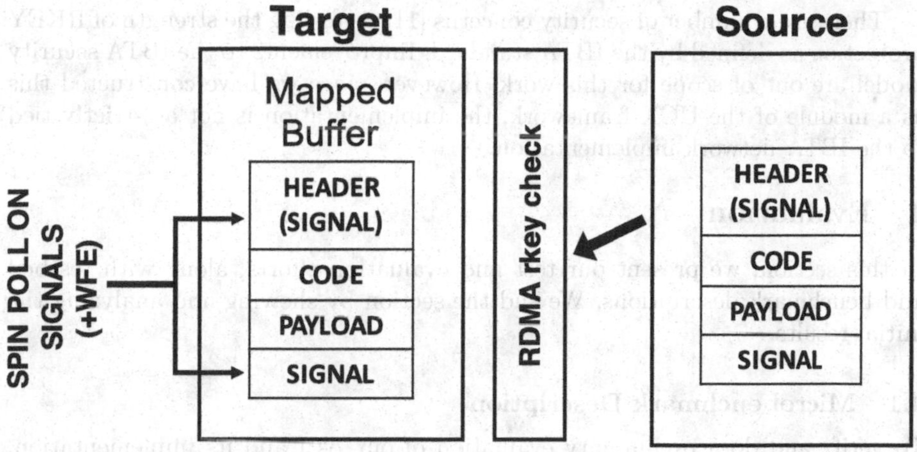

Fig. 2. `ifunc` source-target communication

process can simply load the library and let the system dynamic loader do the GOT construction. In our implementation, the `ucp_poll_ifunc` routine uses the `ifunc`'s name provided by the message header to attempt the auto-registration of any first-seen `ifunc` type. If the corresponding library is found and loaded successfully, the UCX runtime will patch the alternative GOT pointer of the code section of the `ifunc` message with a pointer to the same library's GOT in the local address space, and store the related information in a hash table for subsequent messages of the same type. We plan to implement the dynamic linking and GOT reconstruction mechanism in the future.

3.5 Security Implications and Mitigations

A full security model design and implementation is well beyond the scope of this paper. This section provides an overview of security challenges and directions for security improvements.

For our *Two-Chains* framework implementation, we have relied on the built-in security mechanisms defined by the UCX framework and the IBTA standard [8], which underpins RDMA interconnects. Specifically, we are using a remote access key (RKEY) to register and control remote memory accesses. For IBTA interconnects, the RKEY is defined as a 32-bit value. When the memory is registered for remote memory access, the underlying interconnect generates the RKEY based on a virtual memory address and the permissions (remote read, write, or atomic access). In order to access the memory region over the RDMA interconnect, the target process has to provide the RKEY to the RDMA initiator through an out-of-band channel. Then, the remote memory access initiator uses the RKEY to remotely read and write to the target process memory. If the process accesses the memory with an invalid RKEY, the request gets rejected at the hardware level.

There are a number of security concerns [11] regarding the strength of RKEY protection as defined by the IBTA standard. Improvements to the IBTA security model are out of scope for this work. However, since we have constructed this as a module of the UCX framework, the implementation is not as strictly tied to the IBTA network implementation.

4 Evaluation

In this section, we present our test and evaluation efforts, along with testbed and benchmark descriptions. We end the section by showing and analyzing the initial results.

4.1 Microbenchmark Description

To verify and do a preliminary evaluation of our API and its implementation, we ran message throughput and ping-pong latency benchmarks with a simple `ifunc` library and we compare them against the same benchmarks written using UCX AM. The results are presented below. In both benchmarks, the `ifunc` main function simply increases a counter on the target process used to count the number of executed messages.

In the `ifunc` message throughput benchmark, a ring buffer is allocated using the `ucp_mem_map` routine so it allows UCP put operations. The source process fills the buffer with `ifunc` messages of a certain size, flushes the UCP endpoint used to send the messages, then waits on the target process's notification indicating that it has finished consuming all the messages before continuing to send the next round of messages. This leads to some overhead but is not significant when the number of messages is large. For the equivalent UCX AM throughput benchmark, since the UCX runtime uses internal buffers to handle the messages, the source process simply sends all the messages in a loop and flushes the endpoint at the end.

The ping-pong benchmark is implemented using the classical approach: each process sends a message, flushes the endpoint and waits for the other process to reply before continuing this process.

4.2 Testbed Platform

The development and evaluation testbed for this work consisted of two servers, each with a 4-core, Arm-based modern superscalar processor with a 1 MB dedicated L2 cache per core, a 1 MB shared L3 cache per 2-core cluster, and a 8 MB shared last level cache (LLC). The core clock is 2.6 GHz and the on-chip interconnect clock is 1.6 GHz. Each server has 16 GB of DDR4-2666 main memory. For the interconnect, we used two Mellanox/Nvidia ConnectX-6 200 Gb/s InfiniBand dual-port HCAs. The two systems were connected back-to-back (no InfiniBand switch) using the first port on each ConnectX-6 HCA. The servers used Ubuntu 20.04, running a custom Linux 5.4 kernel, modified to allow user space control of the CPU prefetching mechanisms. We used the RDMA and InfiniBand drivers that came with Mellanox OFED, versioned `OFED-5.3-1.0.0d`.

4.3 Experimental Results and Analysis

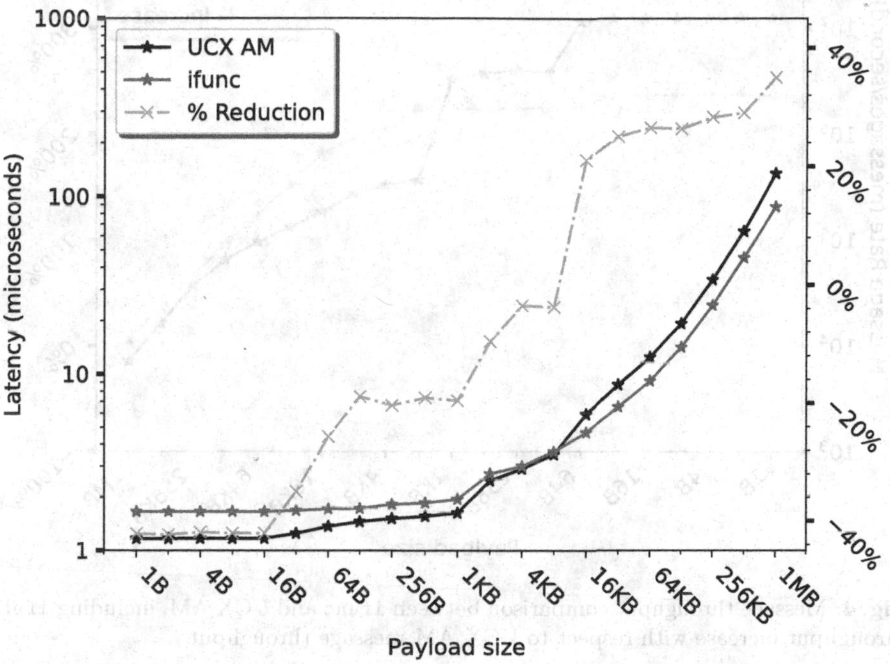

Fig. 3. Latency comparison between `ifunc` and UCX AM, including `ifunc` latency reduction with respect to UCX AM latency

Figure 3 shows the one-way latencies of sending and executing the benchmark function using the `ifunc` and UCX AM APIs. For smaller payloads, the `ifunc` latency is up to 42% slower than the AM latency. As payload (and message) size increases, the `ifunc` latency gets closer to that of AM, crossing over somewhere between payload sizes 8 KB and 16 KB. After this crossover point, the `ifunc` latency keeps improving, reaching a 35% latency reduction for the 1 MB payload size. For small payload sizes, we expected the AM latencies to be better because the code sent in the `ifunc` messages dominate the message size, not the payload. That being said, the performance gap is larger than it needs to be because of the `clear_cache` operation.

To ensure the correct operation of the `ifunc` invocation, the instruction cache needs to be cleared after the runtime confirms the data has arrived because the I-cache could have stale data due to some systems not having coherent I-caches. `glibc`'s Arm64 `clear_cache` implementation avoids clearing the I-cache when it detects a coherent I-cache by reading an architectural register. Our testbed did not have a coherent I-cache, and that is why the arrival of each `ifunc` incurs a performance hit on the target system. This is likely to be the reason why the latencies were not better.

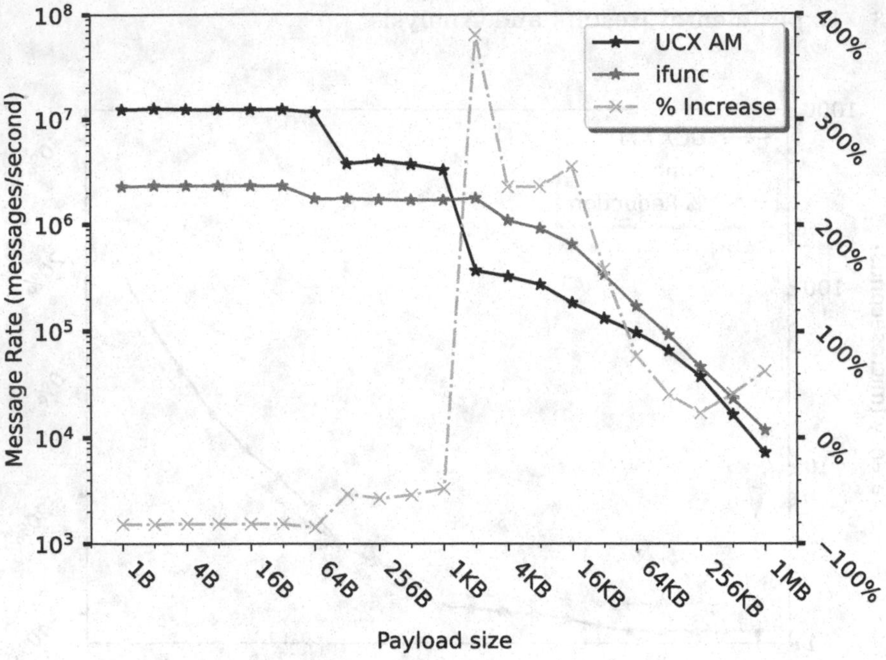

Fig. 4. Message throughput comparison between `ifunc` and UCX AM, including `ifunc` throughput increase with respect to UCX AM message throughput

Figure 4 presents the results of the message throughput benchmarks using both APIs. For 1B payloads, the `ifunc` message rate is 81% lower than that of UCX AMs. The message rate continues to be worse until the payload goes from 1 KB to 2 KB. From this point on, the `ifunc` message rate is superior, first spiking at 380% better, then dropping to 23% and then coming back up to 62% higher.

One interesting observation is the *stepping* experienced by the UCX AM line. These steps are likely due to the change is underlying protocol for moving the active messages. Interestingly, the point where `ifuncs` start performing better coincides with the sharp performance falloff *step* experienced by UCX AM, possibly due to protocol differences between `ifunc` and UCX AM.

As in the latency case, we think that the `ifunc` performance would have been better if we had evaluated using a platform with a coherent I-cache. Another area where we could have extracted more performance is the buffer mechanism used to send messages to the target.

4.4 Takeaways

From these initial benchmarks, we observe that the `ifuncs` perform worse than UCX Active Messages for small payload sizes. The larger the payloads become, the better `ifuncs` behave. This small-payload behavior is expected because, while active messages carry a numerical ID alongside the payload, `ifuncs` actually carry the function binary alongside the payload. Despite the `ifunc` messages being larger, we expected them to be more performant, but the slowdowns could be explained by the need to perform a `clear_cache` operation on the instruction cache because our testbed does not have a coherent I-cache.

Since this is a preliminary evaluation of the `ifunc` API, we plan need to run additional benchmarks to better understand the behavior of the *Two-Chains* framework with a wider set of micro-benchmarks and applications in the future.

5 Conclusion

The `ifunc` API and *Two-Chains* framework provide a high performance mechanism of moving compute and data over networks between a wide class of processing elements. It uses dynamic linking and loading to resolve `ifunc` external symbolic references on a per-process basis. We presented the user-facing side of the API and how developers write `ifunc` libraries. Important differences between `ifuncs` and traditional active messages were also discussed. We provided an overview of the security mechanisms of that *Two-Chains* can leverage. The code is released on GitHub [1]. We will discuss the future steps on the evolution of *Two-Chains* and the `ifunc` API below.

5.1 Future Work

Our *Two-Chains* vision does not require the presence of the `ifunc` dynamic library on the target's filesystem. We implemented it first this way in our prototype because it was going to allow us to have a version working sooner for evaluation. We are looking into ways of removing this requirement so *Two-Chains* target processes are able to handle received `ifunc` messages with the correct dynamic linking mechanism.

We are also working on switching the underlying implementation of *Two-Chains* to use UCX's send-receive semantics instead of RDMA Puts. This change will enable a simpler API because the user would not have to worry about setting up a RWX-enabled buffer on the target process. In addition, the user would not have to tell the source process exactly where to PUT the messages. This change would also eliminate the need for a special polling API and calling it from the target process to process incoming messages, as `ifuncs` will be progressed with other UCX operations by calling `ucp_worker_progress`. The good thing with this change is that the current API will only have minimal changes: we would mostly be removing unnecessary arguments and functions calls.

Currently the payload is tightly packed after the code segment of the `ifunc` message frame so we do not have any data alignment guarantees. This could be undesirable for vectorization and some other applications. We plan to allow the user to specify an alignment requirement on the payload buffer to better support vectorization and other needs.

The compilation toolchain of this work uses a Python script to prepare the `ifunc` code section to accept a patched GOT. We are considering updating the way we do this to make this important step target-process-architecture agnostic.

We are still debugging and stress-testing the *Two-Chains* and its API implementation. We are also working on getting *Two-Chains* in a state where it can be accepted to upstream UCX. Finally, we will test the *Two-Chains* framework with benchmarks that do useful work and on a machine that has a coherent I-cache.

Acknowledgments. The authors would like to thank the Los Alamos National Laboratory for their continued support of this project. In addition, we would like thank Curtis Dunham, Megan Grodowitz, Jon Hermes, and Eric Van Hensbergen for their review of the paper and code.

References

1. Two-Chains source code. https://github.com/openucx/ucx-two-chains
2. Acun, B., et al.: Parallel programming with migratable objects: charm++ in practice. In: SC 2014: Proceedings of the International Conference for High Performance Computing, Networking, Storage and Analysis, pp. 647–658. IEEE (2014). http://charm.cs.illinois.edu/newPapers/14-07/paper.pdf
3. Agache, A., et al.: Firecracker: lightweight virtualization for serverless applications. In: 17th USENIX Symposium on Networked Systems Design and Implementation (NSDI 2020), pp. 419–434. USENIX Association, Santa Clara, CA (2020). https://www.usenix.org/conference/nsdi20/presentation/agache
4. Bonachea, D., Hargrove, P.H.: Gasnet-ex: a high-performance, portable communication library for exascale. In: International Workshop on Languages and Compilers for Parallel Computing, pp. 138–158. Springer (2018). https://bytebucket.org/berkeleylab/upcxx/wiki/pubs/gasnet-ex-lcpc18-6da6911-tech.pdf
5. Dragojević, A., Narayanan, D., Castro, M., Hodson, O.: Farm: fast remote memory. In: 11th {USENIX} Symposium on Networked Systems Design and Implementation ({NSDI} 14), pp. 401–414 (2014)
6. Fouladi, S., et al.: From laptop to lambda: outsourcing everyday jobs to thousands of transient functional containers. In: 2019 USENIX Annual Technical Conference (USENIX ATC 19), pp. 475–488. USENIX Association, Renton, WA (2019). https://www.usenix.org/conference/atc19/presentation/fouladi
7. Grodowitz, M., Peña, L.E., Dunham, C., Zhong, D., Shamis, P., Poole, S.: Two-chains: high performance framework for function injection and execution. In: (To appear in) 2021 IEEE International Conference on Cluster Computing (CLUSTER). IEEE (2021). https://arxiv.org/abs/2108.02253
8. Infiniband trade association specification. https://www.infinibandta.org
9. Klinkenberg, J., Samfass, P., Bader, M., Terboven, C., Müller, M.S.: Chameleon: Reactive load balancing for hybrid MPI+openmp task-parallel applications. J. Parallel Distrib. Comput. **138**, 55–64 (2020). https://doi.org/10.1016/j.jpdc.2019.12.005, http://www.sciencedirect.com/science/article/pii/S0743731519305180, https://gauss-allianz.de/files/projects/Chameleon_Reactive_Task_Migration_for_Hybrid_MPI__OpenMP_Applications_9_HPCStatusKonferenz_191128083805.pdf

10. Marty, M., et al.: Snap: a microkernel approach to host networking. In: Proceedings of the 27th ACM Symposium on Operating Systems Principles, pp. 399–413. SOSP 2019, Association for Computing Machinery, New York, NY, USA (2019). https://doi.org/10.1145/3341301.3359657, http://pages.cs.wisc.edu/~yxy/cs839-s20/papers/snap.pdf
11. Rothenberger, B., Taranov, K., Perrig, A., Hoefler, T.: ReDMArk: bypassing RDMA Security Mechanisms. In: Software for Exascale Computing - SPPEXA 2016–2019. USENIX (2021)
12. Shamis, P., et al.: Ucx: an open source framework for HPC network APIS and beyond. In: 2015 IEEE 23rd Annual Symposium on High-Performance Interconnects, pp. 40–43. IEEE (2015)
13. Von Eicken, T., Culler, D.E., Goldstein, S.C., Schauser, K.E.: Active messages: a mechanism for integrated communication and computation. ACM SIGARCH Comput. Arch. News **20**(2), 256–266 (1992)

Can Deferring Small Messages Enhance the Performance of OpenSHMEM Applications?

David Ozog[1](✉), Md. Wasi-ur-Rahman[2], and Kieran Holland[2]

[1] Intel Corporation, Hudson, MA, USA
david.m.ozog@intel.com
[2] Intel Corporation, Austin, TX, USA

Abstract. This work examines the small-message problem in OpenSHMEM applications, and proposes a new software interface that helps alleviate its detrimental performance impacts. We summarize the state-of-the-art in transport middleware that defers and bundles communication to reduce small-message overheads. These techniques increase small-message transmission rates by *chaining* together many small messages in favor of fewer coarse messages and fewer exchanges ("doorbell rings") with the network interface card (NIC). For OpenSHMEM, we focus on the relatively simple approach of chaining only remote memory access (RMA) and atomic memory operations (AMOs).

Theoretically, the performance benefit from small-message chaining should not scale well with the number of processing elements (PEs), because more diverse target PEs typically lead to less opportunity for chaining. However, this paper will show that in practice, there are still good reasons to support this optimization. For instance, many OpenSHMEM users have no need to scale past thousands or even hundreds of clustered compute nodes, and at these scales there is still plenty of benefit from chaining - this paper will show message rate speedups of up to 2.6× in standard benchmarks. Our measurements also show comparable speedups without noticeable degradation at scale for the critical benchmark, Giga Updates Per Second (GUPS). Although micro-benchmarks like GUPS are not entirely indicative of more sophisticated applications, even small portions of small-message random accesses can have significant performance effects on the application overall, suggesting that the small-message problem is worth addressing.

1 Introduction

Some critical OpenSHMEM applications, communication patterns, and benchmarks rely on the performance of small-sized point-to-point operations. Examples include distributed table lookups/updates, certain sparse matrix and graph analytics operations, and any application doing collective/reduction operations where the `nelems` argument is relatively small. In the world of benchmarking,

*Other names and brands may be claimed as the property of others.

S. Poole et al. (Eds.): OpenSHMEM 2021, LNCS 13159, pp. 160–177, 2022.
https://doi.org/10.1007/978-3-031-04888-3_10

important examples that highlight small-message performance include the Giga Updates Per Second (GUPS) benchmark [1], histogram/index-gather benchmarks [2], and the plethora of micro-benchmarks used for analyzing, evaluating, and marketing networking platforms in terms of latency, bandwidth, and message rate.

It is well-known that network interface devices generally transfer at a lower throughput when handling small messages. Consider a simple performance model, $Throughput \approx N/(L + N/B)$, where N is the size of the message (in bytes), B is the maximum network bandwidth, and L is the latency. From this model, we see that the small-message bottleneck is due to the fact that N is small and L dominates, so throughput is limited to $\sim 1/L$. For large-messages, N is large and throughput is $\sim B$. An opposite pattern applies to messaging *rates*: small messages exhibit the highest message rate, because large messages are bottlenecked by streaming constraints within the networking platform to enqueue/dequeue segments the length of a maximum transmission unit (MTU).

A general strategy for increasing throughput of small messages is to reduce the number of transactions with the networking interface. A simple example of this strategy is to combine or *chain* multiple small messages into a single coarse message to be transmitted all at once. Several existing OpenSHMEM implementations utilize transport layer libraries that support such mechanisms (see Background Sect. 3), but there is a catch - the performance benefit of deferring messages is only considerable when there is a sufficiently large number of messages to be chained together in a sufficiently short amount of time. There is currently no way for an OpenSHMEM implementation to accurately determine whether or not the application will initiate enough small messages within a short enough amount of time to reap any benefit from chaining messages. For this reason, OpenSHMEM implementations would benefit from users providing *hints* suggesting that a series of RMA/AMO operations are about to start or end, but currently no standard interface for this exists.

The goal of this paper is to summarize the existing transport-level mechanisms for chaining and to present evidence that these mechanisms can improve the throughput of OpenSHMEM implementations. We first describe related work and background in Sects. 2 and 3. We then describe a simple API for user-provided hints regarding chaining in Sect. 4. We then present some benchmarking measurements that motivate this API in terms of performance improvement in Sect. 5. Finally, we describe future work and conclude in Sect. 6.

2 Related Work

This section briefly summarizes existing work related to small-message optimizations. Some of this related work warrants a closer look and is described in more detail in Background Sect. 3. Readers familiar with these concepts can safely proceed to Sect. 4.

2.1 Nagle's Algorithm

Although TCP/IP is not particularly applicable to most modern high-performance computing (HPC) networking stacks, the idea of deferring communication to improve small-message throughput is not at all new to TCP/IP. *Nagle's algorithm* was first published as an Request for Comments (RPC) in 1984 as a way to provide congestion control for TCP implementations. RPC 896 defined the (even then) well-known "small-packet problem" and observed that it had been first addressed in the Tymnet dial-up communication network as early as the late 1960s [3]. Nagle's algorithm defers sending TCP segments until all previously sent segments are acknowledged. Nagle's algorithm is described in more detail in Subsect. 3.1.

2.2 DMAPP Bundled Puts

An existing interface that implicitly chains non-blocking puts is the bundled put function, `dmapp_bput_nbi`, which is provided by the Distributed Memory Application API (DMAPP) [4]. DMAPP's `bput` function targets use-cases in which several non-contiguous transfers are destined for the same target PE. This provides a useful alternative to packing the data into a contiguous buffer for the simpler `dmapp_put_nbi` function, because packing may require additional memory allocation and copying.

The DMAPP API User Guide [5] suggests there are two important restrictions when using `shmem_bput_nbi`: 1) each put within a series of bundled puts must target a constant destination PE and 2) the series of puts must not be broken by another non-`bput` operation. The first constraint likely limits opportunity for bundling random access benchmarks like GUPS, where there is a diverse range of targets in the main communication loop. The second constraint also motivates the API described in Sect. 4: since implementations do not know when a chain ends or a non-compatible operation will break a chain, user-provided hints would help avoid the implementation from having to detect such events on the RMA critical path.

2.3 Bale: Exstack and Conveyor

A highly influential software project that tackles the small-message problem is found in the `bale` package, which includes the modules `exstack`, `exstack2`, and `conveyor`, as well as several relevant Partitioned Global Address Space (PGAS) mini-apps, such as histogram (`histo`), index-gather, topological sort, distributed matrix transpose, and several more [2]. The `exstack`, `exstack2`, and `conveyor` modules include variations of a novel API that enables writing PGAS programs with potentially much better performance than if they were written more simply using direct Atomics, Gets, and Puts (AGP), in other words written as you would find in a textbook or "as God intended". The `bale` modules present a unique `push`, `pull`, and `advance` programming model which goes beyond the simple OpenSHMEM chaining interface proposed in this paper. We provide more details about `bale` and a simple performance evaluation in Subsect. 3.2.

2.4 Libfabric (FI_MORE)

The OpenFabrics Interface (OFI) is a framework that exposes fabric communication services to applications [6]. OpenSHMEM implementations can access services through the `libfabric` library, which implements a rich set of portable, user-level software interfaces for utilizing high-speed communication fabrics. `Libfabric` has been designed to support multithreaded communication models and to address new fabric resource management challenges introduced by modern high performance fabrics. There are several interesting publications describing particular utilizations of libfabric providers for OpenSHMEM implementations [7–10].

`Libfabric` provides users with the `FI_MORE` [8] optimization flag, which is used to indicate that additional communication requests will be immediately posted after the current call returns. This would allow the provider to chain multiple requests (doorbell rings) to the NIC into one. The semantic behind this feature is remarkably similar to the intent of the proposed API described in Sect. 4.1. It could prove extremely useful for OpenSHMEM implementations to easily support chained RMA and AMO operations. The only downside is that there are currently very few `libfabric` providers that support the `FI_MORE` optimization. It appears that libfabric's `GNI` provider is the only one to support `FI_MORE` as of this writing.

2.5 IB Verbs Postlists

The InfiniBand (IB) Architecture Specification [11] defines a set of "Base Queue Management Extensions" (in §11.1.1) that enable a list of Work Requests (WRs) to be submitted to the Send or Receive Queue. In the implementation of the IB verbs API (`libibverbs`), this feature is exposed as a linked list of work requests passed to the `ibv_post_send()` function. This capability is commonly referred to as the IB *postlist*, which allows applications to post a linked list of WRs with only a single call to `ibv_post_send()`. This optimization potentially reduces the number of NIC doorbell rings for a collection of send operations to only one.

It seems that existing OpenSHMEM implementations running over `libibverbs` typically post non-blocking RMA/AMO requests eagerly. For example, each non-blocking put operation involves an individual call to `ibv_post_send()`. In other words, for n back-to-back OpenSHMEM puts, there would be n calls to `ibv_post_send()`. However, it would be compliant with the OpenSHMEM specification to defer these non-blocking puts and append them together into a list of WRs. Although we are not aware of any OpenSHMEM implementations that make such usage of IB postlists, the results in Sect. 5.2 strongly suggest that applications could benefit from the overhead reduction. It would be particularly helpful if applications could easily indicate that a chain of non-blocking RMA/AMO is beginning and/or ending.

Section 5.2 will present performance measurements using standard IB postlists benchmarks over `libibverbs`.

3 Background

This section provides extra background information on select topics from the related work in Sect. 2. In particular, Subsect. 3.1 described Nagle's algorithm and some important caveats and Sect. 3.2 goes into more detail about the `bale` modules with some informative performance measurements. Finally Sect. 3.3 provides a brief summary of OpenSHMEM communication contexts, which is required background for the proposed API design discussion in Sect. 4.

3.1 How Nagle's Algorithm Works and Its Caveats

Nagle's algorithm works by simply deferring the transmission of TCP data segments if any previously transmitted segments are so far unacknowledged. In other words, the algorithm buffers all outgoing TCP segments until all previously sent segments receive an acknowledgement (ACK); then, the collection of outgoing segments are all sent simultaneously. This optimization can show excellent performance improvement, especially for applications which send lots of small messages (a classic example is Telnet).

However, there is an important caveat to Nagle's algorithm: it may exhibit very poor performance when combined with other congestion optimizations, such as delayed/piggybacked ACKs. ACKs can be delayed with a timeout (up to 500 ms for TCP) to reduce the round-trip time overheads associated with the TCP protocol. However, if the sender is *also* deferring messages until that delayed ACK arrives, the sender may incur a delay proportional to the timeout [12].

This algorithm is certainly different than the mechanisms for OpenSHMEM proposed in this paper; after all, it is primarily targeting congestion reduction as opposed to network interface transactions. However, we mention the concept due to its interesting history in encountering and remedying the small-packet problem in networking. Also, it is possibly prudent for OpenSHMEM implementers to be mindful of the negative interaction between deferred communication and delayed ACKs. For instance, the throughput of small-message chaining in OpenSHMEM will likely suffer if the underlying transport runtime simultaneously delays ACKs on the target PE.

3.2 The Bale Programming Model and a Performance Summary

The `bale` package includes three modules (`exstack`, `exstack2`, and `conveyor`) that roughly share the same high-level programming model. While there are subtle (but important) differences between the three implementations, we will keep this discussion concise by referring to these generally as "`bale`" modules, but the `conveyor` model is the newest and has advanced optimizations, such as asynchronous progress and multi-hop routing [2].

The `bale` modules provide a capability the authors refer to as *aggregation* of PGAS operations, which roughly refers to the packing of "coalesced" messages on the initiator side and the unpacking of these aggregated buffers on the target side. To facilitate this aggregation, the `bale` modules maintain an object on each

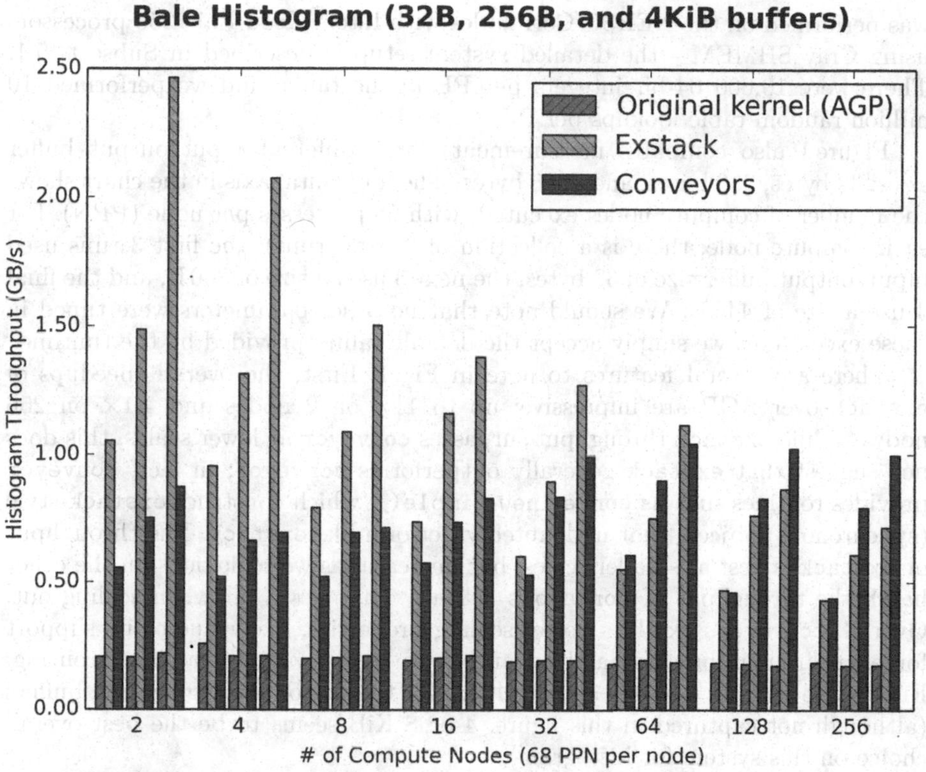

Fig. 1. Bale histogram performance for 3 different packed buffer sizes: 32 bytes, 256 bytes, and 4096 bytes. For each compute node, there is a collection of 9 bars (runs): the first 3 runs used input/output buffer size of 32 bytes, the next 3 used a size of 256 B, and the final 3 use a size of 4 KiB.

PE that includes a collection of input and output buffers for every other PE in the application. When the user issues a `push` operation, a data item is packed into the output buffer for the appropriate target PE. If the buffer ever reaches maximum capacity (the buffer size is user-defined and defaults to ~8 KiB), then the runtime automatically transfers the aggregated buffer. Meanwhile, PEs can `pull` individual items from the input buffers, and can call `advance` (or `proceed`) to flush the output buffers to the appropriate target PE's input buffers. This is done in bulk-synchronous parallel fashion in `exstack`, but asynchronously in `conveyors`.

Figure 1 shows a performance experiment comparing the `exstack`, `conveyor`, and the original (atomics, gets, puts: AGP) variations of the histogram (`histo`) micro-benchmark. The `histo` benchmark is extremely simple, consisting of a single loop of n random lookups in a distributed table using an atomic add operation. This is essentially a weak scaling experiment where the size of the table and number of lookups is proportional to the number of PEs. The experiment was performed on the NERSC Cori nodes with Intel®Xeon Phi 7250 processors using Cray SHMEM - the detailed system setup is described in Subsect. 5.1. There were 10,000 64-bit integers per PE in the table, and we performed 10 million random table lookups per PE.

Figure 1 also compares measurements for 3 different input/output buffer sizes: 32 bytes, 256 bytes, and 4096 bytes. The horizontal axis in the chart shows the number of compute nodes executed, with 68 processes per node (PPN). For each compute node, there is a collection of 9 bars (runs): the first 3 runs used input/output buffer size of 32 bytes, the next 3 used a size of 256 B, and the final 3 use a size of 4 KiB. We should note that no other parameters were tuned in these executions, we simply accept the default values provided by the runtime.

There are several features to note in Fig. 1. First, the overall speedups of `exstack` over AGP are impressive: up to 11× on 2 nodes and 4.1× on 256 nodes. While `exstack` throughput surpasses `conveyor` at lower scales, this does not suggest that `exstack` generally outperforms `conveyor`; in fact, `conveyor` provides routines such as `convey_new_simple()`, which construct `exstack`-style (synchronous) objects that undoubtedly perform like `exstack`. The throughput of `exstack` is best at smaller scales, but decreases as we scale out. On the other hand, the throughput of `conveyors` actually improves a bit when scaling out. Overall, `conveyors` exhibits better scaling properties, likely due to its support for asynchronous progress and advanced topology-aware/hierarchical routing. Finally, we see that 4 KiB is a good choice for the size of the aggregation buffers (although not captured in this figure, 4 or 8 KiB seems to be the best overall choice on this system for histogram).

Inherent to the `bale` programming model is the participation of all remote PEs throughout the execution phase. In other words, the execution phase is effectively collective - target PEs need to pull data from their input buffers until the `bale` object no longer needs to advance. (For this reason, users should be cautious when calling OpenSHMEM routines during this phase.) This collective pattern is important for performance, however, as it enables the impressive speedups shown in Fig. 1. For the `histo` benchmark in particular, this programming model constraint allows the application and middleware to completely avoid calling the atomic routines, which make up the core of the original AGP version of `histo`. Instead, the participating target PEs can simply increment their local values because they have complete control over when the `pull` operations occur with no chance for contention from remote PEs.

A separate but related question is whether comparable performance gains can be made without the collective participation of all PEs in the aggregation phase. We attempt to address this question in Sect. 5 below.

3.3 OpenSHMEM Contexts

Section 4 will argue that RMA/AMO chaining hints are best associated with OpenSHMEM communication contexts, so this section provides a brief overview of these contexts and a collection of citations for the interested reader. However, the most direct source of information regarding the OpenSHMEM context API is the latest version (1.5) of the specification itself [13] in §9.5.

In essence, OpenSHMEM communication contexts are objects affiliated with RMA, AMO, and memory ordering operations that provide independent ordering and completion properties. In multi-threaded OpenSHMEM applications, users can potentially improve performance by using *private* contexts across threads that call OpenSHMEM RMA/AMO routines simultaneously, thereby reducing the underlying overhead in the runtime related to threads sharing resources. In single-threaded OpenSHMEM applications, multiple *shared* contexts can be used to pipeline/overlap communication and computation.

There is a rich collection of research literature describing OpenSHMEM context implementations and other details [14–16]. For this paper, it suffices to say that the chaining operations mentioned in related work (`FI_MORE`, IB postlists, the `bale` modules, and DMAPP bundled puts) are most directly affiliated with RMA/AMO operations, suggesting that OpenSHMEM contexts are an obvious candidate for affiliated user-provided chaining hints. As we will see in Sect. 4, a very simple interface to enable user-provided chaining hints is done on the OpenSHMEM context.

4 Design and Discussion

This section presents a tentative and simple API that would provide users a way to inform the OpenSHMEM runtime about the imminent occurrence of chainable operations. It also briefly describes some speculative follow-on APIs that would support collective operations and/or aggregation. Please note that the discussion below uses the generic term, "chain", in the proposed function names, but there are certainly other viable candidates for a final standardized API including session, bundle, batch, group, chain and more.

4.1 Proposed API

There are several viable interface designs that would enable chained operations in OpenSHMEM programs. For example, it is possible to add a new set of RMA/AMO routines, named something like `shmem_(op)_chain_nbi`. However, this approach would require OpenSHMEM implementations to support chaining across a large number of routines, and the semantics could be difficult to define portably across all these routines. This could also expose non-portable performance behaviors across implementations; for instance, if an implementation is unable to support performant chaining on a particular network. After discussion among the OpenSHMEM specification working groups, we opted for a simpler *hint-based* API that would not change any semantics of a program if the chaining optimization were either unsupported or removed.

A very simple chaining API would consist of only two routines, a routine to indicate the *start* of a chain and a routine to indicate the *end* of a chain. In between the chain start and stop routines, the user could make any OpenSHMEM calls, but only certain calls are viable candidates for chaining. Here is a rough example of a chained code block:

```
shmem_ctx_t ctx;
shmem_chain_start(ctx);
/* Any non-blocking RMA routines, non-blocking AMO routine, and/or
   non-fetching blocking AMO routines could be chained here. */
shmem_chain_stop(ctx);
/* Users need to include any necessary memory ordering routines (fence
   or quiet) regardless of whether chaining hints are included or not. */
```

Our central proposal for this hint-based chaining API is that the communication semantics of the enclosed code region are unchanged regardless of whether the chain start/stop calls are included. We can use this guiding principle to deduce whether an OpenSHMEM routine is a candidate for chaining (but specific chaining support and methods are ultimately implementation-defined). For example, with this hint-based chaining API, all non-blocking RMA and non-blocking AMOs are candidates for chaining, because local and remote completion are not guaranteed immediately after returning from these routines. Therefore, the OpenSHMEM runtime has the opportunity to chain non-blocking operations without affecting the completion semantics when adding or removing the start/stop routines. Additionally, blocking *non-fetching* atomics (such as `shmem_atomic_inc` and `shmem_atomic_and`) as well as scalar puts (`shmem_p`) could be chained. These non-fetching operations have no buffer to update or reuse on the initiator PE immediately after returning, so an OpenSHMEM implementations may freely chain these operations without affecting the completion semantics of the enclosed code region.

On the other hand, blocking RMA (except `shmem_p`), blocking fetching AMOs, and scalar gets would *not* be chained, because these routines have completion semantics indicating that the initiator's local object (i.e., the source buffer for puts and the destination buffer for gets) can be used immediately after returning. For now, we do not consider point-to-point synchronization routines (like `shmem_wait` and `shmem_test`) for chaining, because they do not occur on a OpenSHMEM context, and far richer capabilities are provided by the *vector* point-to-point synchronization API in OpenSHMEM version 1.5.

Stopping a chain should not affect memory ordering or completion semantics, it only provides a hint to the runtime that a collection of chainable operations has finished. Chaining requirements for memory ordering and synchronization is relatively simple with this hint-based API: the inclusion of `shmem_chain_start()` and `shmem_chain_stop()` should not affect the application's requirements for invoking fence, quiet, sync, and barrier operations. In other words, if the application requires a fence and/or a quiet operation for correctness, then it should be included with or without the chaining start/stop routines. With this straightforward API design, we hope users and implementers can easily deduce which OpenSHMEM operations are suitable candidates for chaining optimizations, while maintaining correctness and portability across different implementations and platforms.

4.2 API Extensions (Items up for Discussion)

To generate interesting discussion, we briefly describe two other hypothetical API extensions that may or may not eventually be worthy of OpenSHMEM standardization: collective routines and aggregation APIs.

Collectives. In general, it is more challenging to reap benefits from chaining multiple collective operations than it is for RMAs and AMOs. One reason for this is that the underlying transport mechanisms and interfaces are more geared towards chaining RDMA network "primitive" operations, like send/receive, put/get, and network atomics operations. So OpenSHMEM implementations can easily chain RMAs and/or AMOs within a *single* collective, but it is far more challenging to determine whether *multiple* application-layer collectives operations are chainable. However, this is not to say that it is theoretically impossible to chain collectives. One can imagine a future network in which collectives operations can be encapsulated as a single work request. In this hypothetical scenario, a challenge for OpenSHMEM is in designing a valid chaining interface that is compatible with OpenSHMEM teams. However, contexts do belong to a team in OpenSHMEM v1.5, so perhaps one can safely and productively group collective operations in the future. Furthermore, the hint-based semantic proposed above may require *non-blocking* collectives in OpenSHMEM, which are currently a work-in-progress for standardization.

Aggregation. The simple API design in this section considered chaining only, not the *aggregation* capability that was discussed in the related work and background sections summarizing the `bale` modules (Sects. 2.3 and 3.2). It is certainly possible to standardize an interface that accomplishes aggregation in OpenSHMEM (think `shmem_push`, `shmem_pull`, and `shmem_advance`) with semantics similar to the `bale` interfaces. However, there are matters to consider: The `bale` modules show us that the push/pull/advance programming model leads to a very complex runtime with a rich set of tunable parameters and execution options (buffer sizes, multi-hop routing, asynchronous/synchronous, etc.). There may not be much advantage to requiring all OpenSHMEM implementation vendors to implement these intricate features when there is an impressive implementation already like `convey`. On the other hand, as networks evolve towards having more programmable computational power, like they currently do with Infrastructure Processing Units (IPUs) and SmartNICs, there may be vendor-specific concerns at play when it comes to doing efficient aggregation. There is no doubt that the performance benefits of the push, pull, advance model are substantial, so there may come a day when it makes sense to standardize this type of interface.

5 Performance Evaluation

We now examine performance measurements that quantify the expected benefit of a chaining interface for OpenSHMEM. Section 5.1 describes the experimental setup and system configurations. Section 5.2 shows the expected increase in message rate between processes when they vary the size of the underlying InfiniBand (IB) Verbs postlist. Section 5.3 uses the OSU non-blocking put message rate micro-benchmark to show the benefit of automatic/implicit chaining with Cray SHMEM over DMAPP. Finally, Sect. 5.4 examines the benefit of Cray SHMEM's implicit chaining for the GUPS benchmark.

5.1 Experimental Setup

In Sect. 5.2, the IB postlist experiment was conducted on two separate systems: one with an Intel® Columbiaville E810-C NIC, and the other with a Mellanox* ConnectX-6 MT28908A0 NIC.

The system with an Intel® Columbiaville (CVL) NIC is an internal cluster named Diamond, where each compute node contains a 2-socket Intel® Xeon® Platinum 8170 CPU with 35.75 MB L3 cache at 2.10 GHz (Skylake). Intel® Hyper-Threading Technology and Intel® Turbo Boost Technology are enabled. The operating system (OS) was Red Hat Enterprise Linux 8.1 (Ootpa) with kernel 4.18.0-147.el8.x86_64. The system memory was 12xDDR4, 196608 MB, 2666 MT/s. Diamond was configured with irdma version 1.3.19, ice version 1.4.11, CVL firmware-version 2.15 0x800049c3 1.2789.0, and Intel microcode 0x2000065. We used the Open Fabrics Enterprise Distribution (OFED) Performance Tests `peftools` version 5.5, with the `ib_write_bw` benchmark. The network consisted of an Intel® Colubmiaville E810-C NIC, an Arista DCS-7170-32CD-F switch, 4.22.1FX-CLI, and Mellanox MCP1600-E002 cables.

The system with a Mellanox ConnectX-6 NIC is an internal cluster name Endeavour, where each compute node contains a 2-socket Intel® Xeon® Platinum 8358 CPU with 48 MB cache at 2.60 GHz (Ice Lake). Intel® Hyper-Threading and Intel® Turbo Boost Technology are enabled. The OS is CentOS Linux release 8.3.2011 with kernel 4.18.0-240.22.1.el8_3.crt2.x86_64. The system memory is 256 GB 16*16 GB 3200 MT/s DDR4. We also use the OFED Performance Tests `peftools` version 5.93, with the `ib_write_bw` benchmark. The network consists of a Mellanox ConnectX-6 MT28908A0 interconnect with a Mellanox MQM8790-HS2F HDR InfiniBand switch and MCX654105A-HCAT host bus adapter.

In Sects. 5.3 and 5.4 the experiments are run on NERSC's Cori supercomputer, which is a Cray* XC40 system [17]. Cori contains 2,388 Intel®Xeon E5-2698 v3 (Haswell) processor nodes at 2.3 GHz and 9,688 Intel®Xeon Phi 7250 (Knights Landing) processor nodes with 68 cores per node at 1.4 GHz. The Haswell (HSW) nodes each have 128 GB of DDR4 2133 MHz RAM. Each CPU has 2-way Intel® Hyper-Threading Technology with 32 cores, providing 32 physical cores and 64 hardware thread contexts per compute node. Each Knights Landing (KNL) node has a single socket with 68 cores at 1.4 GHz. The KNL nodes each have 96 GB of DDR4 2400 MHz RAM with 16 GB of MCDRAM. All the Cori compute nodes run a light-weight Cray* Linux Environment based on the SuSE* Linux Enterprise Server distribution. Cori deploys the Aries interconnect with a dragonfly topology [18].

In Sects. 5.3 and 5.4 we use Cray SHMEM [19] version 7.7.16, which is the best-in-class OpenSHMEM implementation for the Cori platform. It is also convenient to do chaining comparison experiments with Cray SHMEM, because it uses DMAPP for transport where we can use the `DMAPP_PUT_NBI_CHAIN_OFF` environment variable to turn automatic chaining on and off. The benchmarks used are the OSU micro-benchmarks version 5.7 and the Giga Updates Per Second (GUPS) application [1] that is included in Sandia OpenSHMEM version 1.5.0 [20].

5.2 Perftools Measurement of IB Verbs Message Rates

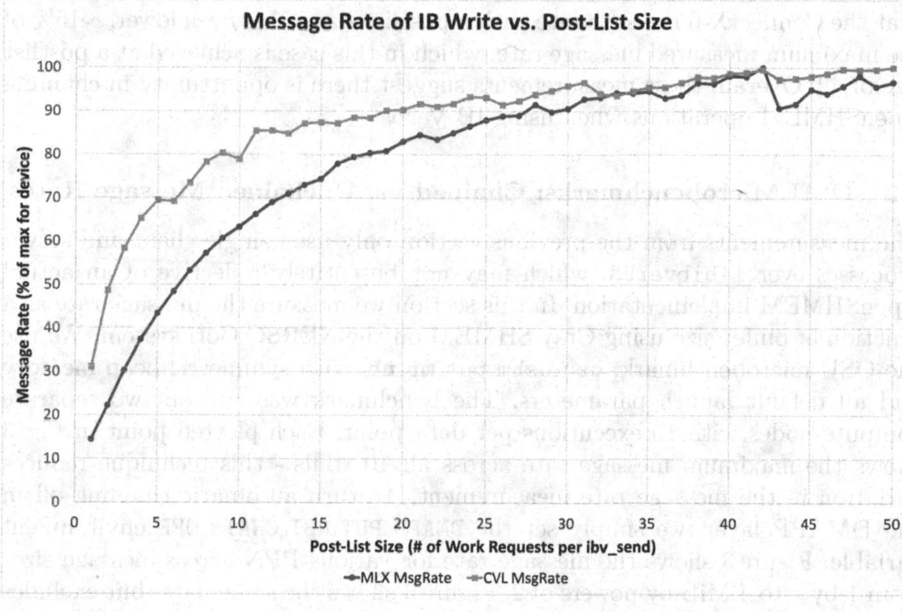

Fig. 2. Single PE message rate (relative to the maximum rate) on Intel® Columbiaville (CVL) and Mellanox* ConnectX-6 HDR (MLX). Each datapoint shows the percent of the maximum message rate with respect to the NIC itself. The graph does not directly compare message rates, instead it shows how the rate is affected by the IB postlist size.

Figure 2 shows the message rate of the `ib_write_bw` benchmark as a function of the size of the IB Verbs postlist (described in Sect. 2.5). Each point in the graph is a single run of the benchmark with the postlist size explicitly set. All benchmark executions transferred work requests with a size of 8 bytes, because this is the size which most often exhibits the highest message rate. We also increased the number of iterations to 1 million to ensure a steady state and reduce measurement variation. For both graphs, we set the number of queue pairs (QPs) to 4, which helps to saturate the NIC to achieve higher message rates, and all QPs are reliably connected (RC). We avoid publishing the raw message rate in Fig. 2 and instead focus on the improvement relative to the maximum message rate measured on each system. This is simply because the data we are trying to highlight is the potential performance benefit of chaining, not any differences in message rate between the two platform (which have very different CPUs in addition to fabrics).

Figure 2 shows that Columbiaville's message rate with a postlist size of 1 is only 31% of the maximum measured message rate, which is achieved at a postlist size of 50. As far as we are a aware, OpenSHMEM implementations over `libibverbs` typically perform a single non-blocking RMA or AMO operation with a postlist size of 1, suggesting that there may be considerable room for improvement by increasing the postlist size, at least when there are many small messages initiated within a sufficiently short amount of time. Figure 2 also shows that the ConnectX-6 message rate with a postlist size of 1 is even lower, ~15% of the maximum measured message rate, which in this case is achieved at a postlist size of 42. Overall, these measurements suggest there is opportunity in chaining OpenSHMEM operations when using IB Verbs.

5.3 OSU Microbenchmarks: Chained vs. Unchained Message Rates

The measurements from the previous section only used single client and server processes over `libibverbs`, which may not be entirely reflective of an actual OpenSHMEM implementation. In this section we measure the message rate as a function of buffer size using Cray SHMEM on the NERSC Cori system. We use the OSU microbenchmark, `osu_oshm_put_mr_nb`, with symmetric heap memory and all default launch parameters. The benchmark was run on two separate compute nodes with 10 executions per data point. Each plotted point in Fig. 3 shows the maximum message rate across all 10 trials - this technique reduces variation in the message rate measurement. To turn automatic chaining off in the DMAPP layer, we simply set the `DMAPP_PUT_NBI_CHAIN_OFF` environment variable. Figure 3 shows the message rate for various PPN across message sizes from 1 byte to 4 MiB by powers of 2. Figure 3 shows the same data, but excludes measurements below 1 million messages/second to focus on the region of interest.

Curves sharing the same color in Fig. 3 were executed with the same PPN. The only difference between two curves sharing the same color is whether chaining was enabled or disabled. Curves with the empty diamonds correspond to executions where chaining was enabled (the default case), and curves with the filled squares correspond to executions where chaining was disabled (by setting the environment variable).

The major takeaway from these graphs is that the chaining optimization for message rate is already done in practice in Cray SHMEM, and with impressive effect. For transfer sizes less than 128 bytes, message rate improvement is consistently in the 1.5–2× range. For 4 and 8 bytes messages, the improvement is upwards of 2.6×. More investigation and/or instrumentation of the source code is needed to explain the 4–8 byte bump. We also see that the message rate scales up well to 16 PPN on these nodes. However, Table 1 shows that 22 PPN and higher begins to suffer poor message rate scaling, likely due to over-subscription effects. Despite this, the highest message rate is seen with 20 PPN, as highlighted in Table 1.

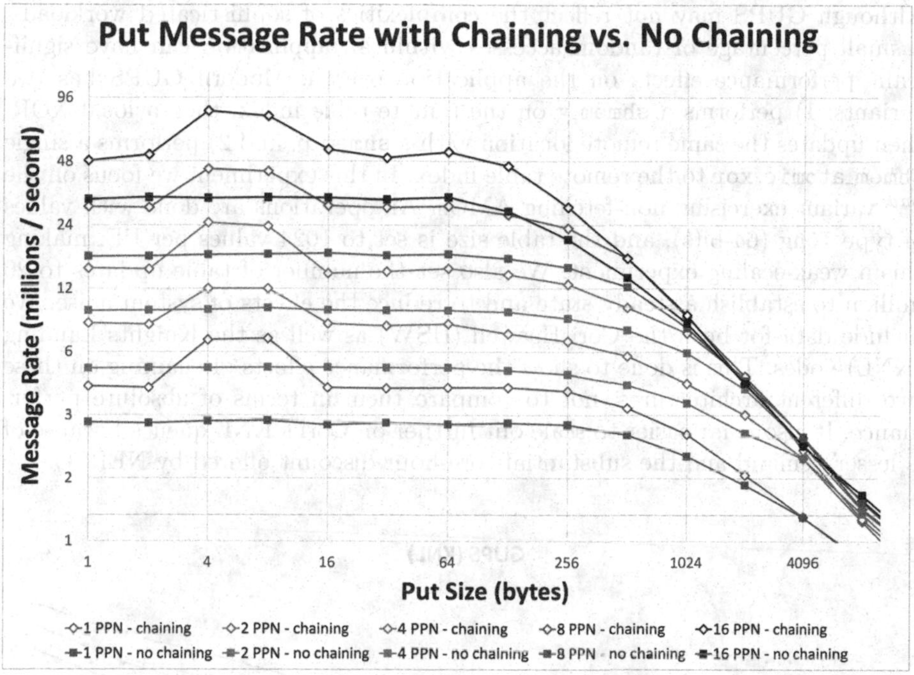

Fig. 3. Message rate of Cray SHMEM with and without chaining for various processes per node (PPN) excluding data with a message rate lower than 1 million per second on two Cori HSW nodes.

Table 1. Message rates (in millions/second) not shown in Fig. 3. The underlined values emphasize performance degradation that is likely due to over-subscription effects, and the ⋆ measurement shows the maximum rate measured.

Size	Chaining	16 PPN	18 PPN	20 PPN	22 PPN	24 PPN
1 byte	Enabled	48.3	53.4	62.4	<u>28.7</u>	<u>11.4</u>
1 byte	Disabled	31.7	35.4	36.3	37.0	37.4
8 bytes	Enabled	78.5	88.8	91.0⋆	<u>78.0</u>	<u>36.2</u>
8 bytes	Disabled	32.3	35.9	36.7	37.3	37.6
32 bytes	Enabled	54.5	60.3	65.8	<u>63.8</u>	<u>47.3</u>
32 bytes	Disabled	31.6	35.3	35.8	35.8	36.0
64 bytes	Enabled	53.1	56.7	64.8	69.4	<u>69.3</u>
64 bytes	Disabled	32.5	34.7	35.4	35.8	36.2

5.4 GUPS with and Without Chaining

We now quantify the performance effects of chaining non-fetching AMOs using the GUPS benchmark [1]. In short, GUPS quantifies the number of random memory locations that can be updated across a distributed table per second. Although GUPS may not reflect the complexities of sophisticated workloads, a small percentage of random accesses within an application can have significant performance effects on the application overall. Modern GUPS has two variants: 1) performs a `shmem_g` on the remote table index, then a local XOR, then updates the same remote location with a `shmem_p`, and 2) performs a single `shmem_atomic_xor` to the remote table index. In this experiment we focus on the 2nd variant exercising non-fetching AMOs. All operations are done with values of type `long` (64-bits), and the table size is set to 1024 values per PE, making this a weak-scaling experiment. We also set the number of table updates to 20 million to establish a steady state and to reduce the effects of system noise. We include data for both the Cori Haswell (HSW) as well as the Knights Landing (KNL) nodes. This is done to show the performance effects of chaining on these two different architectures, not to compare them in terms of absolute performance. It also is far easier to scale out further on Cori's KNL queues because of is lesser demand and the substantial core-hour discount offered by NERSC.

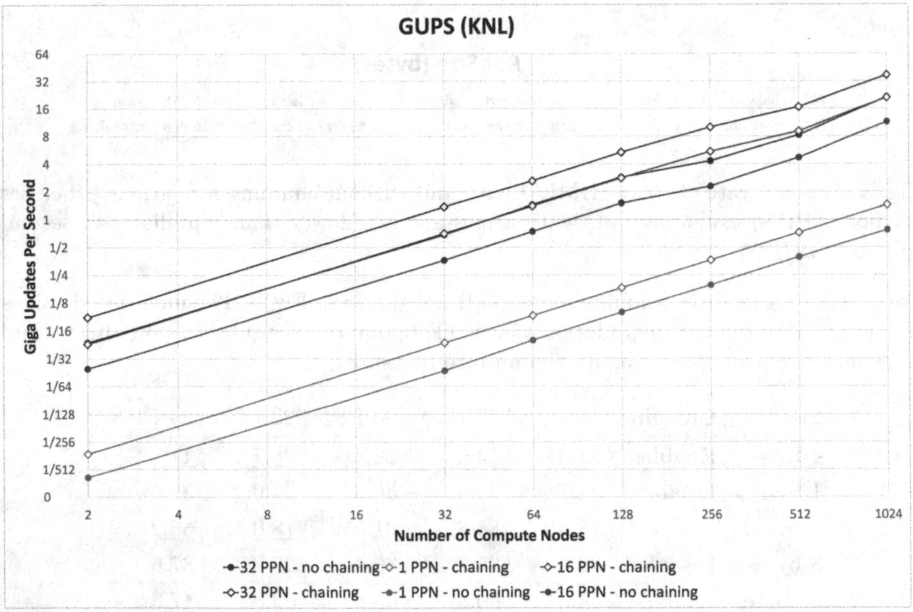

Fig. 4. GUPS chaining vs. no-chaining on KNL.

Figures 4 and 5 show the GUPS measurement across several different numbers of compute nodes. We ran the benchmark 10 times for each datapoint, and recorded the maximum measured GUPS value in the figure. The speedups comparing chaining with no chaining are considerable, varying between 1.7× and 2.7× depending on the architecture, number of compute nodes, and values of PPN. In general, speedups appear to decrease as we increase the number of total PEs. However, even at the largest scales (32,768 PEs on KNL and 4,096 PEs on HSW), speedups are still considerable enough to motivate this optimization (1.7× and 2.0×, respectively).

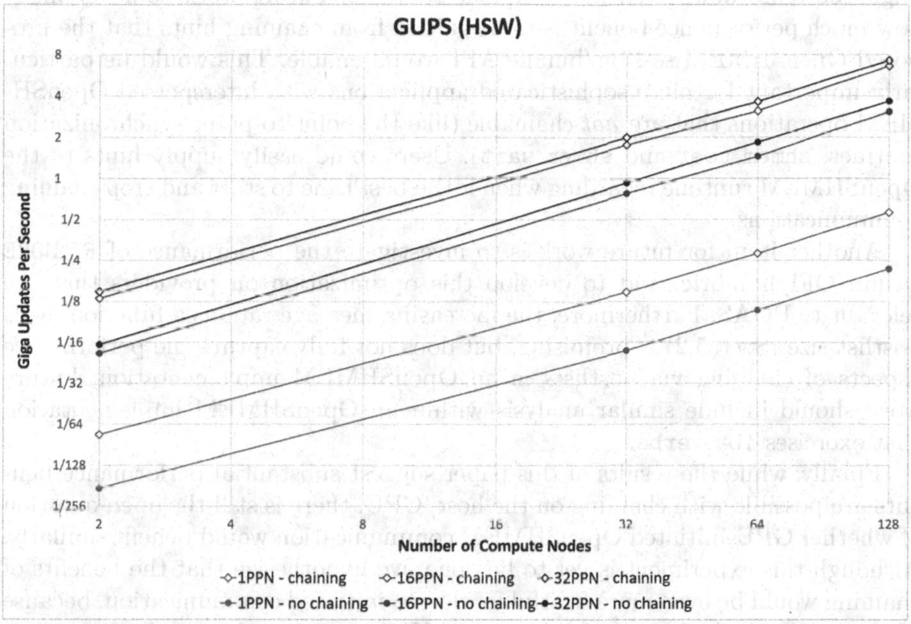

Fig. 5. GUPS chaining vs. no-chaining on HSW.

It is important to note that the observed increase in message rate was accomplished by an OpenSHMEM implementation that *detects* whether a chain is in progress. In other words, Cray SHMEM was given no hints in either the OSU benchmark or in GUPS that a chain is in progress. We can only expect better performance if the runtime was informed that a chain is taking place. For instance, the OpenSHMEM runtime may not have to do any chain continuity checks on the performance-critical path if the user can supply a hint that a chain is in progress. Also, the runtime would not have to detect that a chain is complete if the user can supply a hint to stop the chain.

6 Future Work and Conclusion

The experiments throughout Sect. 5 prove that an OpenSHMEM implementation can substantially increase message rate for benchmarks in which many small messages are sent back-to-back. While the benchmarks in Sect. 5 do not entirely reflect more complex "real-world" PGAS applications, they certainly highlight common latency-bound communication patterns that can dramatically hinder the performance of critical application components.

Because the experiments in Sect. 5 leverage an *implicit* chaining feature in Cray SHMEM, they do not fully capture the potential benefit of more explicit chaining based on user-provided hints. For instance, it is likely that implicit chaining requires a branching instruction on the RMA/AMO critical path, which might be removable given more explicit chaining. Future work could quantify how much performance benefit is to be gained from chaining hints that the proposed OpenSHMEM session/bundle API would enable. This would be particularly important for more sophisticated applications with interspersed OpenSHMEM operations that are *not* chainable (like the point-to-point synchronization routines, `shmem_test` and `shmem_wait`). Users could easily supply hints to the OpenSHMEM runtime regarding when is the best time to start and stop chaining communications.

Another item for future work is to investigate the performance of `FI_MORE` within OFI/libfabric, and to develop this optimization on providers that are relevant to PGAS. Furthermore, the increasing message rate as a function of IB postlist size (Sect. 5.2) is promising, but does not fully capture the performance aspects of chaining via postlists in an OpenSHMEM implementation. Future work should include similar analysis within an OpenSHMEM implementation that exercises `ibv_verbs`.

Finally, while the results of this paper suggest substantial performance benefits are possible with chaining on the host/CPU, there is still the open question of whether GPU-initiated OpenSHMEM communication would benefit similarly. Although this experiment is yet to be done, we hypothesize that the benefits of chaining would be even more fruitful for device-initiated communication, because of the relatively high cost of initiating a NIC operation from a PCI-attached device (i.e., ringing the NIC doorbell for every single RMA/AMO operation). We leave this investigation as future work.

References

1. RandomAccess GUPS (Giga Updates Per Second). http://icl.cs.utk.edu/projectsfiles/hpcc/RandomAccess/
2. Maley, F.M., DeVinney, J.G.: Conveyors for streaming many-to-many communication. In: 2019 IEEE/ACM 9th Workshop on Irregular Applications: Architectures and Algorithms (IA3), pp. 1–8 (2019)
3. Nagle, J.: RFC0896: congestion control in IP/TCP internetworks (1984)
4. ten Bruggencate, M., Roweth, D.: DMAPP - an API for one-sided program models on baker systems. In: Cray User Group Conference (2010)
5. Cray. XC Series GNI and DMAPP API User Guide. https://support.hpe.com/hpesc/public/docDisplay?docId=a00114945en_us&page=dmapp_bput_nbi.html
6. Grun, P., et al.: A brief introduction to the OpenFabrics interfaces - a new network API for maximizing high performance application efficiency. In: 2015 IEEE 23rd Annual Symposium on High-Performance Interconnects, pp. 34–39. IEEE (2015)

7. Pritchard, H., Harvey, E., Choi, S.-E., Swaro, J., Tiffany, Z.: The GNI provider layer for OFI libfabric. In: Proceedings of Cray User Group Meeting, CUG, vol. 2016 (2016)
8. Choi, S.-E., Pritchard, H., Shimek, J., Swaro, J., Tiffany, Z., Turrubiates, B.: An implementation of OFI libfabric in support of multithreaded PGAS solutions. In: 2015 9th International Conference on Partitioned Global Address Space Programming Models, pp. 59–69. IEEE (2015)
9. Ozog, D., Rahman, M.W., Seager, K., Dinan, J.: Design and optimization of OpenSHMEM 1.4 for the Intel® omni-path fabric 100 series. In: Pophale, S., Imam, N., Aderholdt, F., Gorentla Venkata, M. (eds.) OpenSHMEM 2018. LNCS, vol. 11283, pp. 22–40. Springer, Cham (2019). https://doi.org/10.1007/978-3-030-04918-8_2
10. Venkata, G., Imam, N., Yu, W., Bhattacharya, S., Kundnani, H., Salman, S., et al.: An initial implementation of libfabric conduit for OpenSHMEM-X. Technical report, Oak Ridge National Lab. (ORNL), Oak Ridge, TN (United States) (2018)
11. InfiniBand Trade Association. InfiniBand Architecture Specification, Volume 1, Release 1.5 (2021)
12. Cheshire, S.: TCP Performance problems caused by interaction between Nagle's Algorithm and Delayed ACK (2005). http://stuartcheshire.org/papers/NagleDelayedAck/
13. OpenSHMEM Application Programming Interface, Version 1.5 (2020). http://www.openshmem.org
14. Bouteiller, A., Pophale, S., Boehm, S., Baker, M.B., Venkata, M.G.: Evaluating contexts in OpenSHMEM-X reference implementation. In: Gorentla Venkata, M., Imam, N., Pophale, S. (eds.) OpenSHMEM 2017. LNCS, vol. 10679, pp. 50–62. Springer, Cham (2018). https://doi.org/10.1007/978-3-319-73814-7_4
15. Namashivayam, N., Knaak, D., Cernohous, B., Radcliffe, N., Pagel, M.: An evaluation of thread-safe and contexts-domains features in cray SHMEM. In: Gorentla Venkata, M., Imam, N., Pophale, S., Mintz, T.M. (eds.) OpenSHMEM 2016. LNCS, vol. 10007, pp. 163–180. Springer, Cham (2016). https://doi.org/10.1007/978-3-319-50995-2_11
16. Grossman, M., Doyle, J., Dinan, J., Pritchard, H., Seager, K., Sarkar, V.: Implementation and evaluation of OpenSHMEM contexts using OFI libfabric. In: Gorentla Venkata, M., Imam, N., Pophale, S. (eds.) OpenSHMEM 2017. LNCS, vol. 10679, pp. 19–34. Springer, Cham (2018). https://doi.org/10.1007/978-3-319-73814-7_2
17. Antypas, K., Wright, N., Cardo, N.P., Andrews, A., Cordery, M.: Cori: a cray XC pre-exascale system for NERSC. In: Cray User Group Proceedings. Cray (2014)
18. Alverson, B., Froese, E., Kaplan, L., Roweth, D.: Cray XC Series Network. Cray Inc., White Paper WP-Aries01-1112 (2012)
19. Cray Research Inc.: SHMEM Technical Note for C, SG-2516 2.3 (1994)
20. Sandia OpenSHMEM. https://github.com/Sandia-OpenSHMEM/SOS

Remote Programmability Model for SmartNICs in HPC Workloads

Morad Horany(✉) and Alex Margolin

Toga Networks, a Huawei Company, Hod Hasharon, Israel
{morad.horany,alex.margolin}@huawei.com

Abstract. HPC workloads experience significant overhead due to handling network-related tasks on the CPU. Some tasks could be offloaded to a SmartNIC, thus reducing the run-time of the workload, but this typically requires explicit support in the application. Moreover, several SmartNIC models available today expose different APIs for offloading tasks. In this paper we present a model for SmartNIC programmability, including a proposed system design for allocating and utilizing network-wide SmartNIC resources. Unlike existing APIs for programming accelerators, our proposal focuses on access to resources over the network: large-scale deployments imply a network-based mechanism for allocating, and offloading to, SmartNIC devices. While a SmartNIC is often characterized by its embedded processor, the proposed system is also applicable to NICs based on ASIC or FPGA, aided by the host CPU.

1 Introduction

The growing throughput of modern interconnect technologies increases the rate of traffic reaching the server: both internal, between processes or virtual machines, and external - targeting other servers or appliances, e.g. storage. Both create memory-intensive tasks on the CPU and typically impact application performance. Tasks that can be performed on incoming or outgoing messages and only require limited local state are good candidates for offloading to a SmartNIC. Part of the challenge in offloading operations from the host CPU is the various APIs provided by accelerator vendors. Accelerators are common in data-centers, targeting workloads such as image processing and machine learning, but a standardized programming API standard does not exist. As a result many applications are written for a specific hardware platform, impairing or preventing the same run on a different platform. OpenSNAPI is a collaborative effort to form a standard API for utilizing the capabilities of SmartNICs across the network. Such API would allow programming SmartNICs from different vendors, with the goal of performing processing operations on compute engines on the network, possibly in parallel with a workload on the host CPUs. In this paper, we will present our proposal for the OpenSNAPI standard.

The rest of this paper is organized as follows: Sect. 2 outlines the proposed design for SmartNIC programming, Sect. 3 discusses scalability aspects, Sect. 4 covers related work and Sect. 5 summarizes the remote SmartNIC programmability model.

S. Poole et al. (Eds.): OpenSHMEM 2021, LNCS 13159, pp. 178–186, 2022.
https://doi.org/10.1007/978-3-031-04888-3_11

2 Proposed System Design

The problem statement outlined in the previous section requires a flexible design, accommodating the various use-cases. In this section we propose a design for this system, followed by an example. In order to describe the interactions within this system, we define the following roles:

Initiator	A process which requires the service of a SmartNIC.
SmartNIC	The SmartNIC to be used by the initiator.
SmartNIC Host	The host where the SmartNIC is physically installed.
Manager	A central entity in the network that manages SmartNIC resources.

The interaction between these roles is divided into four stages, as illustrated with a typical flow in Fig. 1. We note that while the initiator is expected to run on a host CPU in most cases, it could potentially run on a SmartNIC in the manner described below, creating a chain of SmartNICs collaborating on a task.

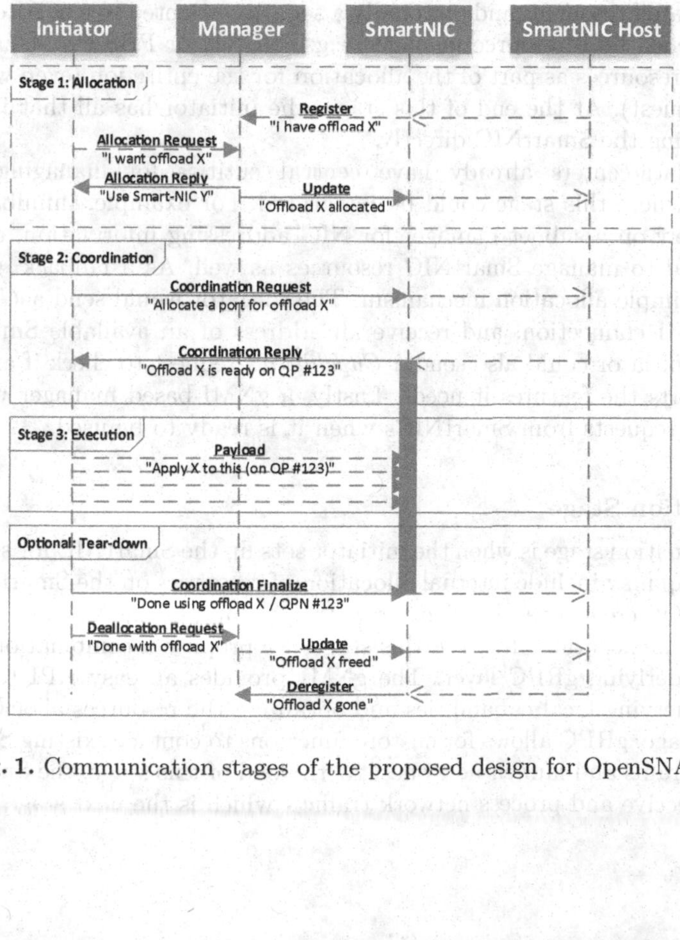

Fig. 1. Communication stages of the proposed design for OpenSNAPI

2.1 Rationale

In contrast to traditional accelerator APIs invoked on the host, we propose SmartNIC programming over the network. Section 3 elaborates on the motivation for this difference, making this API resemble RPC designs. The technology to facilitate this RPC must be flexible, performant and suitable to run on embedded systems. In light of these factors, we chose gRPC and gNMI as the framework to be extended by SmartNIC vendors.

Allocation Stage

During this preliminary stage, SmartNICs make their presence and capabilities known to a central entity. These include hardware offloads present (e.g. compression or MPI tag-matching), consumed resources (e.g. memory or storage space) and API information (i.e. supported RPC calls for the upcoming coordination stage). This central entity, the *Manager* from Fig. 1, is responsible for tracking network-wide resources and allocating them upon request.

Before a process can use SmartNIC resources, be it on the same host or elsewhere, it sends an *allocation request* to the manager with its identification and a list of requirements. In return, the manager sends an *allocation reply* with a list of allocated resources and optionally a security-oriented token. Alternatively, a job launched by a resource manager, e.g. SLURM or PBS Pro, could receive SmartNIC resources as part of the allocation for the entire job (even without an explicit request). At the end of this stage, the initiator has all that is required for contacting the SmartNIC directly.

Most data-centers already have central entities for managing network resources, where this stage could be integrated. For example, Infiniband interconnects rely on a subnet manager for NIC addressing information, and it can be extended to manage SmartNIC resources as well. As a fallback, gNMI can provide a simple allocation mechanism. The initiator would send a *Get* request over a gNMI connection, and receive an address of an available SmartNIC in reply. An initiator could also send a *Capabilities* request to check if any SmartNIC supports the features it needs. Lastly, a gNMI-based manager would also accept *Set* requests from SmartNICs when it is ready to be used.

Coordination Stage

The coordination stage is when the initiator sets up the SmartNIC for subsequent usage. Setup may include internal allocation of resources on the SmartNIC, such as RDMA QP creation and memory registration, and in the general case launching a custom executable file. For this stage, we propose a combination of gNMI and its underlying gRPC layer. The gNMI provides an easy API to interface with for querying local capabilities and obtaining the resources allocated in the previous stage. gRPC allows for custom functions to contact existing SmartNIC-based programs and launch new ones. At the end of this stage, the SmartNIC is ready to receive and process network traffic - which is the next stage.

This stage is when the SmartNIC programmability is exercised. SmartNICs are expected to expose some built-in features, such as packet filtering or stream operations (e.g. compression). These features could be loaded using gNMI *Get* requests, and remain active as long as the connection to the initiator remains open. For custom features, some SmartNICs allow running executables on the embedded processor - this could be achieved by a gNMI *Set* request containing the binary executable. On simpler NICs, which cannot run executables, the host CPU can facilitate the coordination stage and control the NIC.

Execution Stage

This stage is when the initiator makes use of the SmartNICs it had set up in the previous stage. During this stage either a built-in feature or a custom program is consuming SmartNIC resources to aid the initiator and offload some of its tasks. This stage is not limited to a specific interconnect technology or software stack, though it is expected to use existing low-latency solutions (e.g. *UCX* [1]).

Tear-Down Stage

Once the execution is finished, and the resources on the SmartNIC are no longer required, the initiator messages the SmartNIC to indicate tear-down can take place. This stage is considered optional since many use-cases would not require explicit termination.

2.2 Example: SmartNIC-Based Storage

In order to demonstrate the proposed design we implement a simple storage service to run on a SmartNIC. The initiator uses this storage for caching requests, and even simple NICs can provide this capability. The demonstration code uses gRPC and focuses on the coordination and execution stages.

Allocation Stage. For systems using gNMI to manage SmartNIC resources, a YANG model describes the capabilities an initiator can request. Below is a YANG file excerpt demonstrating possible features. For example, if a SmartNIC can offload the MPI's *Alltoall* collective operations then a gNMI *Get* request on `cap-alltoall` would return `true`.

```
module: smartnic
  +--rw smartnic-config
  |  +--ro fw-version? uint32
  |  +--rw enable-offload? boolean
  |  +--ro supported-mpi-functions
  |  |  +--ro cap-allreduce? boolean
  |  |  +--ro cap-alltoall? boolean
  ...
```

Coordination Stage. During this stage the initiator opens a gRPC connection to the SmartNIC and asks for a buffer of a given size by invoking the `AllocRequest` gRPC call. Upon invocation, the SmartNIC allocates the buffer and replies with a message containing the fields which the initiator needs for the execution stage. Because the demonstration uses UCX, the reply consists of fields it later requires for one-sided operations on the new buffer - including the address of the UCX Worker. To complete the stage, the initiator uses UCX to connect to the newly created worker.

To use gRPC for coordination, we define the offloaded function prototypes for buffer allocation and deallocation in a protocol buffer file: .

```
service ServiceAPI {
  rpc AllocateBuffer   (AllocRequest)   returns (AllocReply)
  rpc DeallocateBuffer (DeallocRequest) returns (DeallocReply)
}
```

Next, we add the four messages passed between the initiator and the SmartNIC for calling these two functions via gRPC: .

```
message AllocRequest {
  int32 size = 1;
}

message AllocReply {
  uint64 targetPtr = 1;
  uint32 rkeyLen = 2;
  uint32 ucpAddrLen = 3;
  bytes  rkey = 4;
  bytes  ucpAddr = 5;
}

message DeallocRequest {
  int32 size = 1;
}

message DeallocReply {
  string message = 1;
}
```

Execution Stage. At this point, the initiator is free to access the buffer using one-sided operations. We used the UCX calls equivalent to RDMA Read and Write operations: `ucp_get_nbx` and `ucp_put_nbx`.

Tear-Down Stage. To finish the execution, the initiator uses gRPC to invoke `DeallocRequest`, the service instance on the SmartNIC then releases the buffer and responds, which indicates to the initiator it can now close the gRPC connection and terminate.

3 Scalability

A critical aspect of OpenSNAPI and the deployment of SmartNICs in a datacenter is the aspect of scale. This includes both technological considerations and commercial ones. One technological consideration is the overhead of coordinating among multiple SmartNICs, and another is handling faults brought on by the increasing number of components. Commercial considerations may include the trade-off between cost and computational power, however those are outside the scope of this paper. This section explores a range of SmartNIC deployment options in relation to the typical job using them, focusing on the resource management considerations.

The density of SmartNICs in the data-center determines the availability of a SmartNIC for a given process and the expected distance between the two. Density may be as high as multiple SmartNICs in each host (e.g. a SmartNIC per accelerator), however a single SmartNIC per-rack may also prove advantageous for some cases. Next, we will explore the range of possible density and how it would effect the usage.

SmartNIC per Accelerator. In this scenario, each accelerator has a dedicated SmartNIC - either sharing the same board or accessible over the system bus. HPC systems commonly host GPU and TPU devices as accelerators. While the simplest case is a 1:1 ratio, some vendors suggest one SmartNIC for every two GPUs. This scenario diminishes the significance of SmartNIC resource allocation: process affinity dictates the SmartNIC to be chosen for it, making resource allocation for both the job and the process trivial. SmartNIC programming would be likely be carried out by either the process itself or some central per-host entity.

SmartNIC per Host. This scenario is expected to be the typical one, where each host contains a SmartNIC for all the processing on its CPUs and accelerators. Much like with the previous case, clearly all tasks will run on the same SmartNIC - keeping SmartNIC usage local and making resource allocation moot.

SmartNIC per Rack. This scenario addresses the need to reduce the overall cost of the system while still benefiting from SmartNIC offloads. One suitable use-case is MPI collective operations, many of which have an explicit (root process is specified) or implicit logical tree topology. For example, a reduction operation could use the SmartNIC in each rack to aggregate the vectors from its hosts.

SmartNIC Pool. This scenario is especially relevant for cloud providers, where resources are often pooled and allocated towards compute instances on multi-tenant data-centers. It could be viewed as a generalization of the previous scenario, with the key difference of disassociating the process and SmartNIC locations. Here the SmartNIC is allocated based on resource availability and supported offload features rather than location, and the process should not make assumptions about the proximity of the SmartNIC it was allocated.

To conclude this section, Table 1 reviews the combinations of job span and the aforementioned SmartNIC density, with the following variables in mind:

- Resource Usage: the distance between the SmartNIC and the process which explicitly uses it, including both the initial programming and the run-time processing. This could be either local (process and SmartNIC on the same host), remote (process and SmartNIC on different nodes) or both.
- Resource Allocation: the distance between the process and the entity allocating SmartNIC resources for subsequent usage. This could be either "internal" or "external" with respect to the processes composing the job.
- Resource Sharing: the likelihood of having to share the resources on a single SmartNIC with other jobs.

Table 1. SmartNIC resource management aspects for deployment parameters

Density	Multiple jobs per host			Few hosts per job			Large-scale jobs		
Per Accelerator	local	external	[a]	local	internal	unlikely	local	internal	unlikely
Per Host	local	external	likely	local	internal	unlikely	local	internal	unlikely
Per Rack	remote	external	likely	remote	external	likely	[b]	external	unlikely
Pool	remote	external	likely	remote	external	likely	remote	external	likely

[a] An accelerator along with its associated SmartNIC might be either completely allocated to one of the jobs (no resource sharing) or split among them.
[b] Job is assumed to span across multiple groups, racks and SmartNICs. However, an in-job allocation mechanism would require knowledge of the network topology and job layout, and may interfere with the central allocation mechanisms for smaller jobs. Thus, it is likely that SmartNICs belonging to a network group or rack will be allocated by a central entity, similarly to the pool scenario.

The main conclusion from this table is the need to support various methods for both the allocation and the sharing of SmartNIC resources. Namely, methods for an efficient in-host SmartNIC usage as well as obtaining and using remote SmartNICs over the network. While the former may be easier and better suited for existing SmartNIC APIs, e.g. IB Verbs, we estimate that the latter is critical for large-scale deployments on SmartNICs in a data-center.

4 Related Work

Numerous studies [7,8] demonstrate the utilization of programmable NICs to accelerate applications by offloading tasks to the NIC. Such offloading significantly reduces both host CPU and memory usage. For example, *Lynx* [2] provides a system to implement direct networking services which need access to accelerators, e.g. GPUs, without involving the host CPU - for over 4x higher throughput on GPU-centric face verification. *λ-NIC* [3] exposes an event-based programming abstraction, Match+lambda, for SmartNICs. Porting the Key-value store use-case to run on SmartNICs [4,5] has been shown to achieve a significant improvement in terms of requests per second compared to a popular host-based KVS implementation. *sPIN* is a programming model proposed by Hoefler et al.: it extends the RDMA and message matching concepts to enable the offloading of simple packet processing functions to the NIC. sPIN acceleration results in a significant speedup for real-world applications, and a follow-up work by Di Girolamo et al. [9] expands these concepts to a new SmartNIC design - tailored for offloading packet processing functionality using sPIN. While previous research on SmartNIC programmability focused on developing the program to match NIC hardware, our work focuses on how to allocate SmartNIC resources and facilitate the execution of any program compatible with the target SmartNIC.

5 Conclusions and Summary

In this paper we presented a software design for programming SmartNICs over the network, which aligns with the goals of OpenSNAPI. A successful implementation should take into account the requirements that come with scale and facilitate the offloading of tasks to the SmartNIC. This system would rely on the gRPC and gNMI software frameworks to communicate between the SmartNIC and the host-based processes offloading tasks to it. Both frameworks are already used for RPC and configuring network devices, and can be extended to accommodate the flows required for SmartNIC programming. With several SmartNIC models already available, the challenge is to balance performance and portability across these and future models.

References

1. Shamis, P., et al.: UCX: an open source framework for HPC network APIs and beyond. In: 23rd IEEE Annual Symposium on High-Performance Interconnects (HOTI), pp. 40–43 (2015). https://doi.org/10.1109/HOTI.2015.13
2. Tork, M., Maudlej, L, Silberstein, M.: Lynx: a SmartNIC-driven accelerator-centric architecture for network servers. In: 25th International Conference on Architectural Support for Programming Languages and Operating Systems (ASPLOS), pp. 117–131 (2020). https://doi.org/10.1145/3373376.3378528
3. Choi, S., Shahbaz, M., Prabhakar, B., Rosenblum, M.: λ-NIC: interactive serverless compute on SmartNICs. In: Proceedings of the ACM Special Interest Group on Data Communication (SIGCOMM), pp. 151–152 (2019). https://doi.org/10.1145/3342280.3342341
4. Siracusano, G., Bifulco, R.: Is it a SmartNIC or a key-value store? Both! In: Proceedings of the ACM Special Interest Group on Data Communication (SIGCOMM), pp. 138–140 (2017). https://doi.org/10.1145/3123878.3132014
5. Li, B., et al.: KV-direct: high-performance in-memory key-value store with programmable NIC. In: 26th ACM Symposium on Operating Systems Principles (SOSP), pp. 137–152 (2017). https://doi.org/10.1145/3132747.3132756
6. Biswas, R., Lu, X., Panda, D.K.: Accelerating TensorFlow with adaptive RDMA-based gRPC. In: 25th IEEE International Conference on High Performance Computing (HiPC), pp. 2–11 (2018). https://doi.org/10.1109/HiPC.2018.00010
7. Arashloo, M.T., Lavrov, A., Ghobadi, M., Rexford, J., Walker, D., Wentzlaff, D.: Enabling programmable transport protocols in high-speed NICs. In: 17th USENIX Symposium on Networked Systems Design and Implementation (NSDI) (2020)

8. Eran, H., Zeno, L., Tork, M., Malka, G., Silberstein, M.: NICA: an infrastructure for inline acceleration of network applications. In: USENIX Annual Technical Conference (ATC), pp. 345–361 (2019). https://doi.org/10.5555/3358807.3358838
9. Girolamo, S.D., et al.: A RISC-V in-network accelerator for flexible high-performance low-power packet processing. In: 48th Annual International Symposium on Computer Architecture (ISCA) (2021)

Dynamic Symmetric Heap Allocation in NVSHMEM

Akhil Langer(✉), Seth Howell, Sreeram Potluri, Jim Dinan, and Jiri Kraus

NVIDIA Corporation, Santa Clara, USA
{alanger,sethh,spotluri,jdinan,jkraus}@nvidia.com

Abstract. The OpenSHMEM programming model encourages application developers to partition memory into local and symmetric segments through the use of the `SHMEM_SYMMETRIC_SIZE` environment variable. While this can lead to improved communication efficiency, it requires applications to partition the available memory. Setting this value requires that users calculate the amount of memory an application requires for a given dataset or problem. It also presents challenges to applications that progress through phases where OpenSHMEM is not used in every phase and the full memory capacity is needed when OpenSHMEM is not in use. This work presents a dynamic mapping approach to establishing the symmetric heap in NVSHMEM, an OpenSHMEM library for clusters of NVIDIA GPUs. Results indicate that this approach obviates the need for static partitioning of memory with low overheads, significantly improving the usability and flexibility of the NVSHMEM library.

Keywords: NVIDIA GPU · PGAS · High performance computing · OpenSHMEM · NVSHMEM · CUDA Virtual Memory Management

1 Introduction

OpenSHMEM is a Partitioned Global Address Space (PGAS) library that provides an API for doing one-sided communication, atomic operations, and collective operations. These operations are performed on remotely accessible memory that is allocated on each Processing Element (PE). For efficient reference to remotely accessible memory it is organized as symmetric memory. That means that a remotely accessible memory allocation has the same size on each PE which enables to compute references to the symmetric memory on a remote PE without involving the remote PE. All information needed is the local object's reference and the remote PE index. From this information, symmetry allows the OpenSHMEM library to calculate the corresponding location in the remote PEs memory by adding the local objects offset to the remote PE's symmetric memory base address.

In an OpenSHMEM program, remotely accessible memory is allocated with the call `shmem_malloc`. To ensure symmetry, i.e., that each local object is placed at the same offset relative to the PE's base, this is a collective operation that

S. Poole et al. (Eds.): OpenSHMEM 2021, LNCS 13159, pp. 187–198, 2022.
https://doi.org/10.1007/978-3-031-04888-3_12

requires special management of the underlying heap. In NVSHMEM the approach was to preallocate an equally sized symmetric heap during library initialization. That provides an equally sized Virtual Address (VA) range reservation backed by physical memory on each PE and therefore allows the required heap management during `shmem_malloc`. However, it requires a sufficiently large symmetric heap to serve all allocations done by an OpenSHMEM application. Because the preallocated heap competes with local memory allocations for capacity, it is necessary to limit the size of the preallocated symmetric heap. This is possible by setting the environment variable `SHMEM_SYMMETRIC_SIZE` prior to starting an OpenSHMEM application. Setting `SHMEM_SYMMETRIC_SIZE` to too low will cause `shmem_malloc` to fail with an out of memory error, while setting it too high might cause regular local allocations to fail with an out of memory error even if the total physical memory capacity is sufficient. The amount of required symmetric memory in an OpenSHMEM program often depends on the program's input, the number of PEs participating in a run and other runtime parameters. It is therefore not always easy to determine the right value of `SHMEM_SYMMETRIC_SIZE`. Furthermore, when symmetric memory is deallocated it is only returned to the symmetric heap not to the system. This further limits the memory capacity available to local allocations of the same program or other concurrently running programs.

In this paper we describe an approach to avoid specifying `SHMEM_SYMMETRIC_SIZE` by only reserving a sufficiently large virtual address (VA) range during library initialization. Within this VA range, NVSHMEM allocates and maps physical pages on demand during `shmem_malloc`. This is enabled by the CUDA Virtual Memory Management (VMM) API introduced with CUDA 10.2 [13]. Besides avoiding the described issues this also allows to simplify calculation of remote pointers of peer-to-peer connected GPUs. In most cases it is possible to reserve a VA range that is large enough to cover the aggregate available memory of all peer GPUs so that the memory of each peer can be mapped at fixed offsets. During calculation of remote references to peer GPUs this can avoid a round-trip memory access that is otherwise necessary to fetch the mapped base address of the peer GPU.

The paper is organized as follows. In Sect. 2, we introduce NVSHMEM and how it implements the symmetric heap. Section 3 introduces the CUDA VMM API. Section 4 describes the implementation of dynamic symmetric heap. Experimental results are presented in Sect. 5, and related work is discussed in Sect. 6. Finally, we conclude the paper in Sect. 7.

2 NVSHMEM

The OpenSHMEM specification [12] defines a standard API for the SHMEM programming model, which was first introduced for the Cray T3D system [2]. OpenSHMEM is a single program, multiple data (SPMD) programming model that defines symmetric memory segments. Symmetric memory is globally addressable and may be physically distributed, forming a partitioned global address space

(PGAS). Objects in symmetric memory are allocated collectively, such that every processing element (PE) allocates space for an object of the given size. OpenSHMEM treats the local address of a given symmetric object as a symmetric address, which can be used to reference any location in the same object at any peer PE. In the OpenSHMEM model, a tuple containing a symmetric address and PE index represents a global address that can be used to access any location in the PGAS.

NVSHMEM is an implementation of the OpenSHMEM specification for clusters with NVIDIA GPUs. NVSHMEM provides APIs for initiating communication from kernels executing on the device, enqueueing operations on CUDA streams, embedding operations as nodes in CUDA graphs, and for initiating communication from host CPU processes. NVSHMEM is optimized for GPU centric communication and all symmetric objects are located within GPU device memory. While APIs for most operations are provided for both CPU and GPU usage, some operations are not supported from the CPU because CPU bindings would be inefficient. For example, the wait APIs are not supported on the CPU because they would incur high overhead from the CPU polling device memory. Instead, users can enqueue a wait operation on a CUDA stream and wait for completion of the enqueued wait operation.

NVSHMEM supports peer-to-peer communication between GPUs using NVLink or PCI Express, as well as communication over a network, such as InfiniBand or RoCE Ethernet. Device-side functions in NVSHMEM are inlined in order to allow the compiler to optimize for peer-to-peer memory access. NVSHMEM provides thread, warp, and block level data transfer functions, which enable threads to parallelize peer-to-peer data copies. Network transfers in NVSHMEM are facilitated through a proxy thread running on the CPU. Kernels running on the GPU submit work requests through a circular queue to the proxy thread and interactions between the GPU and CPU are optimized to minimize the number of memory barriers required to submit the request. Relative to the overhead of submitting work requests directly to the NIC, work submission to the proxy thread incurs significantly lower overhead to the calling thread. The NVSHMEM proxy thread, in turn, submits communication request to a lower-level communication layer, presently either Verbs or UCX.

2.1 NVSHMEM Symmetric Memory

NVSHMEM supports dynamically allocated symmetric objects through a symmetric heap located in GPU device memory. Symmetric memory access in NVSHMEM has been optimized to minimize address translation and memory registration overheads. Prior to this work, PEs allocate a slab of `NVSHMEM_SYMMETRIC_SIZE` bytes of memory during initialization and the starting address (or base address) of the memory is shared with rest of the PEs. The address of the symmetric object on remote PE (remote_pe) can then be calculated as

$$remote\_addr = base\_addr[remote\_pe] + (addr - base\_addr[local\_pe]) \quad (1)$$

where $base\_addr[remote\_pe]$ is the starting address of the symmetric heap on $remote\_pe$, $base\_addr[local\_pe]$ is the starting address of the local symmetric heap, and $addr$ is the local address of the remote object being referenced.

The remote GPU can be connected either via a peer-to-peer (P2P) connection (e.g., NVLink or PCIe) or via a network interconnect (e.g., Infiniband (IB) or RDMA over Converged Ethernet (RoCE)). Memory access setup is performed for each connection type as detailed in the next sections.

2.2 Peer-to-Peer Memory Access

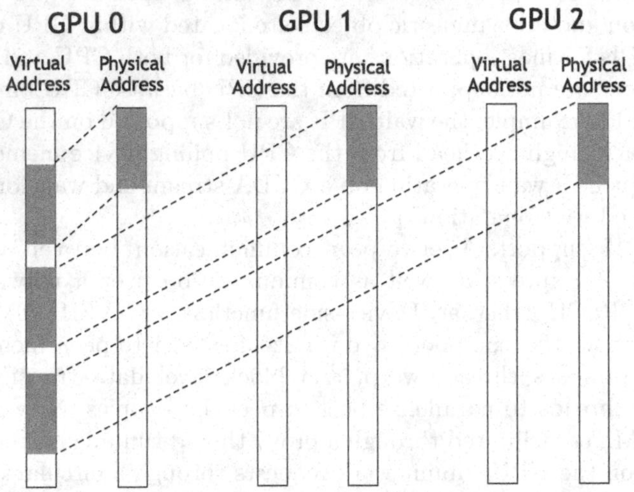

Fig. 1. Memory mapping of P2P connected GPUs using CUDA IPC API

When the peer GPU is P2P connected via NVLink or PCIe, a pointer to its memory location can be obtained and direct loads or stores can be performed to that location. NVSHMEM uses the CUDA IPC API to map memory of P2P connected GPUs to local virtual address space, as shown in Listing 1.1. The resulting mapping is shown in Fig. 1.

2.3 Network Interconnect

For GPUs connected via a network interconnect like IB or RoCE, the local symmetric heap is registered with the networking layer. For example, when using the NVSHMEM IB Verbs transport, memory is registered with the RDMA core layer by calling `ibv_reg_mr`. The memory handle returned by this operation is then shared with all other processes, so that it can be used when issuing communication operations.

Listing 1.1. Using CUDA IPC API to map memory of P2P connected GPUs

```
/* Obtain IPC handle of symmetric heap */
CUipcMemHandle ipc_handle;
CUdeviceptr heap_addr; /* pointer to symmetric heap */
cuIpcGetMemHandle(&ipc_handle, heap_addr);

/* Peer PE maps the IPC handle to a local virtual address */
cuIpcOpenMemHandle(&peer_heap_addr, ipc_handle,
    CU_IPC_MEM_LAZY_ENABLE_PEER_ACCESS);
```

3 CUDA Virtual Memory Management (VMM) API

CUDA 10.2 introduced the new virtual memory mangement functions that enable the programmers to have better control of GPU memory usage. There are many applications where it is hard to guess how big the initial allocation should be. A classic example of this is the `vector` class in C++ Standard Template Library (STL) where the amount of memory that the vector will require cannot always be determined in advance. Hence, the vector may need to grow as it runs out of memory to add new elements. However, one cannot afford the performance and development cost of pointer-chasing through a specialized data-structure from the GPU. An alternative is to maintain virtual address contiguity by allocating new memory that is large enough and copying the data from old memory to new memory. This has memory copying overheads and also limits the maximum memory usage to half of total available memory. What is ideal in such a scenario is that the application can grow the allocation as more memory is needed and yet have the contiguous address range as it was before. The CUDA VVM API allows the programmer to do just that (Article [13]). There are six primary functions in the VMM API:

`cuMemCreate`
: Creates a physical memory handle representing a memory allocation of a given size described by the given properties.

`cuMemAddressReserve`
: Reserves a virtual address range.

`cuMemMap`
: Maps a physical memory handle to a virtual address range.

`cuMemSetAccess`
: Sets the memory access rights for each device to the allocation.

`cuMemExportToShareableHandle`
: Exports an allocation to a requested shareable handle type.

`cuMemImportFromShareableHandle`
: Imports an allocation from a requested shareable handle type.

Listing 1.2 shows example usage of the VMM API. This example shows how physical memory is allocated, how VA range is reserved, and mapping of the

Listing 1.2. Low-level Virtual Memory Management CUDA API since CUDA 10.2

```
size_t granularity = 0;
CUmemGenericAllocationHandle allocHandle;
CUmemAllocationProp prop = {};
prop.type          = CU_MEM_ALLOCATION_TYPE_PINNED;
prop.location.type = CU_MEM_LOCATION_TYPE_DEVICE;
prop.location.id   = currentDev;
cuMemGetAllocationGranularity(&granularity, &prop,
   CU_MEM_ALLOC_GRANULARITY_MINIMUM);
padded_size = ROUND_UP(size, granularity);
cuMemCreate(&allocHandle, padded_size, &prop, 0);

/* Reserve a virtual address range */
cuMemAddressReserve(&ptr, padded_size, 0, 0, 0);

/* Map the VA range to the physical allocation */
cuMemMap(ptr, padded_size, 0, allocHandle, 0);

CUmemAccessDesc accessDesc = {};
accessDesc.location.type= CU_MEM_LOCATION_TYPE_DEVICE;
accessDesc.location.id  = currentDev;
accessDesc.flags        = CU_MEM_ACCESS_FLAGS_PROT_READWRITE;
cuMemSetAccess(ptr, size, &accessDesc, 1);
```

physical memory to a desired location in the VA range. We discuss the usage of this API for implementing dynamic symmetric heap management in NVSHMEM in the following section.

4 Using VMM for Dynamic Heap Allocation

While the VMM API has been available since CUDA 10.2, NVSHMEM requires VMM features available since CUDA 11.3 to support dynamic heap allocation. Dynamic heap allocation can be enabled or disabled in NVSHMEM using the `NVSHMEM_DISABLE_CUDA_VMM` environment variable. Without dynamic heap allocation, NVSHMEM relies on a statically allocated heap whose size is specified using the `NVSHMEM_SYMMETRIC_SIZE` environment variable.

The default allocation size for the static symmetric heap is 1 GiB per PE plus a small memory for internal structures used in the implementation of collective operations. The entire slab is allocated during NVSHMEM initialization and all future calls to `nvshmem_malloc` will be reserved from this slab. Once the static heap is exhausted, all calls to `nvshmem_malloc` will return `NULL` until sufficient memory is released back to the symmetric heap from other allocations using `nvshmem_free`.

In the dynamic heap implementation, during NVSHMEM initialization first the Virtual Address (VA) space is reserved using the `cuMemAddressReserve` API. The amount of VA space reserved is equal to the following.

$$\text{(Num. of P2P connected GPUs)} * \text{(Max. Symmetric Heap Size Per GPU)} \quad (2)$$

The `cuMemAddressReserve` API returns the starting address of the VA range (*heap_base*). The memory of ith P2P GPU is then mapped starting at address as follows.

$$\text{heap\_base} + i * \text{(Max. Symmetric Heap Size Per GPU)} \quad (3)$$

During NVSHMEM initialization, some amount of symmetric memory is allocated which is required for implementing collective operations. More memory is allocated during `nvshmem_malloc` when there is not sufficient memory left to service the `nvshmem_malloc` request. The new memory is allocated using the `cuMemCreate` API which returns a handle to the physical memory object. The physical memory objects may be discontinuously located in physical memory but they are mapped to contiguous locations in the VA space using the `cuMemMap` API. We implemented a custom allocator to manage the allocated memory. This allocator can add new VA space to its memory pool. Whenever new physical memory is allocated and mapped to the PEs VA space, the new VA space is added to the allocator's available memory pool.

Figure 2 shows the mapping of two physical memory objects onto the VA space. A shareable handle of type `CU_MEM_HANDLE_TYPE_POSIX_FILE_DESCRIPTOR` for a memory object can be created using the `cuMemExportToShareableHandle` API. The returned file descriptor is then exchanged with other P2P connected PEs using a Unix domain socket. The PEs then import the file descriptor into CUDA memory allocation handle using the `cuMemImportShareableHandle` API. This is followed by a call to `cuMemMap` API to map the imported allocation handle onto the VA space reserved for the peer GPU as shown in Fig. 2.

For data transfer over networks such as IB or RoCE, the symmetric heap has to be registered with the network using the `ibv_reg_mr` API from the ibverbs library [8]. The `ibv_reg_mr` API in turn calls `nv-p2p` APIs to register the memory for GPUDirect RDMA [6], and returns a Memory Region (MR) (of type `struct ibv_mr *`) corresponding to the given buffer address and size.

Today, support for PCI Express Base Address Register 1 (PCIe BAR1) mappings of VA space that spans multiple memory objects does not exist. This implies that NVSHMEM has to maintain an MR for every new physical memory object that is added to the NVSHMEM symmetric heap. The physical memory allocations are done at a certain granularity that is determined by the `cuMemGetAllocationGranularity` API and can also be set to a larger value via the `NVSHMEM_CUMEM_GRANULARITY` environment variable. The allocation mapping makes it possible to store mappings from addresses to MRs in such a way that an MR for any address can be looked up in O(1) time by using bit masks. The communication API in ibverbs takes one MR each for the source and destination

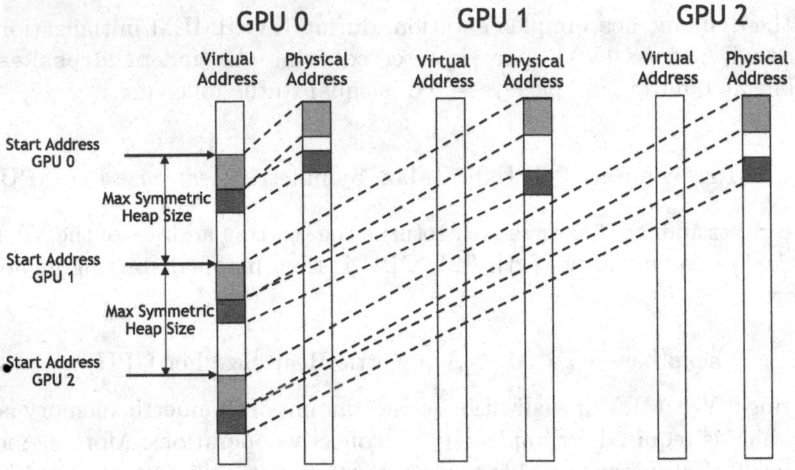

Fig. 2. Memory mapping of P2P connected GPUs using CUDA VMM API

buffers. This means that a given communication operation may have to be split into multiple communication operations depending on the number of MRs (or physical allocations) registered by the source and destination buffer. Listing 1.3 shows the pseudo-code for a communication operation.

When `nvshmem_free` is called, the memory is not returned back to the system but is returned to the NVSHMEM allocator. Subsequent `nvshmem_malloc` calls will therefore be faster if available memory is sufficient to serve the request.

5 Experimental Results

The experiments were performed on Nvidia's Selene supercomputer. Selene is made up of Nvidia DGX A100 nodes. A DGX A100 node consists of 2 AMD EPYC 7742/2.25 GHz CPUs, 8 Nvidia A100 GPUs, and 8×200 Gbps HDR Infiniband network adapters. As of the time of obtaining these results the nodes have CUDA Display Driver 470.57.02 installed, and CUDA version 11.4 was used for obtaining the results.

5.1 Register Count

Usage of the VMM API makes peer address calculation faster and simpler. Prior to VMM API, memory of peer GPUs is mapped by the `cuIpcOpenMemHandle` API, and the returned address is stored in an array in global memory. Peer address calculation involves loading the start address from this array in global memory:

$$\_\_ldg(peer\_heap\_base\_addr[remote\_pe]) \qquad (4)$$

CUDA VMM API makes it possible to map the peer GPUs memory to the desired address using the `cuMemMap` API. Peer address calculation then involves

Listing 1.3. Implementation of Communication Operation

```
void *src, *dst;
while(size_remaining) {
    chunk_size = min(size_remaining,
                     get_chunk_size(src),
                     get_chunk_size(dst));
    /* where, get_chunk_size(void *ptr) returns size of
    remaining portion of ptr in current physical object
    with (O(1) lookup overhead */
    ib_send(sptr, dptr, get_mr(src), get_mr(dst), ..);
    src += chunk_size;
    dst += chunk_size;
    size_remaining -= chunk_size;
}
```

loading the starting address of the VA range from constant memory and then doing a bit-shift operation and an addition.

$$heap\_base + (remote\_pe << 37) \tag{5}$$

where $37 = log_2(128 \text{ GB})$, and 128 GB is the maximum heap memory per GPU. PTXAS (Parallel Thread Execution Optimizing Assembler) analysis of the `bw`[1] kernel having the above two different ways of calculating the peer base address showed that the latter uses 2 fewer registers compared to the former method.

5.2 Memory Allocation Time

We compare `nvshmem_malloc` times without and with dynamic heap feature. In static heap runs, during NVSHMEM initialization, `NVSHMEM_SYMMETRIC_SIZE` sized memory is allocated and memory of peer GPUs is mapped using the CUDA IPC API. Since all the memory allocation and setup has already happened, `nvshmem_malloc` only calls the allocator to find a chunk of requested size. On the other hand, in dynamic heap runs, physical memory allocation and mapping happens during `nvshmem_malloc` using the CUDA VMM API.

Table 1 shows the memory allocation times on 8 GPUs of NVIDIA DGX A100 server in which all the GPUs are NVLink connected to each other. In addition to dynamic allocation, the difference in allocation times is also attributed to the different APIs used by the two setups. NVSHMEM initialization times for static and dynamic heap were 300 ms and 120 ms, respectively.

[1] perftest/device/pt-to-pt/shmem_p_bw.cu in the NVSHMEM distribution [11].

Table 1. Latency of `nvshmem_malloc` for different allocation sizes, using the static and dynamic heap management methods.

Malloc size (GB)	Time (ms)	
	Static heap	Dynamic heap
1	0.023	98
2	0.023	159.9
4	0.023	299.7
8	0.023	568.8
16	0.023	1133.4

6 Related Work

OpenSHMEM 1.5 memory allocation is collective across all PEs and must also allocate an identical buffer size at every PE. While a symmetric heap is not a requirement, this is the approach that most OpenSHMEM libraries have taken for supporting symmetric memory allocation. As shown in Sect. 5.2 this can significantly reduce runtime overheads. However, reserving memory for the symmetric heap can be challenging for applications, which may have difficulty specifying the total symmetric heap size ahead of time, or may go through phases where memory is used only locally. Welch et al. [14] and Ravichandrasekaran et al. [10], have proposed the concept of memory spaces for OpenSHMEM that allows for collective allocation of symmetric memory on an OpenSHMEM team. This proposed extension to OpenSHMEM would allow users better control over memory usage, in comparison with the current method of symmetric memory allocation that is performed across all PEs.

The symmetry requirement of OpenSHMEM memory allocation also poses a challenge to applications with irregular data distributions. Relaxing the symmetry of OpenSHMEM allocations was proposed by Ionkov and Young [7]. This work identified that the OpenSHMEM symmetric pointer addressing model can require internal lookups to support asymmetric registration and it explored the relationship between latency and number of registrations for the symmetric pointer addressing model. As an alternative to the OpenSHMEM symmetric pointer addressing model, the MPI Remote Memory Access (RMA) [9] addressing model uses an opaque object, called a window, and a displacement into the window's memory. An existing memory allocation can be exposed in a window, or new memory can be allocated as part of window creation. The window object provides a reference to communication metadata, eliminating lookup overheads. The displacement-based addressing model can also avoid the challenges associated with symmetric pointer arithmetic when a remote PE exposes more memory than the local PE.

UPC (Unified Parallel C) [4] is a C language extension that provides a Partitioned Global Address Space (PGAS) programming model for writing parallel programs. In addition to collective shared memory allocation, UPC also allows a single thread to allocate distributed, shared memory from the PGAS that is accessible by all other processes. In this way, UPC also allows asymmetric allocation of shared memory. UPC libraries provide an environment variable (for example, UPC_SHARED_HEAP_SIZE in Berkeley UPC [3] or XT_SYMMETRIC_HEAP_SIZE in Cray UPC [5]) that can be tuned at run-time to set the per-thread maximum amount of memory in bytes that can be allocated dynamically by `upc_alloc()` and other shared array allocation functions. UPC++ [1,15] is a C++11 library that supports a UPC-like PGAS model in C++. Upon startup, each UPC++ rank creates a fixed-size shared memory heap from which calls to shared memory allocation API are satisfied. The amount of shared memory on a rank cannot exceed the size of the heap. The heap size can be adjusted by passing `-shared-heap` parameter to the UPC++ run script. The approach of dynamic symmetric heap management presented in this paper, can also be applied to the shared memory heap in UPC and UPC++.

7 Conclusion and Future Work

This work identified static symmetric allocation as a challenge to applications and proposed a dynamic symmetric heap allocation method that takes advantage of virtual addressing to split symmetric heap management into separate virtual and physical address allocation stages using the CUDA VMM API. During initialization, enough VA space is reserved to map the local PE's symmetric heap, as well as all peer-to-peer accessible symmetric heaps into a contiguous VA range, up to a maximum size for each PE's symmetric heap. During memory allocation, additional physical address space is allocated and mapped as needed by each PE. In addition, P2P and network registrations are created to enable communication on the newly mapped physical memory.

Dynamic mapping of the symmetric heap enabled a simplified layout of peer symmetric heap mappings in memory, allowing this approach to improve peer-to-peer communication overheads by eliminating base address lookup and reducing register usage. However, an analysis of the overhead involved in growing the symmetric heap revealed some overheads. In particular, the need to separately register each physical memory allocation with RDMA core layer leads to splitting of a communication operation into multiple communication operations. This overhead can be addressed by enabling registration of VA space backed with multiple physical objects. Finally, while this work has enabled dynamic growing of the symmetric heap, dynamic shrinking of the symmetric heap and effective heuristics to balance resource availability with runtime overheads remains unexplored.

Dynamic symmetric heap allocation addresses the usability challenges associated with static partitioning of memory into symmetric and non-symmetric regions. However, global allocation by all PEs and symmetric allocation size requirements present challenges to applications whose data layouts don't fit easily into this memory management model. Additional work is needed to explore how best to support such applications in the OpenSHMEM model, while still maintaining low overheads and high communication efficiency.

References

1. Bachan, J., et al.: UPC++ programmer's guide, v1.0-2018.3.0, Technical report, LBNL-2001136, Lawrence Berkeley National Laboratory (2018)
2. Barriuso, R., Knies, A.: SHMEM user's guide (1994)
3. Chen, W.-Y., Bonachea, D., Duell, J., Husbands, P., Iancu, C., Yelick, K.: A performance analysis of the Berkeley UPC compiler. In: Proceedings of the 17th Annual International Conference on Supercomputing, pp. 63–73 (2003)
4. El-Ghazawi, T., Carlson, W., Sterling, T., Yelick, K.: UPC: Distributed Shared Memory Programming, vol. 40. Wiley (2005)
5. El-Ghazawi, T.A., Cantonnet, F., Yao, Y., Vetter, J.: Evaluation of UPC on the Cray X1. In: Cray User Group Proceedings. Citeseer (2005)
6. GPUDirect RDMA. https://docs.nvidia.com/cuda/gpudirect-rdma/index.html
7. Ionkov, L., Young, G.: Asymmetric memory extension for Openshmem. In: Proceedings of the 8th International Conference on Partitioned Global Address Space Programming Models, PGAS 2014. Association for Computing Machinery, New York (2014)
8. Linux RDMA core, 8 June 2020. https://github.com/linux-rdma/rdma-core
9. MPI Forum: A message-passing interface standard, version 4.0. Technical report, University of Tennessee, Knoxville, June 2021
10. Namashivayam, N., et al.: Symmetric memory partitions in OpenSHMEM: a case study with Intel KNL. In: Gorentla Venkata, M., Imam, N., Pophale, S. (eds.) OpenSHMEM 2017. LNCS, vol. 10679, pp. 3–18. Springer, Cham (2018). https://doi.org/10.1007/978-3-319-73814-7_1
11. Nvshmem repository. https://developer.download.nvidia.com/compute/redist/nvshmem/2.2.1/. Accessed 9 Sept 2021
12. Openshmem 1.5 specification. http://www.openshmem.org/site/sites/default/site_files/OpenSHMEM-1.5.pdf. Accessed 8 June 2020
13. Perry, C., Sakharnykh, N.: Introducing low-level GPU virtual memory management, 15 April 2020. https://developer.nvidia.com/blog/introducing-low-level-gpu-virtual-memory-management/
14. Welch, A., Pophale, S., Shamis, P., Hernandez, O., Poole, S., Chapman, B.: Extending the Openshmem memory model to support user-defined spaces. In: Proceedings of the 8th International Conference on Partitioned Global Address Space Programming Models, pp. 1–10 (2014)
15. Zheng, Y., Kamil, A., Driscoll, M.B., Shan, H., Yelick, K.: UPC++: A PGAS extension for C++. In: 2014 IEEE 28th International Parallel and Distributed Processing Symposium, pp. 1105–1114. IEEE (2014)

Author Index

Printed in the United States
by Baker & Taylor Publisher Services

Printed in the United States
by Baker & Taylor Publisher Services